MW01534259

Anti-Inflammatory Cookbook for Beginners 2022

*500 Quick & Easy Recipes with 28-Day Meal Plan
to Lose Weight, Balance Hormones
and Reduce Inflammation.*

Gemma Madison

© Copyright 2022 - All rights reserved.

TABLE OF CONTENTS

MEDITERRANEAN DIET SHOPPING LIST

STAPLES

Oils
- ☐ Olive Oil
- ☐ Extra-virgin olive oil

Vinegar
- ☐ Balsamic
- ☐ Red wine
- ☐ White wine

A variety of dried herbs & spices
- ☐ Basil
- ☐ Parsley
- ☐ Oregano
- ☐ Cayenne pepper
- ☐ Cinnamon
- ☐ Cloves
- ☐ Cumin
- ☐ Coriander
- ☐ Dill
- ☐ Fennel seed
- ☐ Ginger
- ☐ Rosemary
- ☐ Red and white wine
- ☐ Garlic

MEAT & SEAFOOD

- ☐ Clams
- ☐ Cod
- ☐ Crab meat
- ☐ Halibut
- ☐ Mussels
- ☐ Salmon
- ☐ Scallops
- ☐ Shrimp
- ☐ Tilapia
- ☐ Tuna
- ☐ Chicken breast*
- ☐ Chicken thighs*
- ☐ Lean red meat**

CANNED & PACKAGED

- ☐ Olives
- ☐ Canned Tomatoes

Dried & canned beans
- ☐ Cannellini beans
- ☐ Navy beans
- ☐ Chickpeas
- ☐ Black beans
- ☐ Kidney beans
- ☐ Lentils
- ☐ Canned tuna

Whole Grains
- ☐ Whole grain pasta
- ☐ Bulgur
- ☐ Whole wheat couscous
- ☐ Quinoa
- ☐ Brown rice
- ☐ Barley
- ☐ Faro
- ☐ Polenta
- ☐ Oats
- ☐ Whole wheat bread or pita
- ☐ Whole grain crackers

Nuts & seeds
- ☐ Almonds
- ☐ Hazelnuts
- ☐ Pine nuts
- ☐ Walnuts
- ☐ Cashews
- ☐ Sunflower seeds
- ☐ Sesame seeds

REFRIGERATED

Cheese
- ☐ Cream cheese
- ☐ Feta
- ☐ Goat cheese
- ☐ Mozzarella
- ☐ Parmesan
- ☐ Ricotta
- ☐ Low-fat milk
- ☐ Plain or Greek yogurt
- ☐ Eggs

PRODUCE

- ☐ Apples
- ☐ Artichokes
- ☐ Asparagus
- ☐ Avocado
- ☐ Bananas
- ☐ Beets
- ☐ Bell peppers
- ☐ Berries (all types)
- ☐ Broccoli
- ☐ Brussels sprouts
- ☐ Cabbage
- ☐ Carrots
- ☐ Celery
- ☐ Cherries
- ☐ Cucumbers
- ☐ Dates
- ☐ Eggplant
- ☐ Fennel
- ☐ Figs
- ☐ Grapes
- ☐ Green beans
- ☐ Kiwi
- ☐ Leafy greens
- ☐ Lemons
- ☐ Lettuce
- ☐ Limes
- ☐ Melons
- ☐ Mushrooms
- ☐ Nectarines
- ☐ Onions
- ☐ Oranges
- ☐ Peas
- ☐ Peaches
- ☐ Pears
- ☐ Plums
- ☐ Pomegranate
- ☐ Potatoes
- ☐ Shallots
- ☐ Spinach
- ☐ Squash
- ☐ Tomatoes
- ☐ Zucchini

* In moderation, once to twice per week
** On rare occasions, once to twice monthly

emeals

INTRODUCTION

"Mediterranean diet" is a generic term based on the traditional eating habits in the countries bordering the Mediterranean Sea. There's not one standard Mediterranean diet. At least 16 countries border the Mediterranean. Eating styles vary among these countries and even among regions within each country because of differences in culture, ethnic background, religion, economy, geography and agricultural production. However, there are some common factors.

Interest in the Mediterranean diet began in the 1960s with the observation that coronary heart disease caused fewer deaths in Mediterranean countries, such as Greece and Italy, than in the U.S. and northern Europe. Subsequent studies found that the Mediterranean diet is associated with reduced risk factors for cardiovascular disease. The Mediterranean diet is a way of eating based on the traditional cuisine of countries bordering the Mediterranean Sea. The foundation of the Mediterranean diet is vegetables, fruits, herbs, nuts, beans and whole grains. Meals are built around these plant-based foods. Moderate amounts of dairy, poultry and eggs are also central to the Mediterranean Diet, as is seafood. In contrast, red meat is eaten only occasionally. Healthy fats are a mainstay of the Mediterranean diet. They're eaten instead of less healthy fats, such as saturated and trans fats, which contribute to heart disease.

Olive oil is the primary source of added fat in the Mediterranean diet. Olive oil provides monounsaturated fat, which has been found to lower total cholesterol and low-density lipoprotein (LDL or "bad") cholesterol levels. The Mediterranean diet typically allows red wine in moderation. Although alcohol has been associated with a reduced risk of heart disease in some studies, it's by no means risk free. Below you can find the shopping list of the most common ingredients in the Mediterranean diet. They are divided by category; they are the most used ingredients but you will also find recipes with ingredients not present in this list.

Chapter 1

The 30-Day Meal Plan

	Breakfast	Lunch	Dinner	Total Calories
DAY 1	Ricotta Toast with Strawberries Calories:274	Black Bean Chili with Mangoes Calories: 430	Roasted Veggies and Brown Rice Bowl Calories: 453	**1157**
DAY 2	Mediterranean Eggs Calories: 223	Italian Sautéd Cannellini Beans Calories: 435	Asian-Inspired Tuna Lettuce Wraps Calories: 270	**928**
DAY 3	Breakfast Yogurt Sundae Calories: 236	Turkish Canned Pinto Bean Salad Calories: 402	Roasted Chicken Thighs With Basmati Rice Calories: 400	**1038**
DAY 4	Savory Breakfast Oatmeal Calories: 197	Bulgur Pilaf with Garbanzo Calories: 462	Quick Chicken Salad Wraps Calories: 428	**1087**
DAY 5	Tomato and Egg Scramble Calories: 260	Mediterranean Lentils Calories: 426	Mango and Coconut Frozen Pie Calories: 426	**1112**
DAY 6	Baked Eggs in Avocado Calories: 301	Tomato Basil Pasta Calories: 415	Potato Lamb and Olive Stew Calories: 309	**1025**
DAY 7	Crustless Tiropita Calories: 181	Ritzy Veggie Chili Calories: 633	Pecan and Carrot Cake Calories: 255	**1069**
DAY 8	Avocado Toast with Goat Cheese Calories: 136	Caprese Fusilli Calories: 589	Zucchini and Artichokes Bowl with Farro Calories: 366	**1091**
DAY 9	Berry and Nut Parfait Calories: 507	Walnut and Ricotta Spaghetti Calories: 264	Garlicky Zucchini Cubes with Mint Calories: 146	**917**
DAY 10	Kale and Apple Smoothie Calories: 177	Chard and Mushroom Risotto Calories: 420	Parsley-Dijon Chicken and Potatoes Calories: 324	**921**
DAY 11	Calo Cinnamon Oatmeal Calories: 107	Pesto Pasta Calories: 1067	Cauliflower Hash with Carrots Calories: 158	**1332**
DAY 12	Breakfast Yogurt Sundae Calories: 236	Grana Padano Risotto Calories: 307	Vegetable and Cheese Lavash Pizza Calories: 431	**974**

DAY 13	Avocado Toast with Goat Cheese Calories: 136	Garlic Shrimp Fettuccine Calories: 615	Sweet Potato and Tomato Curry Calories: 224	975
DAY 14	Banana-Blueberry Breakfast Cookies Calories: 264	Lentil Risotto Calories: 261	Macadamia Pork Calories: 436	961
DAY 15	Blackberry-Yogurt Green Smoothie Calories: 201	Cheesy Tomato Linguine Calories: 311	Glazed Mushroom and Vegetable Fajitas Calories: 403	915
DAY 16	Spinach Cheese Pie Calories: 417	Chicken and Spaghetti Ragù Bolognese Calories: 477	Spicy Tofu Tacos with Cherry Tomato Salsa Calories: 240	1134
DAY 17	Baked Ricotta with Honey Pears Calories: 329 Page:	Black Bean Chili with Mangoes Calories: 430	Roasted Tomato Panini Calories: 323	1082
DAY 18	Breakfast Pancakes with Berry Sauce Calories: 275	Italian Sautéd Cannellini Beans Calories: 435	Vegetable and Cheese Lavash Pizza Calories: 431	1141
DAY 19	Apple-Tahini Toast Calories: 458	Cumin Quinoa Pilaf Calories: 384	Lamb Tagine with Couscous and Almonds Calories: 447	1289
DAY 20	Tomato and Egg Breakfast Pizza Calories: 429	Grana Padano Risotto Calories: 307	Cheesy Sweet Potato Burgers Calories: 290	1026
DAY 21	Avocado and Egg Toast Calories: 297	Mint Brown Rice Calories: 514	Cauliflower Rice Risotto with Mushrooms Calories: 167	978
DAY 22	Ricotta Toast with Strawberries Calories: 274	Tomato Basil Pasta Calories: 415	Baked Salmon with Basil and Tomato Calories: 403	1092
DAY 23	Creamy Vanilla Oatmeal Calories: 117	Ritzy Veggie Chili Calories: 633	Spiced Roast Chicken Calories: 275	1025
DAY 24	Mediterranean Eggs (Shakshuka) Calories: 223	Mediterranean Lentils Calories: 426	Lemony Shrimp with Orzo Salad Calories: 565	1214
DAY 25	Healthy Chia Pudding Calories: 236	Lentil and Vegetable Curry Stew Calories: 530	Grilled Chicken and Zucchini Kebabs Calories: 283	1049
DAY 26	Feta and Spinach Frittata Calories: 529	Wild Rice, Celery, and Cauliflower Pilaf Calories: 214	Roasted Chicken Thighs With Basmati Calories: 400	1143
DAY 27	Kale and Apple Smoothie Calories: 177	Pesto Pasta Calories: 1067	Zucchini Fritters Calories: 113	1357

DAY 28	Spinach Cheese Pie Calories: 417	Walnut and Ricotta Spaghetti Calories: 264	Brussels Sprouts Linguine Calories: 502	1183
DAY 29	Egg Bake Calories: 240	Roasted Ratatouille Pasta Calories: 613	Grilled Vegetable Skewers Calories: 115	968
DAY 30	Pumpkin Pie Parfait Calories: 263	Bean and Veggie Pasta Calories: 565	Sauté ed Green Beans with Tomatoes Calories: 219	1047

Please note: refer to the index to find the number of the page corresponding to the recipe. *We trust that this 30-day nutritional plan is to your liking!*

Chapter 2

Breakfasts

Spinach and Egg Breakfast Wraps

Prep time: 10 minutes | Cook time: 7 minutes | Serves 2

1 tablespoon olive oil
¼ cup minced onion
3 to 4 tablespoons minced sun-dried tomatoes in olive oil and herbs
3 large eggs, whisked
1½ cups packed baby spinach
1 ounce (28 g) crumbled feta cheese
Salt, to taste
2 (8-inch) whole-wheat tortillas

1. Heat the olive oil in a large skillet over medium-high heat.
2. Sauté the onion and tomatoes for about 3 minutes, stirring occasionally, until softened.
3. Reduce the heat to medium. Add the whisked eggs and stir-fry for 1 to 2 minutes.
4. Stir in the baby spinach and scatter with the crumbled feta cheese. Season as needed with salt.
5. Remove the egg mixture from the heat to a plate. Set aside.
6. Working in batches, place 2 tortillas on a microwave-safe dish and microwave for about 20 seconds to make them warm.
7. Spoon half of the egg mixture into each tortilla. Fold them in half and roll up, then serve.

Per Serving

calories: 434 | fat: 28.1g | protein: 17.2g | carbs: 30.8g | fiber: 6.0g | sodium: 551mg

Pumpkin Pie Parfait

Prep time: 5 minutes | Cook time: 0 minutes | Serves 4

1 (15-ounce / 425-g) can pure pumpkin purée
4 teaspoons honey
1 teaspoon pumpkin pie spice
¼ teaspoon ground cinnamon
2 cups plain Greek yogurt
1 cup honey granola

1. Combine the pumpkin purée, honey, pumpkin pie spice, and cinnamon in a large bowl and stir to mix well.
2. Cover the bowl with plastic wrap and chill in the refrigerator for at least 2 hours.
3. Make the parfaits: Layer each parfait glass with ¼ cup pumpkin mixture in the bottom. Top with ¼ cup of yogurt and scatter each top with ¼ cup of honey granola. Repeat the layers until the glasses are full.
4. Serve immediately.

Per Serving

calories: 263 | fat: 8.9g | protein: 15.3g | carbs: 34.6g | fiber: 6.0g | sodium: 91mg

Mediterranean Eggs (Shakshuka)

Prep time: 5 minutes | Cook time: 20 minutes | Serves 4

2 tablespoons extra-virgin olive oil
1 cup chopped shallots
1 teaspoon garlic powder
1 cup finely diced potato
1 cup chopped red bell peppers
1 (14.5-ounce/ 411-g) can diced tomatoes, drained
¼ teaspoon ground cardamom
¼ teaspoon paprika
¼ teaspoon turmeric
4 large eggs
¼ cup chopped fresh cilantro

1. Preheat the oven to 350ºF (180ºC).
2. Heat the olive oil in an ovenproof skillet over medium-high heat until it shimmers.
3. Add the shallots and sauté for about 3 minutes, stirring occasionally, until fragrant.
4. Fold in the garlic powder, potato, and bell peppers and stir to combine.
5. Cover and cook for 10 minutes, stirring frequently.
6. Add the tomatoes, cardamon, paprika, and turmeric and mix well.
7. When the mixture begins to bubble, remove from the heat and crack the eggs into the skillet.
8. Transfer the skillet to the preheated oven and bake for 5 to 10 minutes, or until the egg whites are set and the yolks are cooked to your liking.
9. Remove from the oven and garnish with the cilantro before serving.

Per Serving

calories: 223 | fat: 11.8g | protein: 9.1g | carbs: 19.5g | fiber: 3.0g | sodium: 277mg

Ricotta Toast with Strawberries

Prep time: 10 minutes | Cook time: 0 minutes | Serves 2

½ cup crumbled ricotta cheese
1 tablespoon honey, plus additional as needed
Pinch of sea salt, plus additional as needed
4 slices of whole-grain bread, toasted
1 cup sliced fresh strawberries
4 large fresh basil leaves, sliced into thin shreds

1. Mix together the cheese, honey, and salt in a small bowl until well incorporated.
2. Taste and add additional salt and honey as needed.
3. Spoon 2 tablespoons of the cheese mixture onto each slice of bread and spread it all over.
4. Sprinkle the sliced strawberry and basil leaves on top before serving.

Per Serving calories: 274 | fat: 7.9g | protein: 15.1g | carbs: 39.8g | fiber: 5.0g | sodium: 322mg

Egg Bake

Prep time: 10 minutes | Cook time: 30 minutes | Serves 2

1 tablespoon olive oil	½ teaspoon onion powder
1 slice whole-grain bread	¼ teaspoon garlic powder
4 large eggs	¾ cup chopped cherry tomatoes
3 tablespoons unsweetened almond milk	¼ teaspoon salt
	Pinch freshly ground black pepper

1. Preheat the oven to 375°F (190°C).
2. Coat two ramekins with the olive oil and transfer to a baking sheet. Line the bottom of each ramekin with ½ of bread slice.
3. In a medium bowl, whisk together the eggs, almond milk, onion powder, garlic powder, tomatoes, salt, and pepper until well combined.
4. Pour the mixture evenly into two ramekins. Bake in the preheated oven for 30 minutes, or until the eggs are completely set.
5. Cool for 5 minutes before serving.

Per Serving

calories: 240 | fat: 17.4g | protein: 9.0g | carbs: 12.2g | fiber: 2.8g | sodium: 396mg

Creamy Peach Smoothie

Prep time: 15 minutes | Cook time: 0 minutes | Serves 2

2 cups packed frozen peaches, partially thawed	2 tablespoons flax meal
½ ripe avocado	1 tablespoon honey
½ cup plain or vanilla Greek yogurt	1 teaspoon orange extract
	1 teaspoon vanilla extract

1. Place all the ingredients in a blender and blend until completely mixed and smooth.
2. Divide the mixture into two bowls and serve immediately.

Per Serving

calories: 212 | fat: 13.1g | protein: 6.0g | carbs: 22.5g | fiber: 7.2g | sodium: 40mg

Blueberry Smoothie

Prep time: 5 minutes | Cook time: 0 minutes | Serves 1

1 cup unsweetened almond milk, plus additional as needed	1 tablespoon ground flaxseed or chia seeds
¼ cup frozen blueberries	1 to 2 teaspoons maple syrup
2 tablespoons unsweetened almond butter	½ teaspoon vanilla extract
1 tablespoon extra-virgin olive oil	¼ teaspoon ground cinnamon

1. Blend all the ingredients in a blender until smooth and creamy.
2. You can add additional almond milk to reach your preferred consistency as needed. Serve immediately.

Per Serving

calories: 459 | fat: 40.1g | protein: 8.9g | carbs: 20.0g | fiber: 10.1g | sodium: 147mg

Cauliflower Breakfast Porridge

Prep time: 5 minutes | Cook time: 5 minutes | Serves 2

2 cups riced cauliflower	½ teaspoon almond extract or vanilla extract
¾ cup unsweetened almond milk	½ teaspoon ground cinnamon
4 tablespoons extra-virgin olive oil, divided	⅛ teaspoon salt
2 teaspoons grated fresh orange peel (from ½ orange)	4 tablespoons chopped walnuts, divided
	1 to 2 teaspoons maple syrup (optional)

1. Place the riced cauliflower, almond milk, 2 tablespoons of olive oil, orange peel, almond extract, cinnamon, and salt in a medium saucepan. Stir to incorporate and bring the mixture to a boil over medium-high heat, stirring.
2. Remove from the heat and add 2 tablespoons of chopped walnuts and maple syrup (if desired).Stir again and divide the porridge into bowls. Sprinkle each bowl evenly with remaining 2 tablespoons of walnuts and olive oil.

Per Serving calories: 381 | fat: 37.8g | protein: 5.2g | carbs: 10.9g | fiber: 4.0g | sodium: 228mg

Morning Overnight Oats with Raspberries

Prep time: 5 minutes | Cook time: 0 minutes | Serves 2

⅔ cup unsweetened almond milk	¼ teaspoon turmeric
¼ cup raspberries	⅛ teaspoon ground cinnamon
⅓ cup rolled oats	Pinch ground cloves
1 teaspoon honey	

1. Place the almond milk, raspberries, rolled oats, honey, turmeric, cinnamon, and cloves in a mason jar. Cover and shake to combine. Transfer to the refrigerator for at least 8 hours, preferably 24 hours. Serve chilled.

Per Serving calories: 81 | fat: 1.9g | protein: 2.1g | carbs: 13.8g | fiber: 3.0g | sodium: 97mg

Tomato and Egg Scramble

Prep time: 10 minutes | Cook time: 20 minutes | Serves 4

2 tablespoons extra-virgin olive oil	8 large eggs
¼ cup finely minced red onion	½ teaspoon salt
1½ cups chopped fresh tomatoes	¼ teaspoon freshly ground black pepper
2 garlic cloves, minced	¾ cup crumbled feta cheese
½ teaspoon dried thyme	¼ cup chopped fresh mint leaves
½ teaspoon dried oregano	

1. Heat the olive oil in a large skillet over medium heat.
2. Sauté the red onion and tomatoes in the hot skillet for 10 to 12 minutes, or until the tomatoes are softened. Stir in the garlic, thyme, and oregano and sauté for 2 to 4 minutes, or until the garlic is fragrant. Meanwhile, beat the eggs with the salt and pepper in a medium bowl until frothy. Pour the beaten eggs into the skillet and reduce the heat to low. Scramble for 3 to 4 minutes, stirring constantly, or until the eggs are set. Remove from the heat and scatter with the feta cheese and mint. Serve warm.

Per Serving calories: 260 | fat: 21.9g | protein: 10.2g | carbs: 5.8g | fiber: 1.0g | sodium: 571mg

Baked Eggs in Avocado

Prep time: 5 minutes | Cook time: 10 to 15 minutes | Serves 2

1 ripe large avocado
2 large eggs
Salt and freshly ground black pepper, to taste
4 tablespoons jarred pesto, for serving

2 tablespoons chopped tomato, for serving
2 tablespoons crumbled feta cheese, for serving (optional)

1. Preheat the oven to 425ºF (220ºC).
2. Slice the avocado in half, remove the pit and scoop out a generous tablespoon of flesh from each half to create a hole big enough to fit an egg.
3. Transfer the avocado halves (cut-side up) to a baking sheet.
4. Crack 1 egg into each avocado half and sprinkle with salt and pepper.
5. Bake in the preheated oven for 10 to 15 minutes, or until the eggs are cooked to your preferred doneness.
6. Remove the avocado halves from the oven. Scatter each avocado half evenly with the jarred pesto, chopped tomato, and crumbled feta cheese (if desired). Serve immediately.

Per Serving

calories: 301 | fat: 25.9g | protein: 8.1g | carbs: 9.8g | fiber: 5.0g | sodium: 435mg

Crustless Tiropita (Greek Cheese Pie)

Prep time: 10 minutes | Cook time: 35 to 40 minutes | Serves 6

4 tablespoons extra-virgin olive oil, divided
½ cup whole-milk ricotta cheese
1¼ cups crumbled feta cheese
1 tablespoon chopped fresh dill
2 tablespoons chopped fresh mint

½ teaspoon lemon zest
¼ teaspoon freshly ground black pepper
2 large eggs
½ teaspoon baking powder

1. Preheat the oven to 350ºF (180ºC). Coat the bottom and sides of a baking dish with 2 tablespoons of olive oil. Set aside.
2. Mix together the ricotta and feta cheese in a medium bowl and stir with a fork until well combined. Add the dill, mint, lemon zest, and black pepper and mix well.
3. In a separate bowl, whisk together the eggs and baking powder. Pour the whisked eggs into the bowl of cheese mixture. Blend well.
4. Slowly pour the mixture into the coated baking dish and drizzle with the remaining 2 tablespoons of olive oil.
5. Bake in the preheated oven for about 35 to 40 minutes, or until the pie is browned around the edges and cooked through.
6. Cool for 5 minutes before slicing into wedges.

Per Serving

calories: 181 | fat: 16.6g | protein: 7.0g | carbs: 1.8g | fiber: 0g | sodium: 321mg

Fluffy Almond Flour Pancakes with Strawberries

Prep time: 5 minutes | Cook time: 15 minutes | Serves 4

1 cup plus 2 tablespoons unsweetened almond milk
1 cup almond flour
2 large eggs, whisked ⅓ cup honey

1 teaspoon baking soda
¼ teaspoon salt
2 tablespoons extra-virgin olive oil
1 cup sliced strawberries

1. Combine the almond milk, almond flour, whisked eggs, honey, baking soda, and salt in a large bowl and whisk to incorporate.
2. Heat the olive oil in a large skillet over medium-high heat.
3. Make the pancakes: Pour ⅓ cup of batter into the hot skillet and swirl the pan so the batter covers the bottom evenly. Cook for 2 to 3 minutes until the pancake turns golden brown around the edges. Gently flip the pancake with a spatula and cook for 2 to 3 minutes until cooked through. Repeat with the remaining batter.
4. Serve the pancakes with the sliced strawberries on top.

Per Serving

calories: 298 | fat: 11.7g | protein: 11.8g | carbs: 34.8g | fiber: 3.9g | sodium: 195mg

Breakfast Yogurt Sundae

Prep time: 5 minutes | Cook time: 0 minutes | Serves 1

¾ cup plain Greek yogurt
¼ cup fresh mixed berries (blueberries, strawberries, blackberries)

2 tablespoons walnut pieces
1 tablespoon ground flaxseed
2 fresh mint leaves, shredded

1. Pour the yogurt into a tall parfait glass and sprinkle with the mixed berries, walnut pieces, and flaxseed.
2. Garnish with the shredded mint leaves and serve immediately.

Per Serving

calories: 236 | fat: 10.8g | protein: 21.1g | carbs: 15.9g | fiber: 4.1g | sodium: 63mg

Avocado Toast with Goat Cheese

Prep time: 5 minutes | Cook time: 2 to 3 minutes | Serves 2

2 slices whole-wheat thin-sliced bread
½ avocado

2 tablespoons crumbled goat cheese
Salt, to taste

1. Toast the bread slices in a toaster for 2 to 3 minutes on each side until browned.
2. Scoop out the flesh from the avocado into a medium bowl and mash it with a fork to desired consistency. Spread the mash onto each piece of toast.
3. Scatter the crumbled goat cheese on top and season as needed with salt.
4. Serve immediately.

Per Serving

calories: 136 | fat: 5.9g | protein: 5.0g | carbs: 17.5g | fiber: 5.1g | sodium: 194mg

Banana-Blueberry Breakfast Cookies

Prep time: 10 minutes | Cook time: 13 minutes | Serves 4

2 medium bananas, sliced	1 teaspoon vanilla extract
4 tablespoons almond butter	⅔ cup coconut flour
4 large eggs, lightly beaten	¼ teaspoon salt
½ cup unsweetened applesauce	1 cup fresh or frozen blueberries

1. Preheat the oven to 375ºF (190ºC). Line a baking sheet with parchment paper.
2. Stir together the bananas and almond butter in a medium bowl until well incorporated.
3. Fold in the beaten eggs, applesauce, and vanilla and blend well.
4. Add the coconut flour and salt and mix well. Add the blueberries and stir to just incorporate.
5. Drop about 2 tablespoons of dough onto the parchment paper-lined baking sheet for each cookie. Using your clean hand, flatten each into a rounded biscuit shape, until it is 1 inch thick.
6. Bake in the preheated oven for about 13 minutes, or until the top is golden brown and a toothpick inserted in the center comes out clean.
7. Let the cookies cool for 5 to 10 minutes before serving.

Per Serving (3 cookies)

calories: 264 | fat: 13.9g | protein: 7.3g | carbs: 27.6g | fiber: 5.2g | sodium: 219mg

Blackberry-Yogurt Green Smoothie

Prep time: 5 minutes | Cook time: 0 minutes | Serves 2

1 cup plain Greek yogurt	½ cup unsweetened almond milk
1 cup baby spinach	
½ cup frozen blackberries	½ teaspoon peeled and grated fresh ginger
	¼ cup chopped pecans

1. Process the yogurt, baby spinach, blackberries, almond milk, and ginger in a food processor until smoothly blended.
2. Divide the mixture into two bowls and serve topped with the chopped pecans.

Per Serving

calories: 201 | fat: 14.5g | protein: 7.1g | carbs: 14.9g | fiber: 4.3g | sodium: 103mg

Buckwheat Porridge

Prep time: 5 minutes | Cook time: 40 minutes | Serves 4

3 cups water	Pinch sea salt
2 cups raw buckwheat groats	1 cup unsweetened almond milk

1. In a medium saucepan, add the water, buckwheat groats, and sea salt and bring to a boil over medium-high heat.
2. Once it starts to boil, reduce the heat to low. Cook for about 20 minutes, stirring occasionally, or until most of the water is absorbed.
3. Fold in the almond milk and whisk well. Continue cooking for about 15 minutes, or until the buckwheat groats are very softened. Ladle the porridge into bowls and serve warm.

Per Serving calories: 121 | fat: 1.0g | protein: 6.3g | carbs: 21.5g | fiber: 3.0g | sodium: 47mg

Healthy Chia Pudding

Prep time: 5 minutes | Cook time: 0 minutes | Serves 4

4 cups unsweetened almond milk	1 teaspoon ground cinnamon
¾ cup chia seeds	Pinch sea salt

1. In a medium bowl, whisk together the almond milk, chia seeds, cinnamon, and sea salt until well incorporated.
2. Cover and transfer to the refrigerator to thicken for about 1 hour, or until a pudding-like texture is achieved.
3. Serve chilled.

Per Serving calories: 236 | fat: 9.8g | protein: 13.1g | carbs: 24.8g | fiber: 11.0g | sodium: 133mg

Creamy Vanilla Oatmeal

Prep time: 5 minutes | Cook time: 40 minutes | Serves 4

4 cups water	¾ cup unsweetened almond milk
Pinch sea salt	
1 cup steel-cut oats	2 teaspoons pure vanilla extract

1. Add the water and salt to a large saucepan over high heat and bring to a boil.
2. Once boiling, reduce the heat to low and add the oats. Mix well and cook for 30 minutes, stirring occasionally.
3. Fold in the almond milk and vanilla and whisk to combine. Continue cooking for about 10 minutes, or until the oats are thick and creamy.
4. Ladle the oatmeal into bowls and serve warm.

Per Serving calories: 117 | fat: 2.2g | protein: 4.3g | carbs: 20.0g | fiber: 3.8g | sodium: 38mg

Cheesy Broccoli and Mushroom Egg Casserole

Prep time: 10 minutes | Cook time: 40 minutes | Serves 4

2 tablespoons extra-virgin olive oil	¼ cup unsweetened almond milk
½ sweet onion, chopped	1 tablespoon chopped fresh basil
1 teaspoon minced garlic	
1 cup sliced button mushrooms	1 cup shredded Cheddar cheese
1 cup chopped broccoli	Sea salt and freshly ground black pepper, to taste
8 large eggs	

1. Preheat the oven to 375ºF (190ºC).
2. Heat the olive oil in a large ovenproof skillet over medium-high heat.
3. Add the onion, garlic, and mushrooms to the skillet and sauté for about 5 minutes, stirring occasionally.
4. Stir in the broccoli and sauté for 5 minutes until the vegetables start to soften.
5. Meanwhile, beat the eggs with the almond milk and basil in a small bowl until well mixed.
6. Remove the skillet from the heat and pour the egg mixture over the top. Scatter the Cheddar cheese all over.
7. Bake uncovered in the preheated oven for about 30 minutes, or until the top of the casserole is golden brown and a fork inserted in the center comes out clean.
8. Remove from the oven and sprinkle with the sea salt and pepper. Serve hot.

Per Serving

calories: 326 | fat: 27.2g | protein: 14.1g | carbs: 6.7g | fiber: 0.7g | sodium: 246mg

Quinoa Breakfast Bowls

Prep time: 5 minutes | Cook time: 17 minutes | Serves 1

¼ cup quinoa, rinsed
¾ cup water, plus additional as needed
1 carrot, grated
½ small broccoli head, finely chopped
¼ teaspoon salt
1 tablespoon chopped fresh dill

1. Add the quinoa and water to a small pot over high heat and bring to a boil. Once boiling, reduce the heat to low. Cover and cook for 5 minutes, stirring occasionally.
2. Stir in the carrot, broccoli, and salt and continue cooking for 1o to 12 minutes, or until the quinoa is cooked though and the vegetables are fork- tender. If the mixture gets too thick, you can add additional water as needed.
3. Add the dill and serve warm.

Per Serving calories: 219 | fat: 2.9g | protein: 10.0g | carbs: 40.8g | fiber: 7.1g | sodium: 666mg

Warm Bulgur Breakfast Bowls with Fruits

Prep time: 5 minutes | Cook time: 15 minutes | Serves 6

2 cups unsweetened almond milk
1½ cups uncooked bulgur
1 cup water
½ teaspoon ground cinnamon
2 cups frozen (or fresh, pitted) dark sweet cherries
8 dried (or fresh) figs, chopped
½ cup chopped almonds
¼ cup loosely packed fresh mint, chopped

1. Combine the milk, bulgur, water, and cinnamon in a medium saucepan, stirring, and bring just to a boil.
2. Cover, reduce the heat to medium-low, and allow to simmer for 10 minutes, or until the liquid is absorbed.
3. Turn off the heat, but keep the pan on the stove, and stir in the frozen cherries (no need to thaw), figs, and almonds. Cover and let the hot bulgur thaw the cherries and partially hydrate the figs, about 1 minute.
4. Fold in the mint and stir to combine, then serve.

Per Serving

calories: 207 | fat: 6.0g | protein: 8.0g | carbs: 32.0g | fiber: 4.0g | sodium: 82mg

Spinach Cheese Pie

Prep time: 5 minutes | Cook time: 25 minutes | Serves 8

2 tablespoons extra-virgin olive oil
1 onion, chopped
1 pound (454 g) frozen spinach, thawed
¼ teaspoon ground nutmeg
¼ teaspoon garlic salt
¼ teaspoon freshly ground black pepper
4 large eggs, divided
1 cup grated Parmesan cheese, divided
2 puff pastry doughs, at room temperature
4 hard-boiled eggs, halved
Nonstick cooking spray

1. Preheat the oven to 350ºF (180ºC). Spritz a baking sheet with nonstick cooking spray and set aside.
2. Heat a large skillet over medium-high heat. Add the olive oil and onion and sauté for about 5 minutes, stirring occasionally, or until translucent. Squeeze the excess water from the spinach, then add to the skillet and cook, uncovered, so that any excess water from the spinach can evaporate.
3. Season with the nutmeg, garlic salt, and black pepper. Remove from heat and set aside to cool.
4. Beat 3 eggs in a small bowl. Add the beaten eggs and ½ cup of Parmesan cheese to the spinach mixture, stirring well. Roll out the pastry dough on the prepared baking sheet. Layer the spinach mixture on top of the dough, leaving 2 inches around each edge.
5. Once the spinach is spread onto the pastry dough, evenly place the hard-boiled egg halves throughout the pie, then cover with the second pastry dough. Pinch the edges closed. Beat the remaining 1 egg in the bowl. Brush the egg wash over the pastry dough. Bake in the preheated oven for 15 to 20 minutes until golden brown. Sprinkle with the remaining ½ cup of Parmesan cheese. Cool for 5 minutes before cutting and serving.

Per Serving

calories: 417 | fat: 28.0g | protein: 17.0g | carbs: 25.0g | fiber: 3.0g | sodium: 490mg

Baked Ricotta with Honey Pears

Prep time: 5 minutes | Cook time: 22 to 25 minutes | Serves 4

1 (1-pound / 454-g) container whole-milk ricotta cheese
2 large eggs
¼ cup whole-wheat pastry flour
1 tablespoon sugar
1 teaspoon vanilla extract
¼ teaspoon ground nutmeg
1 pear, cored and diced
2 tablespoons water
1 tablespoon honey
Nonstick cooking spray

1. Preheat the oven to 400ºF (205ºC). Spray four ramekins with nonstick cooking spray.
2. Beat together the ricotta, eggs, flour, sugar, vanilla, and nutmeg in a large bowl until combined. Spoon the mixture into the ramekins.Bake in the preheated oven for 22 to 25 minutes, or until the ricotta is just set.
3. Meanwhile, in a small saucepan over medium heat, simmer the pear in the water for 10 minutes, or until slightly softened. Remove from the heat, and stir in the honey.
4. Remove the ramekins from the oven and cool slightly on a wire rack. Top the ricotta ramekins with the pear and serve.

Per Serving calories: 329 | fat: 19.0g | protein: 17.0g | carbs: 23.0g | fiber: 3.0g | sodium: 109mg

Cinnamon Pistachio Smoothie

Prep time: 5 minutes | Cook time: 0 minutes | Serves 1

½ cup unsweetened almond milk, plus more as needed
½ cup plain Greek yogurt
Zest and juice of ½ orange
1 tablespoon extra-virgin olive oil
1 tablespoon shelled pistachios, coarsely chopped
¼ to ½ teaspoon ground allspice
¼ teaspoon vanilla extract
¼ teaspoon ground cinnamon

1. In a blender, combine ½ cup almond milk, yogurt, orange zest and juice, olive oil, pistachios, allspice, vanilla, and cinnamon. Blend until smooth and creamy, adding more almond milk to achieve your desired consistency.
2. Serve chilled.

Per Serving calories: 264 | fat: 22.0g | protein: 6.0g | carbs: 12.0g | fiber: 2.0g | sodium: 127mg

Breakfast Pancakes with Berry Sauce

Prep time: 5 minutes | Cook time: 10 minutes | Serves 4

Pancakes:
1 cup almond flour
1 teaspoon baking powder
¼ teaspoon salt
6 tablespoon extra-virgin olive oil, divided
2 large eggs, beaten

Zest and juice of 1 lemon
½ teaspoon vanilla extract
Berry Sauce:
1 cup frozen mixed berries
1 tablespoon water, plus more as needed
½ teaspoon vanilla extract

Make the Pancakes

1. In a large bowl, combine the almond flour, baking powder, and salt and stir to break up any clumps.
2. Add 4 tablespoons olive oil, beaten eggs, lemon zest and juice, and vanilla extract and stir until well mixed.
3. Heat 1 tablespoon of olive oil in a large skillet. Spoon about 2 tablespoons of batter for each pancake. Cook until bubbles begin to form, 4 to 5 minutes. Flip and cook for another 2 to 3 minutes. Repeat with the remaining 1 tablespoon of olive oil and batter.

Make the Berry Sauce

4. Combine the frozen berries, water, and vanilla extract in a small saucepan and heat over medium-high heat for 3 to 4 minutes until bubbly, adding more water as needed. Using the back of a spoon or fork, mash the berries and whisk until smooth. Serve the pancakes with the berry sauce.

Per Serving calories: 275 | fat: 26.0g | protein: 4.0g | carbs: 8.0g | fiber: 2.0g | sodium: 271mg

Banana Corn Fritters

Prep time: 5 minutes | Cook time: 10 minutes | Serves 2

½ cup yellow cornmeal
¼ cup flour
2 small ripe bananas, peeled and mashed
2 tablespoons unsweetened almond milk
1 large egg, beaten

½ teaspoon baking powder
¼ to ½ teaspoon ground chipotle chili
¼ teaspoon ground cinnamon
¼ teaspoon sea salt
1 tablespoon olive oil

1. Stir together all ingredients except for the olive oil in a large bowl until smooth.
2. Heat a nonstick skillet over medium-high heat. Add the olive oil and drop about 2 tablespoons of batter for each fritter. Cook for 2 to 3 minutes until the bottoms are golden brown, then flip. Continue cooking for 1 to 2 minutes more, until cooked through. Repeat with the remaining batter. Serve warm.

Per Serving calories: 396 | fat: 10.6g | protein: 7.3g | carbs: 68.0g | fiber: 4.8g | sodium: 307mg

Apple-Tahini Toast

Prep time: 5 minutes | Cook time: 0 minutes | Serves 1

2 slices whole-wheat bread, toasted
2 tablespoons tahini

1 small apple of your choice, cored and thinly sliced
1 teaspoon honey

1. Spread the tahini on the toasted bread.
2. Place the apple slices on the bread and drizzle with the honey. Serve immediately.

Per Serving
calories: 458 | fat: 17.8g | protein: 11.0g | carbs: 63.5g | fiber: 10.5g | sodium: 285mg

Marinara Poached Eggs

Prep time: 5 minutes | Cook time: 15 minutes | Serves 6

1 tablespoon extra-virgin olive oil
1 cup chopped onion
2 garlic cloves, minced
2 (14.5-ounce / 411-g) cans no-salt-added

Italian diced tomatoes, undrained
6 large eggs
½ cup chopped fresh flat-leaf parsley

1. Heat the olive oil in a large skillet over medium-high heat.
2. Add the onion and sauté for 5 minutes, stirring occasionally. Add the garlic and cook for 1 minute more.
3. Pour the tomatoes with their juices over the onion mixture and cook for 2 to 3 minutes until bubbling.
4. Reduce the heat to medium and use a large spoon to make six indentations in the tomato mixture. Crack the eggs, one at a time, into each indentation.
5. Cover and simmer for 6 to 7 minutes, or until the eggs are cooked to your preference.
6. Serve with the parsley sprinkled on top.

Per Serving
calories: 89 | fat: 6.0g | protein: 4.0g | carbs: 4.0g | fiber: 1.0g | sodium: 77mg

Avocado Smoothie

Prep time: 2 minutes | Cook time: 0 minutes | Serves 2

1 large avocado
1½ cups unsweetened coconut milk

2 tablespoons honey

1. Place all ingredients in a blender and blend until smooth and creamy.
2. Serve immediately.

Per Serving
calories: 686 | fat: 57.6g | protein: 6.2g | carbs: 35.8g | fiber: 10.7g | sodium: 35mg

Savory Breakfast Oatmeal

Prep time: 5 minutes | Cook time: 15 minutes | Serves 2

½ cup steel-cut oats
1 cup water
1 medium cucumber, chopped
1 large tomato, chopped
1 tablespoon olive oil

Pinch freshly grated Parmesan cheese
Sea salt and freshly ground pepper, to taste
Flat-leaf parsley or mint, chopped, for garnish

1. Combine the oats and water in a medium saucepan and bring to a boil over high heat, stirring continuously, or until the water is absorbed, about 15 minutes.
2. Divide the oatmeal between 2 bowls and scatter the tomato and cucumber on top. Drizzle with the olive oil and sprinkle with the Parmesan cheese.
3. Season with salt and pepper to taste. Serve garnished with the parsley.

Per Serving
calories: 197| fat: 8.9g | protein: 6.3g | carbs: 23.1g | fiber: 6.4g | sodium: 27mg

Feta and Olive Scrambled Eggs

Prep time: 5 minutes | Cook time: 5 minutes | Serves 2

4 large eggs	¼ cup crumbled feta cheese
1 tablespoon unsweetened almond milk	10 Kalamata olives, pitted and sliced
Sea salt and freshly ground pepper, to taste	Small bunch fresh mint, chopped, for garnish
1 tablespoon olive oil	

1. Beat the eggs in a bowl until just combined. Add the milk and a pinch of sea salt and whisk well.
2. Heat a medium nonstick skillet over medium-high heat and add the olive oil.
3. Pour in the egg mixture and stir constantly, or until they just begin to curd and firm up, about 2 minutes. Add the feta cheese and olive slices, and stir until evenly combined. Season to taste with salt and pepper.
4. Divide the mixture between 2 plates and serve garnished with the fresh chopped mint.

Per Serving

calories: 244 | fat: 21.9g | protein: 8.4g | carbs:3.5g | fiber: 0.6g | sodium: 339mg

Feta and Spinach Frittata

Prep time: 10 minutes | Cook time: 15 minutes | Serves 2

4 large eggs, beaten	1 cup fresh spinach, arugula, kale, or other leafy greens
2 tablespoons fresh chopped herbs, such as rosemary, thyme, oregano, basil or 1 teaspoon dried herbs	4 ounces (113 g) quartered artichoke hearts, rinsed, drained, and thoroughly dried
¼ teaspoon salt	
Freshly ground black pepper, to taste	8 cherry tomatoes, halved
4 tablespoons extra-virgin olive oil, divided	½ cup crumbled soft goat cheese

1. Preheat the broiler to Low.
2. In a small bowl, combine the beaten eggs, herbs, salt, and pepper and whisk well with a fork. Set aside.
3. In an ovenproof skillet, heat 2 tablespoons of olive oil over medium heat. Add the spinach, artichoke hearts, and cherry tomatoes and sauté until just wilted, 1 to 2 minutes.
4. Pour in the egg mixture and let it cook undisturbed over medium heat for 3 to 4 minutes, until the eggs begin to set on the bottom.
5. Sprinkle the goat cheese across the top of the egg mixture and transfer the skillet to the oven.
6. Broil for 4 to 5 minutes, or until the frittata is firm in the center and golden brown on top.
7. Remove from the oven and run a rubber spatula around the edge to loosen the sides. Slice the frittata in half and serve drizzled with the remaining 2 tablespoons of olive oil.

Per Serving

calories: 529 | fat: 46.5g | protein: 21.4g | carbs: 7.1g | fiber: 3.1g | sodium: 762mg

Avocado and Egg Toast

Prep time: 5 minutes | Cook time: 8 minutes | Serves 2

2 tablespoons ground flaxseed	½ teaspoon garlic powder, sesame seed, caraway seed, or other dried herbs (optional)
½ teaspoon baking powder	
2 large eggs, beaten	
1 teaspoon salt, plus additional for serving	3 tablespoons extra-virgin olive oil, divided
½ teaspoon freshly ground black pepper, plus additional for serving	1 medium ripe avocado, peeled, pitted, and sliced
	2 tablespoons chopped ripe tomato

1. In a small bowl, combine the flaxseed and baking powder, breaking up any lumps in the baking powder.
2. Add the beaten eggs, salt, pepper, and garlic powder (if desired) and whisk well. Let sit for 2 minutes.
3. In a small nonstick skillet, heat 1 tablespoon of olive oil over medium heat. Pour the egg mixture into the skillet and let cook undisturbed until the egg begins to set on bottom, 2 to 3 minutes.
4. Using a rubber spatula, scrape down the sides to allow uncooked egg to reach the bottom. Cook for an additional 2 to 3 minutes.
5. Once almost set, flip like a pancake and allow the top to fully cook, another 1 to 2 minutes.
6. Remove from the skillet and allow to cool slightly, then slice into 2 pieces.
7. Top each piece with avocado slices, additional salt and pepper, chopped tomato, and drizzle with the remaining 2 tablespoons of olive oil. Serve immediately.

Per Serving

calories: 297 | fat: 26.1g | protein: 8.9g | carbs: 12.0g | fiber: 7.1g | sodium: 1132mg

Tomato and Egg Breakfast Pizza

Prep time: 5 minutes | Cook time: 15 minutes | Serves 2

2 (6- to 8-inch-long) slices of whole-wheat naan bread	1 medium tomato, sliced
	2 large eggs
2 tablespoons prepared pesto	

1. Heat a large nonstick skillet over medium-high heat. Place the naan bread in the skillet and let warm for about 2 minutes on each side, or until softened.
2. Spread 1 tablespoon of the pesto on one side of each slice and top with tomato slices.
3. Remove from the skillet and place each one on its own plate.
4. Crack the eggs into the skillet, keeping them separated, and cook until the whites are no longer translucent and the yolk is cooked to desired doneness.
5. Using a spatula, spoon one egg onto each bread slice. Serve warm.

Per Serving

calories: 429 | fat: 16.8g | protein: 18.1g | carbs: 12.0g | fiber: 4.8g | sodium: 682mg

Classic Shakshuka

Prep time: 15 minutes | Cook time: 30 minutes | Serves 2

1 tablespoon olive oil	1 (14.5-ounce / 411-g) can
½ red pepper, diced	fire-roasted tomatoes
½ medium onion, diced	¼ teaspoon salt
2 small garlic cloves, minced	Pinch freshly ground black
½ teaspoon smoked paprika	pepper
½ teaspoon cumin	1 ounce (28 g) crumbled feta
Pinch red pepper flakes	cheese (about ¼ cup)
	3 large eggs
	3 tablespoons minced fresh
	parsley

1. Heat the olive oil in a skillet over medium-high heat and add the pepper, onion, and garlic. Sauté until the vegetables start to turn golden.
2. Add the paprika, cumin, and red pepper flakes and stir to toast the spices for about 30 seconds. Add the tomatoes with their juices.
3. Reduce the heat and let the sauce simmer for 10 minutes, or until it starts to thicken. Add the salt and pepper. Taste the sauce and adjust seasonings as necessary.
4. Scatter the feta cheese on top. Make 3 wells in the sauce and crack one egg into each well.
5. Cover and let the eggs cook for about 7 minutes. Remove the lid and continue cooking for 5 minutes more, or until the yolks are cooked to desired doneness.
6. Garnish with fresh parsley and serve.

Per Serving

calories: 289 | fat: 18.2g | protein: 15.1g | carbs: 18.5g | fiber: 4.9g | sodium: 432mg

Parmesan Oatmeal with Greens

Prep time: 10 minutes | Cook time: 18 minutes | Serves 2

1 tablespoon olive oil	1½ cups water, or low-
¼ cup minced onion	sodium chicken stock
2 cups greens (arugula, baby spinach, chopped kale, or Swiss chard)	2 tablespoons Parmesan cheese
¾ cup gluten-free old-fashioned oats	Salt, to taste
	Pinch freshly ground black pepper

1. Heat the olive oil in a saucepan over medium-high heat. Add the minced onion and sauté for 2 minutes, or until softened.
2. Add the greens and stir until they begin to wilt. Transfer this mixture to a bowl and set aside.
3. Add the oats to the pan and let them toast for about 2 minutes. Add the water and bring the oats to a boil.
4. Reduce the heat to low, cover, and let the oats cook for 10 minutes, or until the liquid is absorbed and the oats are tender.
5. Stir the Parmesan cheese into the oats, and add the onion and greens back to the pan. Add additional water if needed, so the oats are creamy and not dry.
6. Stir well and season with salt and black pepper to taste. Serve warm.

Per Serving

calories: 257 | fat: 14.0g | protein: 12.2g | carbs: 30.2g | fiber: 6.1g | sodium: 262mg

Mediterranean Omelet

Prep time: 8 minutes | Cook time: 15 minutes | Serves 2

2 teaspoons extra-virgin olive oil, divided	2 tablespoons chopped fresh parsley, plus extra for garnish
1 garlic clove, minced	
½ yellow bell pepper, thinly sliced	2 tablespoons chopped fresh basil
½ red bell pepper, thinly sliced	½ teaspoon salt
¼ cup thinly sliced red onion	½ teaspoon freshly ground black pepper
	4 large eggs, beaten

1. In a large, heavy skillet, heat 1 teaspoon of the olive oil over medium heat. Add the garlic, peppers, and onion to the skillet and sauté, stirring frequently, for 5 minutes.
2. Add the parsley, basil, salt, and pepper, increase the heat to medium-high, and sauté for 2 minutes. Slide the vegetable mixture onto a plate and return the skillet to the heat.
3. Heat the remaining 1 teaspoon of olive oil in the skillet and pour in the beaten eggs, tilting the pan to coat evenly. Cook the eggs just until the edges are bubbly and all but the center is dry, 3 to 5 minutes.
4. Spoon the vegetable mixture onto one-half of the omelet and use a spatula to fold the empty side over the top. Slide the omelet onto a platter or cutting board.
5. To serve, cut the omelet in half and garnish with extra fresh parsley.

Per Serving

calories: 206 | fat: 14.2g | protein: 13.7g | carbs: 7.2g | fiber: 1.2g | sodium: 729mg

Berry and Nut Parfait

Prep time: 10 minutes | Cook time: 0 minutes | Serves 2

2 cups plain Greek yogurt	1 cup fresh blueberries
2 tablespoons honey	½ cup walnut pieces
1 cup fresh raspberries	

1. In a medium bowl, whisk the yogurt and honey. Spoon into 2 serving bowls.
2. Top each with ½ cup blueberries, ½ cup raspberries, and ¼ cup walnut pieces. Serve immediately.

Per Serving calories: 507 | fat: 23.0g | protein: 24.1g | carbs: 57.0g | fiber: 8.2g | sodium: 172mg

Creamy Breakfast Bulgur with Berries

Prep time: 2 minutes | Cook time: 10 minutes | Serves 2

½ cup medium-grain bulgur wheat	1 teaspoon pure vanilla extract
1 cup water	¼ teaspoon ground cinnamon
Pinch sea salt	
¼ cup unsweetened almond milk	1 cup fresh berries of your choice

1. Put the bulgur in a medium saucepan with the water and sea salt, and bring to a boil.
2. Cover, remove from heat, and let stand for 10 minutes until water is absorbed.
3. Stir in the milk, vanilla, and cinnamon until fully incorporated. Divide between 2 bowls and top with the fresh berries to serve.

Per Serving calories: 173 | fat: 1.6g | protein: 5.7g | carbs: 34.0g | fiber: 6.0g | sodium: 197mg

Basil Scrambled Eggs

Prep time: 5 minutes | Cook time: 8 minutes | Serves 2

4 large eggs	1 tablespoon plain Greek yogurt
2 tablespoons grated Gruyère cheese	1 tablespoon olive oil
2 tablespoons finely chopped fresh basil	2 cloves garlic, minced
	Sea salt and freshly ground pepper, to taste

1. In a large bowl, beat together the eggs, cheese, basil, and yogurt with a whisk until just combined.
2. Heat the oil in a large, heavy nonstick skillet over medium-low heat. Add the garlic and cook until golden, about 1 minute.
3. Pour the egg mixture into the skillet over the garlic. Work the eggs continuously and cook until fluffy and soft.
4. Season with sea salt and freshly ground pepper to taste. Divide between 2 plates and serve immediately.

Per Serving

calories: 243 | fat: 19.7g | protein: 15.6g | carbs: 3.4g | fiber: 0.1g | sodium: 568mg

Kale and Apple Smoothie

Prep time: 5 minutes | Cook time: 0 minutes | Serves 2

2 cups shredded kale	½ Granny Smith apple, unpeeled, cored and chopped
1 cup unsweetened almond milk	
¼ cup 2 percent plain Greek yogurt	½ avocado, diced 3 ice cubes

1. Put all ingredients in a blender and blend until smooth and thick.
2. Pour into two glasses and serve immediately.

Per Serving

calories: 177 | fat: 6.8g | protein: 8.2g | carbs: 22.0g | fiber: 4.1g | sodium: 112mg

Cinnamon Oatmeal with Dried Cranberries

Prep time: 5 minutes | Cook time: 8 minutes | Serves 2

1 cup almond milk	1 cup old-fashioned oats
1 cup water	½ cup dried cranberries
Pinch sea salt	1 teaspoon ground cinnamon

1. In a medium saucepan over high heat, bring the almond milk, water, and salt to a boil.
2. Stir in the oats, cranberries, and cinnamon. Reduce the heat to medium and cook for 5 minutes, stirring occasionally.
3. Remove the oatmeal from the heat. Cover and let it stand for 3 minutes.
4. Stir before serving.

Per Serving

calories: 107 | fat: 2.1g | protein: 3.2g | carbs: 18.2g | fiber: 4.1g | sodium: 122mg

Chapter 3

Sides, Salads, and Soups

Sumptuous Greek Vegetable Salad

Prep time: 20 minutes | Cook time: 0 minutes | Serves 6

Salad:

1 (15-ounce / 425-g) can chickpeas, drained and rinsed

1 (14-ounce / 397-g) can artichoke hearts, drained and halved

1 head Bibb lettuce, chopped (about 2½ cups)

1 cucumber, peeled deseeded, and chopped (about 1½ cups)

1½ cups grape tomatoes, halved

¼ cup chopped basil leaves

½ cup sliced black olives

½ cup cubed feta cheese

Dressing:

1 tablespoon freshly squeezed lemon juice (from about ½ small lemon)

¼ teaspoon freshly ground black pepper

1 tablespoon chopped fresh oregano

2 tablespoons extra-virgin olive oil

1 tablespoon red wine vinegar

1 teaspoon honey

1. Combine the ingredients for the salad in a large salad bowl, then toss to combine well.
2. Combine the ingredients for the dressing in a small bowl, then stir to mix well.
3. Dress the salad and serve immediately.

Per Serving

calories: 165 | fat: 8.1g | protein: 7.2g | carbs: 17.9g | fiber: 7.0g | sodium: 337mg

Brussels Sprout and Apple Slaw

Prep time: 15 minutes | Cook time: 0 minutes | Serves 4

Salad:

1 pound (454 g) Brussels sprouts, stem ends removed and sliced thinly

1 apple, cored and sliced thinly

½ red onion, sliced thinly

Dressing:

1 teaspoon Dijon mustard

2 teaspoons apple cider vinegar

1 tablespoon raw honey

1 cup plain coconut yogurt

1 teaspoon sea salt

For Garnish:

½ cup pomegranate seeds

½ cup chopped toasted hazelnuts

1. Combine the ingredients for the salad in a large salad bowl, then toss to combine well.
2. Combine the ingredients for the dressing in a small bowl, then stir to mix well.
3. Dress the salad let sit for 10 minutes. Serve with pomegranate seeds and toasted hazelnuts on top.

Per Serving

calories: 248 | fat: 11.2g | protein: 12.7g | carbs: 29.9g | fiber: 8.0g | sodium: 645mg

Butternut Squash and Cauliflower Soup

Prep time: 15 minutes | Cook time: 4 hours | Serves 4 to 6

1 pound (454 g) butternut squash, peeled and cut into 1-inch cubes

1 small head cauliflower, cut into 1-inch pieces

1 onion, sliced

2 cups unsweetened coconut milk

1 tablespoon curry powder

½ cup no-added-sugar apple juice

4 cups low-sodium vegetable soup

2 tablespoons coconut oil

1 teaspoon sea salt

¼ teaspoon freshly ground white pepper

¼ cup chopped fresh cilantro, divided

1. Combine all the ingredients, except for the cilantro, in the slow cooker. Stir to mix well.
2. Cook on high heat for 4 hours or until the vegetables are tender.
3. Pour the soup in a food processor, then pulse until creamy and smooth.
4. Pour the puréed soup in a large serving bowl and garnish with cilantro before serving.

Per Serving

calories: 415 | fat: 30.8g | protein: 10.1g | carbs: 29.9g | fiber: 7.0g | sodium: 1386mg

Cherry, Plum, Artichoke, and Cheese Board

Prep time: 15 minutes | Cook time: 0 minutes | Serves 4

2 cups rinsed cherries

2 cups rinsed and sliced plums

2 cups rinsed carrots, cut into sticks

1 cup canned low-sodium artichoke hearts, rinsed and drained

1 cup cubed feta cheese

1. Arrange all the ingredients in separated portions on a clean board or a large tray, then serve with spoons, knife, and forks.

Per Serving

calories: 417 | fat: 13.8g | protein: 20.1g | carbs: 56.2g | fiber: 3.0g | sodium: 715mg

Artichoke and Arugula Salad

Prep time: 10 minutes | Cook time: 0 minutes | Serves 6

Salad:

6 canned oil-packed artichoke hearts, sliced

6 cups baby arugula leaves

6 fresh olives, pitted and chopped

1 cup cherry tomatoes, sliced in half

Dressing:

1 teaspoon Dijon mustard

2 tablespoons balsamic vinegar

1 clove garlic, minced

2 tablespoons extra-virgin olive oil

For Garnish:

4 fresh basil leaves, thinly sliced

1. Combine the ingredients for the salad in a large salad bowl, then toss to combine well. Combine the ingredients for the dressing in a small bowl, then stir to mix well.
2. Dress the salad, then serve with basil leaves on top.

Per Serving calories: 134 | fat: 12.1g | protein: 1.6g | carbs: 6.2g | fiber: 3.0g | sodium: 65mg

Baby Potato and Olive Salad

Prep time: 10 minutes | Cook time: 20 minutes | Serves 6

2 pounds (907 g) baby potatoes, cut into 1-inch cubes

1 tablespoon low-sodium olive brine

3 tablespoons freshly squeezed lemon juice (from about 1 medium lemon)

¼ teaspoon kosher salt

3 tablespoons extra-virgin olive oil

½ cup sliced olives

2 tablespoons torn fresh mint

1 cup sliced celery (about 2 stalks)

2 tablespoons chopped fresh oregano

1. Put the tomatoes in a saucepan, then pour in enough water to submerge the tomatoes about 1 inch. Bring to a boil over high heat, then reduce the heat to medium-low. Simmer for 14 minutes or until the potatoes are soft. Meanwhile, combine the olive brine, lemon juice, salt, and olive oil in a small bow. Stir to mix well.
2. Transfer the cooked tomatoes in a colander, then rinse with running cold water. Pat dry with paper towels. Transfer the tomatoes in a large salad bowl, then drizzle with olive brine mixture. Spread with remaining ingredients and toss to combine well. Serve immediately.

Per Serving calories: 220 | fat: 6.1g | protein: 4.3g | carbs: 39.2g | fiber: 5.0g | sodium: 231mg

Barley, Parsley, and Pea Salad

Prep time: 10 minutes | Cook time: 10 minutes | Serves 4

2 cups water

1 cup quick-cooking barley

1 small bunch flat-leaf parsley, chopped (about 1 to 1½ cups)

2 cups sugar snap pea pods

Juice of 1 lemon

½ small red onion, diced

2 tablespoons extra-virgin olive oil

Sea salt and freshly ground pepper, to taste

1. Pour the water in a saucepan. Bring to a boil. Add the barley to the saucepan, then put the lid on.
2. Reduce the heat to low. Simmer the barley for 10 minutes or until the liquid is absorbed, then let sit for 5 minutes.
3. Open the lid, then transfer the barley in a colander and rinse under cold running water.
4. Pour the barley in a large salad bowl and add the remaining ingredients. Toss to combine well.
5. Serve immediately.

Per Serving calories: 152 | fat: 7.4g | protein: 3.7g | carbs: 19.3g | fiber: 4.7g | sodium: 20mg

Cheesy Peach and Walnut Salad

Prep time: 10 minutes | Cook time: 0 minutes | Serves 1

1 ripe peach, pitted and sliced

¼ cup chopped walnuts, toasted

¼ cup shredded Parmesan cheese

1 teaspoon raw honey

Zest of 1 lemon

1 tablespoon chopped fresh mint

1. Combine the peach, walnut, and cheese in a medium bowl, then drizzle with honey. Spread the lemon zest and mint on top. Toss to combine everything well. Serve immediately.

Per Serving calories: 373 | fat: 26.4g | protein: 12.9g | carbs: 27.0g | fiber: 4.7g | sodium: 453mg

Greek Chicken, Tomato, and Olive Salad

Prep time: 10 minutes | Cook time: 0 minutes | Serves 2

Salad:

2 grilled boneless, skinless chicken breasts, sliced (about 1 cup)

10 cherry tomatoes, halved

8 pitted Kalamata olives, halved

½ cup thinly sliced red onion

Dressing:

¼ cup balsamic vinegar

1 teaspoon freshly squeezed lemon juice

¼ teaspoon sea salt

¼ teaspoon freshly ground black pepper

2 teaspoons extra-virgin olive oil

For Serving:

2 cups roughly chopped romaine lettuce

½ cup crumbled feta cheese

1. Combine the ingredients for the salad in a large bowl. Toss to combine well. Combine the ingredients for the dressing in a small bowl. Stir to mix well. Pour the dressing the bowl of salad, then toss to coat well. Wrap the bowl in plastic and refrigerate for at least 2 hours.
2. Remove the bowl from the refrigerator. Spread the lettuce on a large plate, then top with marinated salad. Scatter the salad with feta cheese and serve immediately.

Per Serving calories: 328 | fat: 16.9g | protein: 27.6g | carbs: 15.9g | fiber: 3.1g | sodium: 1102mg

Ritzy Summer Fruit Salad

Prep time: 10 minutes | Cook time: 0 minutes | Serves 8

Salad:
1 cup fresh blueberries
2 cups cubed cantaloupe
2 cups red seedless grapes
1 cup sliced fresh strawberries
2 cups cubed honeydew melon
Zest of 1 large lime

½ cup unsweetened toasted coconut flakes
Dressing:
¼ cup raw honey
Juice of 1 large lime
¼ teaspoon sea salt
½ cup extra-virgin olive oil

1. Combine the ingredients for the salad in a large salad bowl, then toss to combine well. Combine the ingredients for the dressing in a small bowl, then stir to mix well.
2. Dress the salad and serve immediately.

Per Serving calories: 242 | fat: 15.5g | protein: 1.3g | carbs: 28.0g | fiber: 2.4g | sodium: 90mg

Roasted Broccoli and Tomato Panzanella

Prep time: 10 minutes | Cook time: 20 minutes | Serves 4

1 pound (454 g) broccoli (about 3 medium stalks), trimmed, cut into 1- inch florets and ½-inch stem slices
2 tablespoons extra-virgin olive oil, divided
1½ cups cherry tomatoes
1½ teaspoons honey, divided
3 cups cubed whole-grain crusty bread

1 tablespoon balsamic vinegar
¼ teaspoon kosher salt
½ teaspoon freshly ground black pepper
¼ cup grated Parmesan cheese, for serving (optional)
¼ cup chopped fresh oregano leaves, for serving (optional)

1. Preheat the oven to 450°F (235°C).
2. Toss the broccoli with 1 tablespoon of olive oil in a large bowl to coat well.
3. Arrange the broccoli on a baking sheet, then add the tomatoes to the same bowl and toss with the remaining olive oil. Add 1 teaspoon of honey and toss again to coat well. Transfer the tomatoes on the baking sheet beside the broccoli.
4. Place the baking sheet in the preheated oven and roast for 15 minutes, then add the bread cubes and flip the vegetables. Roast for an additional 3 minutes or until the broccoli is lightly charred and the bread cubes are golden brown.
5. Meanwhile, combine the remaining ingredients, except for the Parmesan and oregano, in a small bowl. Stir to mix well.
6. Transfer the roasted vegetables and bread cubes to the large salad bowl, then dress them and spread with Parmesan and oregano leaves. Toss and serve immediately.

Per Serving
calories: 162 | fat: 6.8g | protein: 8.2g | carbs: 18.9g | fiber: 6.0g | sodium: 397mg

Grilled Bell Pepper and Anchovy Antipasto

Prep time: 15 minutes | Cook time: 8 minutes | Serves 4

2 tablespoons extra-virgin olive oil, divided
4 medium red bell peppers, quartered, stem and seeds removed
6 ounces (170 g) anchovies in oil, chopped

2 tablespoons capers, rinsed and drained
1 cup Kalamata olives, pitted
1 small shallot, chopped
Sea salt and freshly ground pepper, to taste

1. Heat the grill to medium-high heat. Grease the grill grates with 1 tablespoon of olive oil.
2. Arrange the red bell peppers on the preheated grill grates, then grill for 8 minutes or until charred.
3. Turn off the grill and allow the pepper to cool for 10 minutes.
4. Transfer the charred pepper in a colander. Rinse and peel the peppers under running cold water, then pat dry with paper towels.
5. Cut the peppers into chunks and combine with remaining ingredients in a large bowl. Toss to mix well.
6. Serve immediately.

Per Serving calories: 227 | fat: 14.9g | protein: 13.9g | carbs: 9.9g | fiber: 3.8g | sodium: 1913mg

Marinated Mushrooms and Olives

Prep time: 1 hour 10 minutes | Cook time: 0 minutes | Serves 8

1 pound (454 g) white button mushrooms, rinsed and drained
1 pound (454 g) fresh olives
½ tablespoon crushed fennel seeds
1 tablespoon white wine vinegar

2 tablespoons fresh thyme leaves
Pinch chili flakes
Sea salt and freshly ground pepper, to taste
2 tablespoons extra-virgin olive oil

1. Combine all the ingredients in a large bowl. Toss to mix well.
2. Wrap the bowl in plastic and refrigerate for at least 1 hour to marinate.
3. Remove the bowl from the refrigerator and let sit under room temperature for 10 minutes, then serve.

Per Serving
calories: 111 | fat: 9.7g | protein: 2.4g | carbs: 5.9g | fiber: 2.7g | sodium: 449mg

Root Vegetable Roast

Prep time: 15 minutes | Cook time: 25 minutes | Serves 4 to 6

1 bunch beets, peeled and cut into 1-inch cubes
2 small sweet potatoes, peeled and cut into 1-inch cubes
3 parsnips, peeled and cut into 1-inch rounds
4 carrots, peeled and cut into 1-inch rounds
1 tablespoon raw honey
1 teaspoon sea salt
½ teaspoon freshly ground black pepper
1 tablespoon extra-virgin olive oil
2 tablespoons coconut oil, melted

1. Preheat the oven to 400°F (205°C). Line a baking sheet with parchment paper.
2. Combine all the ingredients in a large bowl. Toss to coat the vegetables well.
3. Pour the mixture in the baking sheet, then place the sheet in the preheated oven.
4. Roast for 25 minutes or until the vegetables are lightly browned and soft. Flip the vegetables halfway through the cooking time.
5. Remove the vegetables from the oven and allow to cool before serving.

Per Serving

calories: 461 | fat: 18.1g | protein: 5.9g | carbs: 74.2g | fiber: 14.0g | sodium: 759mg

Sardines with Lemony Tomato Sauce

Prep time: 10 minutes | Cook time: 40 minutes | Serves 4

2 tablespoons olive oil, divided
4 Roma tomatoes, peeled and chopped, reserve the juice
1 small onion, sliced thinly
Zest of 1 orange
Sea salt and freshly ground pepper, to taste
1 pound (454 g) fresh sardines, rinsed, spine removed, butterflied
½ cup white wine
2 tablespoons whole-wheat breadcrumbs

1. Preheat the oven to 425°F (220°C). Grease a baking dish with 1 tablespoon of olive oil.
2. Heath the remaining olive oil in a nonstick skillet over medium-low heat until shimmering.
3. Add the tomatoes with juice, onion, orange zest, salt, and ground pepper to the skillet and simmer for 20 minutes or until it thickens.
4. Pour half of the mixture on the bottom of the baking dish, then top with the butterflied sardines. Pour the remaining mixture and white wine over the sardines.
5. Spread the breadcrumbs on top, then place the baking dish in the preheated oven. Bake for 20 minutes or until the fish is opaque.
6. Remove the baking sheet from the oven and serve the sardines warm.

Per Serving

calories: 363 | fat: 20.2g | protein: 29.7g | carbs: 9.7g | fiber: 2.0g | sodium: 381mg

Greens, Fennel, and Pear Soup with Cashews

Prep time: 15 minutes | Cook time: 15 minutes | Serves 4 to 6

2 tablespoons olive oil
1 fennel bulb, cut into ¼-inch-thick slices
2 leeks, white part only, sliced
2 pears, peeled, cored, and cut into ½-inch cubes
1 teaspoon sea salt
¼ teaspoon freshly ground black pepper
½ cup cashews
2 cups packed blanched spinach
3 cups low-sodium vegetable soup

1. Heat the olive oil in a stockpot over high heat until shimmering.
2. Add the fennel and leeks, then sauté for 5 minutes or until tender.
3. Add the pears and sprinkle with salt and pepper, then sauté for another 3 minutes or until the pears are soft.
4. Add the cashews, spinach, and vegetable soup. Bring to a boil. Reduce the heat to low. Cover and simmer for 5 minutes.
5. Pour the soup in a food processor, then pulse until creamy and smooth.
6. Pour the soup back to the pot and heat over low heat until heated through.
7. Transfer the soup to a large serving bowl and serve immediately.

Per Serving

calories: 266 | fat: 15.1g | protein: 5.2g | carbs: 32.9g | fiber: 7.0g | sodium: 628mg

Cucumber Gazpacho

Prep time: 10 minutes | Cook time: 0 minutes | Serves 4

2 cucumbers, peeled, deseeded, and cut into chunks
½ cup mint, finely chopped
2 cups plain Greek yogurt
2 garlic cloves, minced
2 cups low-sodium vegetable soup
1 tablespoon no-salt-added tomato paste
3 teaspoons fresh dill
Sea salt and freshly ground pepper, to taste

1. Put the cucumber, mint, yogurt, and garlic in a food processor, then pulse until creamy and smooth.
2. Transfer the puréed mixture in a large serving bowl, then add the vegetable soup, tomato paste, dill, salt, and ground black pepper. Stir to mix well.
3. Keep the soup in the refrigerator for at least 2 hours, then serve chilled.

Per Serving

calories: 133 | fat: 1.5g | protein: 14.2g | carbs: 16.5g | fiber: 2.9g | sodium: 331mg

Veggie Slaw

Prep time: 20 minutes | Cook time: 0 minutes | Serves 4 to 6

Salad:

2 large broccoli stems, peeled and shredded
½ celery root bulb, peeled and shredded
¼ cup chopped fresh Italian parsley
1 large beet, peeled and shredded
2 carrots, peeled and shredded
1 small red onion, sliced thin
2 zucchinis, shredded

Dressing:

1 teaspoon Dijon mustard
½ cup apple cider vinegar
1 tablespoon raw honey
1 teaspoon sea salt
¼ teaspoon freshly ground black pepper
2 tablespoons extra-virgin olive oil

Topping:

½ cup crumbled feta cheese

1. Combine the ingredients for the salad in a large salad bowl, then toss to combine well.
2. Combine the ingredients for the dressing in a small bowl, then stir to mix well.
3. Dress the salad, then serve with feta cheese on top.

Per Serving

calories: 387 | fat: 30.2g | protein: 8.1g | carbs: 25.9g | fiber: 6.0g | sodium: 980mg

Moroccan Lentil, Tomato, and Cauliflower Soup

Prep time: 15 minutes | Cook time: 4 hours | Serves 6

1 cup chopped carrots
1 cup chopped onions
3 cloves garlic, minced
½ teaspoon ground coriander
1 teaspoon ground cumin
1 teaspoon ground turmeric
¼ teaspoon ground cinnamon
¼ teaspoon freshly ground black pepper
1 cup dry lentils

28 ounces (794 g) tomatoes, diced, reserve the juice
1½ cups chopped cauliflower
4 cups low-sodium vegetable soup
1 tablespoon no-salt-added tomato paste
1 teaspoon extra-virgin olive oil
1 cup chopped fresh spinach
¼ cup chopped fresh cilantro
1 tablespoon red wine vinegar (optional)

1. Put the carrots and onions in the slow cooker, then sprinkle with minced garlic, coriander, cumin, turmeric, cinnamon, and black pepper. Stir to combine well.
2. Add the lentils, tomatoes, and cauliflower, then pour in the vegetable soup and tomato paste. Drizzle with olive oil. Stir to combine well.
3. Put the slow cooker lid on and cook on high for 4 hours or until the vegetables are tender.
4. In the last 30 minutes during the cooking time, open the lid and stir the soup, then fold in the spinach.
5. Pour the cooked soup in a large serving bowl, then spread with cilantro and drizzle with vinegar. Serve immediately.

Per Serving

calories: 131 | fat: 2.1g | protein: 5.6g | carbs: 25.0g | fiber: 5.5g | sodium: 364mg

Mushroom and Soba Noodle Soup

Prep time: 15 minutes | Cook time: 10 minutes | Serves 4

2 tablespoons coconut oil
8 ounces (227 g) shiitake mushrooms, stemmed and sliced thin
1 tablespoon minced fresh ginger
4 scallions, sliced thin
1 garlic clove, minced

1 teaspoon sea salt
4 cups low-sodium vegetable broth
3 cups water
4 ounces (113 g) soba noodles
1 bunch spinach, blanched, rinsed and cut into strips
1 tablespoon freshly squeezed lemon juice

1. Heat the coconut oil in a stockpot over medium heat until melted.
2. Add the mushrooms, ginger, scallions, garlic, and salt. Sauté for 5 minutes or until fragrant and the mushrooms are tender. Pour in the vegetable broth and water. Bring to a boil, then add the soba noodles and cook for 5 minutes or until al dente.
3. Turn off the heat and add the spinach and lemon juice. Stir to mix well.
4. Pour the soup in a large bowl and serve immediately.

Per Serving

calories: 254 | fat: 9.2g | protein: 13.1g | carbs: 33.9g | fiber: 4.0g | sodium: 1773mg

Pumpkin Soup with Crispy Sage Leaves

Prep time: 15 minutes | Cook time: 10 minutes | Serves 4

1 tablespoon olive oil
2 garlic cloves, cut into ⅛-inch-thick slices
1 onion, chopped
2 cups freshly puréed pumpkin
4 cups low-sodium vegetable soup

2 teaspoons chipotle powder
1 teaspoon sea salt
½ teaspoon freshly ground black pepper
½ cup vegetable oil
12 sage leaves, stemmed

1. Heat the olive oil in a stockpot over high heat until shimmering.
2. Add the garlic and onion, then sauté for 5 minutes or until the onion is translucent.
3. Pour in the puréed pumpkin and vegetable soup in the pot, then sprinkle with chipotle powder, salt, and ground black pepper. Stir to mix well.
4. Bring to a boil. Reduce the heat to low and simmer for 5 minutes.
5. Meanwhile, heat the vegetable oil in a nonstick skillet over high heat.
6. Add the sage leaf to the skillet and sauté for a minute or until crispy. Transfer the sage on paper towels to soak the excess oil.
7. Gently pour the soup in three serving bowls, then divide the crispy sage leaves in bowls for garnish. Serve immediately.

Per Serving

calories: 380 | fat: 20.1g | protein: 8.9g | carbs: 45.2g | fiber: 18.0g | sodium: 1364mg

Mushroom Barley Soup

Prep time: 5 minutes | Cook time: 20 to 23 minutes | Serves 6

2 tablespoons extra-virgin olive oil
1 cup chopped carrots
1 cup chopped onion
5½ cups chopped mushrooms
6 cups no-salt-added vegetable broth
1 cup uncooked pearled barley
¼ cup red wine
2 tablespoons tomato paste
4 sprigs fresh thyme or ½ teaspoon dried thyme
1 dried bay leaf
6 tablespoons grated Parmesan cheese

1. In a large stockpot over medium heat, heat the oil. Add the onion and carrots and cook for 5 minutes, stirring frequently. Turn up the heat to medium-high and add the mushrooms. Cook for 3 minutes, stirring frequently.
2. Add the broth, barley, wine, tomato paste, thyme, and bay leaf. Stir, cover, and bring the soup to a boil. Once it's boiling, stir a few times, reduce the heat to medium-low, cover, and cook for another 12 to 15 minutes, until the barley is cooked through.
3. Remove the bay leaf and serve the soup in bowls with 1 tablespoon of cheese sprinkled on top of each.

Per Serving

calories: 195 | fat: 4.0g | protein: 7.0g | carbs: 34.0g | fiber: 6.0g | sodium: 173mg

Paella Soup

Prep time: 6 minutes | Cook time: 24 minutes | Serves 6

2 tablespoons extra-virgin olive oil
1 cup chopped onion
1½ cups coarsely chopped green bell pepper
1½ cups coarsely chopped red bell pepper
2 garlic cloves, chopped
1 teaspoon ground turmeric
1 teaspoon dried thyme
2 teaspoons smoked paprika
2½ cups uncooked instant brown rice
2 cups low-sodium or no-salt-added chicken broth
2½ cups water
1 cup frozen green peas, thawed
1 (28-ounce / 794-g) can low-sodium or no-salt-added crushed tomatoes
1 pound (454 g) fresh raw medium shrimp, shells and tails removed

1. In a large stockpot over medium-high heat, heat the oil. Add the onion, bell peppers, and garlic. Cook for 8 minutes, stirring occasionally. Add the turmeric, thyme, and smoked paprika, and cook for 2 minutes more, stirring often. Stir in the rice, broth, and water. Bring to a boil over high heat. Cover, reduce the heat to medium-low, and cook for 10 minutes.
2. Stir the peas, tomatoes, and shrimp into the soup. Cook for 4 minutes, until the shrimp is cooked, turning from gray to pink and white. The soup will be very thick, almost like stew, when ready to serve.
3. Ladle the soup into bowls and serve hot.

Per Serving

calories: 431 | fat: 5.7g | protein: 26.0g | carbs: 69.1g | fiber: 7.4g | sodium: 203mg

Parmesan Roasted Red Potatoes

Prep time: 10 minutes | Cook time: 55 minutes | Serves 2

12 ounces (340 g) red potatoes (3 to 4 small potatoes), scrubbed and diced into 1-inch pieces
1 tablespoon olive oil
½ teaspoon garlic powder
¼ teaspoon salt
1 tablespoon grated Parmesan cheese
1 teaspoon minced fresh rosemary (from 1 sprig)

1. Preheat the oven to 425ºF (220ºC). Line a baking sheet with parchment paper. In a mixing bowl, combine the potatoes, olive oil, garlic powder, and salt. Toss well to coat. Lay the potatoes on the parchment paper and roast for 10 minutes. Flip the potatoes over and roast for another 10 minutes. Check the potatoes to make sure they are golden brown on the top and bottom. Toss them again, turn the heat down to 350ºF (180ºC), and roast for 30 minutes more. When the potatoes are golden brown, scatter the Parmesan cheese over them and toss again. Return to the oven for 3 minutes to melt the cheese.
2. Remove from the oven and sprinkle with the fresh rosemary before serving.

Per Serving calories: 200 | fat: 8.2g | protein: 5.1g | carbs: 30.0g | fiber: 3.2g | sodium: 332mg

Garlic Wilted Greens

Prep time: 10 minutes | Cook time: 5 minutes | Serves 2

1 tablespoon olive oil
2 garlic cloves, minced
3 cups sliced greens (spinach, chard, beet greens, dandelion greens, or a combination)
Pinch salt
Pinch red pepper flakes (or more to taste)

1. Heat the olive oil in a skillet over medium-high heat.
2. Add garlic and sauté for 30 seconds, or just until fragrant.
3. Add the greens, salt, and pepper flakes and stir to combine. Let the greens wilt, but do not overcook.
4. Remove from the skillet and serve on a plate.

Per Serving calories: 93 | fat: 6.8g | protein: 1.2g | carbs: 7.3g | fiber: 3.1g | sodium: 112mg

Sautéed Kale with Olives

Prep time: 10 minutes | Cook time: 10 minutes | Serves 2

1 bunch kale, leaves chopped and stems minced
½ cup celery leaves, roughly chopped, or additional parsley
½ bunch flat-leaf parsley, stems and leaves roughly chopped
4 garlic cloves, chopped
2 teaspoons olive oil
¼ cup pitted Kalamata olives, chopped
Grated zest and juice of 1 lemon
Salt and pepper, to taste

1. Place the kale, celery leaves, parsley, and garlic in a steamer basket set over a medium saucepan. Steam over medium-high heat, covered, for 15 minutes. Remove from the heat and squeeze out any excess moisture. Place a large skillet over medium heat. Add the oil, then add the kale mixture to the skillet. Cook, stirring often, for 5 minutes. Remove from the heat and add the olives and lemon zest and juice. Season with salt and pepper and serve.

Per Serving calories: 86 | fat: 6.4g | protein: 1.8g | carbs: 7.5g | fiber: 2.1g | sodium: 276mg

Balsamic Brussels Sprouts and Delicata Squash

Prep time: 10 minutes | Cook time: 30 minutes | Serves 2

½ pound (227 g) Brussels sprouts, ends trimmed and outer leaves removed
1 medium delicata squash, halved lengthwise, seeded, and cut into 1-inch pieces
1 cup fresh cranberries

2 teaspoons olive oil
Salt and freshly ground black pepper, to taste
½ cup balsamic vinegar
2 tablespoons roasted pumpkin seeds
2 tablespoons fresh pomegranate arils (seeds)

1. Preheat oven to 400°F (205°C). Line a sheet pan with parchment paper. Combine the Brussels sprouts, squash, and cranberries in a large bowl. Drizzle with olive oil, and season lightly with salt and pepper. Toss well to coat and arrange in a single layer on the sheet pan.
2. Roast in the preheated oven for 30 minutes, turning vegetables halfway through, or until Brussels sprouts turn brown and crisp in spots. Meanwhile, make the balsamic glaze by simmering the vinegar for 10 to 12 minutes, or until mixture has reduced to about ¼ cup and turns a syrupy consistency. Remove the vegetables from the oven, drizzle with balsamic syrup, and sprinkle with pumpkin seeds and pomegranate arils before serving.

Per Serving calories: 203 | fat: 6.8g | protein: 6.2g | carbs: 22.0g | fiber: 8.2g | sodium: 32mg

Green Beans with Tahini-Lemon Sauce

Prep time: 5 minutes | Cook time: 10 minutes | Serves 2

1 pound (454 g) green beans, washed and trimmed
2 tablespoons tahini
1 garlic clove, minced

Grated zest and juice of 1 lemon
Salt and black pepper, to taste
1 teaspoon toasted black or white sesame seeds (optional)

1. Steam the beans in a medium saucepan fitted with a steamer basket (or by adding ¼ cup water to a covered saucepan) over medium-high heat. Drain, reserving the cooking water. Mix the tahini, garlic, lemon zest and juice, and salt and pepper to taste. Use the reserved cooking water to thin the sauce as desired.
2. Toss the green beans with the sauce and garnish with the sesame seeds, if desired. Serve immediately.

Per Serving calories: 188 | fat: 8.4g | protein: 7.2g | carbs: 22.2g | fiber: 7.9g | sodium: 200mg

Mixed Salad With Balsamic Honey Dressing

Prep time: 15 minutes | Cook time: 0 minutes | Serves 2

Dressing:
¼ cup balsamic vinegar
¼ cup olive oil
1 tablespoon honey
1 teaspoon Dijon mustard
¼ teaspoon garlic powder
¼ teaspoon salt, or more to taste
Pinch freshly ground black pepper
Salad:
4 cups chopped red leaf lettuce

½ cup cherry or grape tomatoes, halved
½ English cucumber, sliced in quarters lengthwise and then cut into bite-size pieces
Any combination fresh, torn herbs (parsley, oregano, basil, or chives)
1 tablespoon roasted sunflower seeds

Make the Dressing
1. Combine the vinegar, olive oil, honey, mustard, garlic powder, salt, and pepper in a jar with a lid. Shake well.

Make the Salad
2. In a large bowl, combine the lettuce, tomatoes, cucumber, and herbs. Toss well. Pour all or as much dressing as desired over the tossed salad and toss again to coat the salad with dressing. Top with the sunflower seeds before serving.

Per Serving calories: 337 | fat: 26.1g | protein: 4.2g | carbs: 22.2g | fiber: 3.1g | sodium: 172mg

Arugula and Fig Salad

Prep time: 15 minutes | Cook time: 0 minutes | Serves 2

3 cups arugula
4 fresh, ripe figs (or 4 to 6 dried figs), stemmed and sliced
2 tablespoons olive oil

¼ cup lightly toasted pecan halves
2 tablespoons crumbled blue cheese
1 to 2 tablespoons balsamic glaze

1. Toss the arugula and figs with the olive oil in a large bowl until evenly coated. Add the pecans and blue cheese to the bowl. Toss the salad lightly.
2. Drizzle with the balsamic glaze and serve immediately.

Per Serving calories: 517 | fat: 36.2g | protein: 18.9g | carbs: 30.2g | fiber: 6.1g | sodium: 481mg

Rich Chicken and Small Pasta Broth

Prep time: 10 minutes | Cook time: 4 hours | Serves 6

- 6 boneless, skinless chicken thighs
- 4 stalks celery, cut into ½-inch pieces
- 4 carrots, cut into 1-inch pieces
- 1 medium yellow onion, halved
- 2 garlic cloves, minced
- 2 bay leaves
- Sea salt and freshly ground black pepper, to taste
- 6 cups low-sodium chicken stock
- ½ cup stelline pasta
- ¼ cup chopped fresh flat-leaf parsley

1. Combine the chicken thighs, celery, carrots, onion, and garlic in the slow cooker. Spread with bay leaves and sprinkle with salt and pepper. Toss to mix well.
2. Pour in the chicken stock. Put the lid on and cook on high for 4 hours or until the internal temperature of chicken reaches at least 165°F (74°C).
3. In the last 20 minutes of the cooking, remove the chicken from the slow cooker and transfer to a bowl to cool until ready to reserve.
4. Discard the bay leaves and add the pasta to the slow cooker. Put the lid on and cook for 15 minutes or until al dente. Meanwhile, slice the chicken, then put the chicken and parsley in the slow cooker and cook for 5 minutes or until well combined. Pour the soup in a large bowl and serve immediately.

Per Serving calories: 285 | fat: 10.8g | protein: 27.4g | carbs: 18.8g | fiber: 2.6g | sodium: 815mg

Roasted Root Vegetable Soup

Prep time: 10 minutes | Cook time: 35 minutes | Serves 6

- 2 parsnips, peeled and sliced
- 2 carrots, peeled and sliced
- 2 sweet potatoes, peeled and sliced
- 1 teaspoon chopped fresh rosemary
- 1 teaspoon chopped fresh thyme
- 1 teaspoon sea salt
- ½ teaspoon freshly ground black pepper
- 2 tablespoons extra-virgin olive oil
- 4 cups low-sodium vegetable soup
- ½ cup grated Parmesan cheese, for garnish (optional)

1. Preheat the oven to 400°F (205°C). Line a baking sheet with aluminum foil.
2. Combine the parsnips, carrots, and sweet potatoes in a large bowl, then sprinkle with rosemary, thyme, salt, and pepper, and drizzle with olive oil. Toss to coat the vegetables well.
3. Arrange the vegetables on the baking sheet, then roast in the preheated oven for 30 minutes or until lightly browned and soft. Flip the vegetables halfway through the roasting.
4. Pour the roasted vegetables with vegetable broth in a food processor, then pulse until creamy and smooth.
5. Pour the puréed vegetables in a saucepan, then warm over low heat until heated through. Spoon the soup in a large serving bowl, then scatter with Parmesan cheese. Serve immediately.

Per Serving calories: 192 | fat: 5.7g | protein: 4.8g | carbs: 31.5g | fiber: 5.7g | sodium: 797mg

Super Mushroom and Red Wine Soup

Prep time: 40 minutes | Cook time: 35 minutes | Serves 6

- 2 ounces (57 g) dried morels
- 2 ounces (57 g) dried porcini
- 1 tablespoon extra-virgin olive oil
- 8 ounces (227 g) button mushrooms, chopped
- 8 ounces (227 g) portobello mushrooms, chopped
- 3 shallots, finely chopped
- 2 cloves garlic, minced
- 1 teaspoon finely chopped fresh thyme
- Sea salt and freshly ground pepper, to taste
- ⅓ cup dry red wine
- 4 cups low-sodium chicken broth
- ½ cup heavy cream
- 1 small bunch flat-leaf parsley, chopped

1. Put the dried mushrooms in a large bowl and pour in enough water to submerge the mushrooms. Soak for 30 minutes and drain.
2. Heat the olive oil in a stockpot over medium-high heat until shimmering.
3. Add the mushrooms and shallots to the pot and sauté for 10 minutes or until the mushrooms are tender.
4. Add the garlic and sauté for an additional 1 minute or until fragrant. Sprinkle with thyme, salt, and pepper.
5. Pour in the dry red wine and chicken broth. Bring to a boil over high heat.
6. Reduce the heat to low. Simmer for 20 minutes.
7. After simmering, pour half of the soup in a food processor, then pulse until creamy and smooth.
8. Pour the puréed soup back to the pot, then mix in the cream and heat over low heat until heated through.
9. Pour the soup in a large serving bowl and spread with chopped parsley before serving.

Per Serving
calories: 139 | fat: 7.4g | protein: 7.1g | carbs: 14.4g | fiber: 2.8g | sodium: 94mg

Cheesy Roasted Broccolini

Prep time: 5 minutes | Cook time: 10 minutes | Serves 2

- 1 bunch broccolini (about 5 ounces / 142 g)
- 1 tablespoon olive oil
- ½ teaspoon garlic powder
- ¼ teaspoon salt
- 2 tablespoons grated Romano cheese

1. Preheat the oven to 400°F (205°C). Line a sheet pan with parchment paper.
2. Slice the tough ends off the broccolini and put in a medium bowl. Add the olive oil, garlic powder, and salt and toss to coat well. Arrange the broccolini on the prepared sheet pan.
3. Roast in the preheated oven for 7 minutes, flipping halfway through the cooking time.
4. Remove the pan from the oven and sprinkle the cheese over the broccolini. Using tongs, carefully flip the broccolini over to coat all sides.
5. Return to the oven and cook for an additional 2 to 3 minutes, or until the cheese melts and starts to turn golden. Serve warm.

Per Serving
calories: 114 | fat: 9.0g | protein: 4.0g | carbs: 5.0g | fiber: 2.0g | sodium: 400mg

Orange-Honey Glazed Carrots

Prep time: 10 minutes | Cook time: 15 to 20 minutes | Serves 2

½ pound (227 g) rainbow carrots, peeled
2 tablespoons fresh orange juice
1 tablespoon honey
½ teaspoon coriander
Pinch salt

1. Preheat the oven to 400ºF (205ºC).
2. Cut the carrots lengthwise into slices of even thickness and place in a large bowl. Stir together the orange juice, honey, coriander, and salt in a small bowl. Pour the orange juice mixture over the carrots and toss until well coated.
3. Spread the carrots in a baking dish in a single layer. Roast for 15 to 20 minutes until fork-tender.
4. Let cool for 5 minutes before serving.

Per Serving

calories: 85 | fat: 0g | protein: 1.0g | carbs: 21.0g | fiber: 3.0g | sodium: 156mg

Roasted Cauliflower

Prep time: 10 minutes | Cook time: 20 minutes | Serves 2

½ large head cauliflower, stemmed and broken into florets (about 3 cups)
1 tablespoon olive oil
2 tablespoons freshly squeezed lemon juice
2 tablespoons tahini
1 teaspoon harissa paste
Pinch salt

1. Preheat the oven to 400ºF (205ºC). Line a sheet pan with parchment paper. Toss the cauliflower florets with the olive oil in a large bowl and transfer to the sheet pan.
2. Roast in the preheated oven for 15 minutes, flipping the cauliflower once or twice, or until it starts to become golden. Meanwhile, in a separate bowl, combine the lemon juice, tahini, harissa, and salt and stir to mix well.
3. Remove the pan from the oven and toss the cauliflower with the lemon tahini sauce. Return to the oven and roast for another 5 minutes. Serve hot.

Per Serving calories: 205 | fat: 15.0g | protein: 4.0g | carbs: 15.0g | fiber: 7.0g | sodium: 161mg

Sautéed White Beans with Rosemary

Prep time: 10 minutes | Cook time: 12 minutes | Serves 2

1 tablespoon olive oil
2 garlic cloves, minced
1 (15-ounce / 425-g) can white cannellini beans, drained and rinsed
1 teaspoon minced fresh rosemary plus 1 whole fresh rosemary sprig
¼ teaspoon dried sage
½ cup low-sodium chicken stock
Salt, to taste

1. Heat the olive oil in a saucepan over medium-high heat.
2. Add the garlic and sauté for 30 seconds until fragrant.
3. Add the beans, minced and whole rosemary, sage, and chicken stock and bring the mixture to a boil.
4. Reduce the heat to medium and allow to simmer for 10 minutes, or until most of the liquid is evaporated. If desired, mash some of the beans with a fork to thicken them. Season with salt to taste. Remove the rosemary sprig before serving.

Per Serving calories: 155 | fat: 7.0g | protein: 6.0g | carbs: 17.0g | fiber: 8.0g | sodium: 153mg

Moroccan Spiced Couscous

Prep time: 10 minutes | Cook time: 8 minutes | Serves 2

1 tablespoon olive oil
¾ cup couscous
¼ teaspoon cinnamon
¼ teaspoon garlic powder
¼ teaspoon salt, plus more as needed
1 cup water
2 tablespoons minced dried apricots
2 tablespoons raisins
2 teaspoons minced fresh parsley

1. Heat the olive oil in a saucepan over medium-high heat until it shimmers. Add the couscous, cinnamon, garlic powder, and salt. Stir for 1 minute to toast the couscous and spices. Add the water, apricots, and raisins and bring the mixture to a boil.
2. Cover and turn off the heat. Allow the couscous to sit for 4 to 5 minutes and then fluff it with a fork. Sprinkle with the fresh parsley. Season with more salt as needed and serve.

Per Serving

calories: 338 | fat: 8.0g | protein: 9.0g | carbs: 59.0g | fiber: 4.0g | sodium: 299mg

Lemon-Tahini Hummus

Prep time: 15 minutes | Cook time: 0 minutes | Serves 6

1 (15-ounce / 425-g) can chickpeas, drained and rinsed
4 tablespoons extra-virgin olive oil, divided
4 to 5 tablespoons tahini (sesame seed paste)
2 lemons, juiced
1 lemon, zested, divided
1 tablespoon minced garlic
Pinch salt

1. In a food processor, combine the chickpeas, 2 tablespoons of olive oil, tahini, lemon juice, half of the lemon zest, and garlic and pulse for up to 1 minute, scraping down the sides of the food processor bowl as necessary.
2. Taste and add salt as needed. Feel free to add 1 teaspoon of water at a time to thin the hummus to a better consistency. Transfer the hummus to a serving bowl. Serve drizzled with the remaining 2 tablespoons of olive oil and remaining half of the lemon zest.

Per Serving calories: 216 | fat: 15.0g | protein: 5.0g | carbs: 17.0g | fiber: 5.0g | sodium: 12mg

Lemon and Spinach Orzo

Prep time: 5 minutes | Cook time: 10 minutes | Makes 2 cups

1 cup dry orzo
1 (6-ounce / 170-g) bag baby spinach
1 cup halved grape tomatoes
2 tablespoons extra-virgin olive oil
¼ teaspoon salt
Freshly ground black pepper
¾ cup crumbled feta cheese
1 lemon, juiced and zested

1. Bring a medium pot of water to a boil. Stir in the orzo and cook uncovered for 8 minutes. Drain the water, then return the orzo to medium heat. Add the spinach and tomatoes and cook until the spinach is wilted. Sprinkle with the olive oil, salt, and pepper and mix well. Top with the feta cheese, lemon juice and zest, then toss one or two more times and serve.

Per Serving (1 cup) calories: 610 | fat: 27.0g | protein: 21.0g | carbs: 74.0g | fiber: 6.0g | sodium: 990mg

Zesty Spanish Potato Salad

Prep time: 10 minutes | Cook time: 5 to 7 minutes | Serves 6 to 8

4 russet potatoes, peeled and chopped	5 tablespoons pitted Spanish olives
3 large hard-boiled eggs, chopped	½ teaspoon freshly ground black pepper
1 cup frozen mixed vegetables, thawed	½ teaspoon dried mustard seed
½ cup plain, unsweetened, full-fat Greek yogurt	½ tablespoon freshly squeezed lemon juice
	½ teaspoon dried dill Salt, to taste

1. Place the potatoes in a large pot of water and boil for 5 to 7 minutes, until just fork-tender, checking periodically for doneness. You don't have to overcook them. Meanwhile, in a large bowl, mix the eggs, vegetables, yogurt, olives, pepper, mustard, lemon juice, and dill. Season with salt to taste.
2. Once the potatoes are cooled somewhat, add them to the large bowl, then toss well and serve.

   Per Serving
   calories: 192 | fat: 5.0g | protein: 9.0g | carbs: 30.0g | fiber: 2.0g | sodium: 59mg

Greek Salad with Dressing

Prep time: 10 minutes | Cook time: 0 minutes | Serves 4 to 6

1 head iceberg lettuce	1 teaspoon salt
2 cups cherry tomatoes	1 clove garlic, minced
1 large cucumber	1 cup Kalamata olives, pitted
1 medium onion	1 (6-ounce / 170-g) package feta cheese, crumbled
¼ cup lemon juice	
½ cup extra-virgin olive oil	

1. Cut the lettuce into 1-inch pieces and put them in a large salad bowl. Cut the tomatoes in half and add them to the salad bowl. Slice the cucumber into bite-sized pieces and add them to the salad bowl.
2. Thinly slice the onion and add it to the salad bowl. In a separate bowl, whisk together the olive oil, lemon juice, salt, and garlic. Pour the dressing over the salad and gently toss to evenly coat.
3. Top the salad with the Kalamata olives and feta cheese and serve.

   Per Serving calories: 539 | fat: 50.0g | protein: 9.0g | carbs: 18.0g | fiber: 4.0g | sodium: 1758mg

Tricolor Summer Salad

Prep time: 10 minutes | Cook time: 0 minutes | Serves 3 to 4

¼ cup while balsamic vinegar	¼ cup extra-virgin olive oil
2 tablespoons Dijon mustard	1½ cups chopped orange, yellow, and red tomatoes
1 tablespoon sugar	½ cucumber, peeled and diced
½ teaspoon garlic salt	1 small red onion, thinly sliced
½ teaspoon freshly ground black pepper	¼ cup crumbled feta (optional)

1. In a small bowl, whisk the vinegar, mustard, sugar, pepper, and garlic salt. Then slowly whisk in the olive oil. In a large bowl, add the tomatoes, cucumber, and red onion. Add the dressing. Toss once or twice, and serve with the feta crumbles (if desired) sprinkled on top. **Per Serving** calories: 246 | fat: 18.0g | protein: 1.0g | carbs: 19.0g | fiber: 2.0g | sodium: 483mg

Chicken and Pastina Soup

Prep time: 5 minutes | Cook time: 20 minutes | Serves 6

1 tablespoon extra-virgin olive oil	¼ teaspoon freshly ground black pepper
2 garlic cloves, minced	¾ cup uncooked acini de pepe or pastina pasta
3 cups packed chopped kale; center ribs removed	2 cups shredded cooked chicken (about 12 ounces / 340 g)
1 cup minced carrots	
8 cups no-salt-added chicken or vegetable broth	3 tablespoons grated Parmesan cheese
¼ teaspoon kosher or sea salt	

1. In a large stockpot over medium heat, heat the oil. Add the garlic and cook for 30 seconds, stirring frequently. Add the kale and carrots and cook for 5 minutes, stirring occasionally. Add the broth, salt, and pepper, and turn the heat to high. Bring the broth to a boil, and add the pasta. Reduce the heat to medium and cook for 10 minutes, or until the pasta is cooked through, stirring every few minutes so the pasta doesn't stick to the bottom. Add the chicken, and cook for another 2 minutes to warm through.
2. Ladle the soup into six bowls. Top each with ½ tablespoon of cheese and serve.

Per Serving calories: 275 | fat: 19.0g | protein: 16.0g | carbs: 11.0g | fiber: 2.0g | sodium: 298mg

Green Bean and Halloumi Salad

Prep time: 20 minutes | Cook time: 5 minutes | Serves 2

Dressing:	Salad:
¼ cup unsweetened coconut milk	½ pound (227 g) fresh green beans, trimmed
1 tablespoon olive oil	2 ounces (57 g) Halloumi cheese, sliced into 2 (½-inch-thick) slices
2 teaspoons freshly squeezed lemon juice	
¼ teaspoon garlic powder	½ cup halved cherry or grape tomatoes
¼ teaspoon onion powder	¼ cup thinly sliced sweet onion
Pinch salt	
Pinch freshly ground black pepper	

Make the Dressing

1. Combine the coconut milk, olive oil, lemon juice, onion powder, garlic powder, salt, and pepper in a small bowl and whisk well. Set aside.

Make the Salad

2. Fill a medium-size pot with about 1 inch of water and add the green beans. Cover and steam them for about 3 to 4 minutes, or just until beans are tender. Do not overcook. Drain beans, rinse them immediately with cold water, and set them aside to cool.
3. Heat a nonstick skillet over medium-high heat and place the slices of Halloumi in the hot pan. After about 2 minutes, check to see if the cheese is golden on the bottom. If it is, flip the slices and cook for another minute or until the second side is golden. Remove cheese from the pan and cut each piece into cubes (about 1-inch square).
4. Place the green beans, halloumi slices, tomatoes, and onion in a large bowl and toss to combine.
5. Drizzle the dressing over the salad and toss well to combine. Serve immediately.

Per Serving calories: 274 | fat: 18.1g | protein: 8.0g | carbs: 16.8g | fiber: 5.1g | sodium: 499mg

Citrus Salad with Kale and Fennel

Prep time: 15 minutes | Cook time: 0 minutes | Serves 2

Dressing:	Salad:
3 tablespoons olive oil	2 cups packed baby kale
2 tablespoons fresh orange juice	1 medium navel or blood orange, segmented
1 tablespoon blood orange vinegar, other orange vinegar, or cider vinegar	½ small fennel bulb, stems and leaves removed, sliced into matchsticks
1 tablespoon honey	3 tablespoons toasted pecans, chopped
Salt and freshly ground black pepper, to taste	2 ounces (57 g) goat cheese, crumbled

Make the Dressing

1. Mix the olive oil, orange juice, vinegar, and honey in a small bowl and whisk to combine. Season with salt and pepper to taste. Set aside.

Make the Salad

2. Divide the baby kale, orange segments, fennel, pecans, and goat cheese evenly between two plates.
3. Drizzle half of the dressing over each salad and serve.

Per Serving calories: 503 | fat: 39.1g | protein: 13.2g | carbs: 31.2g | fiber: 6.1g | sodium: 156mg

Arugula, Watermelon, and Feta Salad

Prep time: 10 minutes | Cook time: 0 minutes | Serves 2

3 cups packed arugula	2 ounces (57 g) feta cheese, crumbled
2½ cups watermelon, cut into bite-size cubes	
	2 tablespoons balsamic glaze

1. Divide the arugula between two plates.
2. Divide the watermelon cubes between the beds of arugula.
3. Scatter half of the feta cheese over each salad.
4. Drizzle about 1 tablespoon of the glaze (or more if desired) over each salad. Serve immediately.

Per Serving

calories: 157 | fat: 6.9g | protein: 6.1g | carbs: 22.0g | fiber: 1.1g | sodium: 328mg

Mediterranean Tomato Hummus Soup

Prep time: 10 minutes | Cook time: 10 minutes | Serves 2

1 (14.5-ounce / 411-g) can crushed tomatoes with basil	Salt, to taste
2 cups low-sodium chicken stock	¼ cup thinly sliced fresh basil leaves, for garnish (optional)
1 cup roasted red pepper hummus	

1. Combine the canned tomatoes, hummus, and chicken stock in a blender and blend until smooth. Pour the mixture into a saucepan and bring it to a boil. Season with salt to taste. Serve garnished with the fresh basil, if desired.

Per Serving

calories: 147 | fat: 6.2g | protein: 5.2g | carbs: 20.1g | fiber: 4.1g | sodium: 682mg

Vegetable Fagioli Soup

Prep time: 30 minutes | Cook time: 60 minutes | Serves 2

1 tablespoon olive oil	1 (15-ounce / 425-g) can red kidney beans, drained and rinsed
2 medium carrots, diced	
2 medium celery stalks, diced	
½ medium onion, diced	1 (15-ounce / 425-g) can cannellini beans, drained and rinsed
1 large garlic clove, minced	
3 tablespoons tomato paste	
4 cups low-sodium vegetable broth	½ cup chopped fresh basil
1 cup packed kale, stemmed and chopped	Salt and freshly ground black pepper, to taste

1. Heat the olive oil in a stockpot over medium-high heat. Add the carrots, celery, onion, and garlic and sauté for 10 minutes, or until the vegetables start to turn golden.
2. Stir in the tomato paste and cook for about 30 seconds.
3. Add the vegetable broth and bring the soup to a boil. Cover and reduce the heat to low. Cook the soup for 45 minutes, or until the carrots are tender.
4. Using an immersion blender, purée the soup so that it's partly smooth, but with some chunks of vegetables.
5. Add the kale, beans, and basil. Season with salt and pepper to taste, then serve.

Per Serving

calories: 217 | fat: 4.2g | protein: 10.0g | carbs: 36.2g | fiber: 10.2g | sodium: 482mg

Avgolemono (Lemon Chicken Soup)

Prep time: 15 minutes | Cook time: 60 minutes | Serves 2

½ large onion
2 medium carrots
1 celery stalk
1 garlic clove
5 cups low-sodium chicken stock
¼ cup brown rice
1½ cups (about 5 ounces / 142 g) shredded rotisserie chicken

3 tablespoons freshly squeezed lemon juice
1 egg yolk
2 tablespoons chopped fresh dill
2 tablespoons chopped fresh parsley
Salt, to taste

1. Put the onion, carrots, celery, and garlic in a food processor and pulse until the vegetables are minced.
2. Add the vegetables and chicken stock to a stockpot and bring it to a boil over high heat.
3. Reduce the heat to medium-low and add the rice, shredded chicken and lemon juice. Cover and let the soup simmer for 40 minutes, or until the rice is cooked.
4. In a small bowl, whisk the egg yolk lightly. Slowly, while whisking with one hand, pour about ½ of a ladle of the broth into the egg yolk to warm, or temper, the yolk. Slowly add another ladle of broth and continue to whisk.
5. Remove the soup from the heat and pour the whisked egg yolk–broth mixture into the pot. Stir well to combine.
6. Add the fresh dill and parsley. Season with salt to taste and serve.

Per Serving

calories: 172 | fat: 4.2g | protein: 18.2g | carbs: 16.1g | fiber: 2.1g | sodium: 232m

g

Chapter 4

Sandwiches, Pizzas, and Wraps

Falafel Balls with Tahini Sauce

Prep time: 2 hours 20 minutes | Cook time: 20 minutes | Serves 4

Tahini Sauce:
½ cup tahini
2 tablespoons lemon juice
¼ cup finely chopped flat-leaf parsley
2 cloves garlic, minced
½ cup cold water, as needed

Falafel:
1 cup dried chickpeas, soaked overnight, drained
¼ cup chopped flat-leaf parsley

¼ cup chopped cilantro
1 large onion, chopped
1 teaspoon cumin
½ teaspoon chili flakes
4 cloves garlic
1 teaspoon sea salt
5 tablespoons almond flour
1½ teaspoons baking soda, dissolved in 1 teaspoon water
2 cups peanut oil
1 medium bell pepper, chopped
1 medium tomato, chopped
4 whole-wheat pita breads

Make the Tahini Sauce
1. Combine the ingredients for the tahini sauce in a small bowl. Stir to mix well until smooth.
2. Wrap the bowl in plastic and refrigerate until ready to serve.

Make the Falafel
3. Put the chickpeas, parsley, cilantro, onion, cumin, chili flakes, garlic, and salt in a food processor. Pulse to mix well but not puréed.
4. Add the flour and baking soda to the food processor, then pulse to form a smooth and tight dough.
5. Put the dough in a large bowl and wrap in plastic. Refrigerate for at least 2 hours to let it rise.
6. Divide and shape the dough into walnut-sized small balls.
7. Pour the peanut oil in a large pot and heat over high heat until the temperature of the oil reaches 375°F (190°C).
8. Drop 6 balls into the oil each time, and fry for 5 minutes or until golden brown and crispy. Turn the balls with a strainer to make them fried evenly.
9. Transfer the balls on paper towels with the strainer, then drain the oil from the balls.
10. Roast the pita breads in the oven for 5 minutes or until golden brown, if needed, then stuff the pitas with falafel balls and top with bell peppers and tomatoes. Drizzle with tahini sauce and serve immediately.

Per Serving
calories: 574 | fat: 27.1g | protein: 19.8g | carbs: 69.7g | fiber: 13.4g | sodium: 1246mg

Glazed Mushroom and Vegetable Fajitas

Prep time: 20 minutes | Cook time: 20 minutes | Makes 6

Spicy Glazed Mushrooms:
1 teaspoon olive oil
1 (10- to 12-ounce / 284- to 340-g) package cremini mushrooms, rinsed and drained, cut into thin slices
½ to 1 teaspoon chili powder
Sea salt and freshly ground black pepper, to taste
1 teaspoon maple syrup

Fajitas:
2 teaspoons olive oil
1 onion, chopped
Sea salt, to taste
1 bell pepper, any color, deseeded and sliced into long strips
1 zucchini, cut into large matchsticks
6 whole-grain tortilla
2 carrots, grated
3 to 4 scallions, sliced
½ cup fresh cilantro, finely chopped

Make the Spicy Glazed Mushrooms
1. Heat the olive oil in a nonstick skillet over medium heat until shimmering.
2. Add the mushrooms and sauté for 10 minutes or until tender.
3. Sprinkle the mushrooms with chili powder, salt, and ground black pepper. Drizzle with maple syrup. Stir to mix well and cook for 5 to 7 minutes or until the mushrooms are glazed. Set aside until ready to use.

Make the Fajitas
4. Heat the olive oil in the same skillet over medium heat until shimmering.
5. Add the onion and sauté for 5 minutes or until translucent. Sprinkle with salt.
6. Add the bell pepper and zucchini and sauté for 7 minutes or until tender.
7. Meanwhile, toast the tortilla in the oven for 5 minutes or until golden brown.
8. Allow the tortilla to cool for a few minutes until they can be handled, then assemble the tortilla with glazed mushrooms, sautéed vegetables and remaining vegetables to make the fajitas. Serve immediately.

Per Serving
calories: 403 | fat: 14.8g | protein: 11.2g | carbs: 7.9g | fiber: 7.0g | sodium: 230mg

Cheesy Fig Pizzas with Garlic Oil

Prep time: 1 day 40 minutes | Cook time: 10 minutes | Makes 2 pizzas

Dough:
1 cup almond flour
1½ cups whole-wheat flour
¾ teaspoon instant or rapid-rise yeast
2 teaspoons raw honey
1¼ cups ice water
2 tablespoons extra-virgin olive oil
1¾ teaspoons sea salt

Garlic Oil:
4 tablespoons extra-virgin olive oil, divided

½ teaspoon dried thyme
2 garlic cloves, minced
⅛ teaspoon sea salt
½ teaspoon freshly ground pepper

Topping:
1 cup fresh basil leaves
1 cup crumbled feta cheese
8 ounces (227 g) fresh figs, stemmed and quartered lengthwise
2 tablespoons raw honey

Make the Dough

1. Combine the flours, yeast, and honey in a food processor, pulse to combine well. Gently add water while pulsing. Let the dough sit for 10 minutes.
2. Mix the olive oil and salt in the dough and knead the dough until smooth. Wrap in plastic and refrigerate for at least 1 day.

Make the Garlic Oil

3. Heat 2 tablespoons of olive oil in a nonstick skillet over medium-low heat until shimmering.
4. Add the thyme, garlic, salt, and pepper and sauté for 30 seconds or until fragrant. Set them aside until ready to use.

Make the Pizzas

5. Preheat the oven to 500°F (260°C). Grease two baking sheets with 2 tablespoons of olive oil.
6. Divide the dough in half and shape into two balls. Press the balls into 13- inch rounds. Sprinkle the rounds with a tough of flour if they are sticky.
7. Top the rounds with the garlic oil and basil leaves, then arrange the rounds on the baking sheets. Scatter with feta cheese and figs.
8. Put the sheets in the preheated oven and bake for 9 minutes or until lightly browned. Rotate the pizza halfway through. Remove the pizzas from the oven, then discard the bay leaves. Drizzle with honey. Let sit for 5 minutes and serve immediately.

Per Serving (1 pizza)
calories: 1350 | fat: 46.5g | protein: 27.5g | carbs: 221.9g | fiber: 23.7g | sodium: 2898mg

Mashed Grape Tomato Pizzas

Prep time: 10 minutes | Cook time: 20 minutes | Serves 6

3 cups grape tomatoes, halved
1 teaspoon chopped fresh thyme leaves
2 garlic cloves, minced
¼ teaspoon kosher salt
¼ teaspoon freshly ground black pepper
1 tablespoon extra-virgin olive oil
¾ cup shredded Parmesan cheese
6 whole-wheat pita breads

1. Preheat the oven to 425°F (220°C).
2. Combine the tomatoes, thyme, garlic, salt, ground black pepper, and olive oil in a baking pan.
3. Roast in the preheated oven for 20 minutes. Remove the pan from the oven, mash the tomatoes with a spatula and stir to mix well halfway through the cooking time.
4. Meanwhile, divide and spread the cheese over each pita bread, then place the bread in a separate baking pan and roast in the oven for 5 minutes or until golden brown and the cheese melts.
5. Transfer the pita bread onto a large plate, then top with the roasted mashed tomatoes. Serve immediately.

Per Serving calories: 140 | fat: 5.1g | protein: 6.2g | carbs: 16.9g | fiber: 2.0g | sodium: 466mg

Vegetable and Cheese Lavash Pizza

Prep time: 15 minutes | Cook time: 11 minutes | Serves 4

2 (12 by 9-inch) lavash breads
2 tablespoons extra-virgin olive oil
10 ounces (284 g) frozen spinach, thawed and squeezed dry
1 cup shredded fontina cheese
1 tomato, cored and cut into ½-inch pieces
½ cup pitted large green olives, chopped
¼ teaspoon red pepper flakes
3 garlic cloves, minced
¼ teaspoon sea salt
¼ teaspoon ground black pepper
½ cup grated Parmesan cheese

1. Preheat oven to 475°F (246°C).
2. Brush the lavash breads with olive oil, then place them on two baking sheet. Heat in the preheated oven for 4 minutes or until lightly browned. Flip the breads halfway through the cooking time.
3. Meanwhile, combine the spinach, fontina cheese, tomato pieces, olives, red pepper flakes, garlic, salt, and black pepper in a large bowl. Stir to mix well.
4. Remove the lavash bread from the oven and sit them on two large plates, spread them with the spinach mixture, then scatter with the Parmesan cheese on top.
5. Bake in the oven for 7 minutes or until the cheese melts and well browned. Slice and serve warm.

Per Serving calories: 431 | fat: 21.5g | protein: 20.0g | carbs: 38.4g | fiber: 2.5g | sodium: 854mg

Dulse, Avocado, and Tomato Pitas

Prep time: 10 minutes | Cook time: 30 minutes | Makes 4 pitas

2 teaspoons coconut oil
½ cup dulse, picked through and separated
Ground black pepper, to taste
2 avocados, sliced
2 tablespoons lime juice
¼ cup chopped cilantro

2 scallions, white and light green parts, sliced
Sea salt, to taste
4 (8-inch) whole wheat pitas, sliced in half
4 cups chopped romaine
4 plum tomatoes, sliced

1. Heat the coconut oil in a nonstick skillet over medium heat until melted. Add the dulse and sauté for 5 minutes or until crispy. Sprinkle with ground black pepper and turn off the heat. Set aside. Put the avocado, lime juice, cilantro, and scallions in a food processor and sprinkle with salt and ground black pepper. Pulse to combine well until smooth.
2. Toast the pitas in a baking pan in the oven for 1 minute until soft.
3. Transfer the pitas to a clean work surface and open. Spread the avocado mixture over the pitas, then top with dulse, romaine, and tomato slices. Serve immediately.

Per Serving (1 pita) calories: 412 | fat: 18.7g | protein: 9.1g | carbs: 56.1g | fiber: 12.5g | sodium: 695mg

Greek Vegetable Salad Pita

Prep time: 10 minutes | Cook time: 0 minutes | Serves 4

½ cup baby spinach leaves
½ small red onion, thinly sliced
½ small cucumber, deseeded and chopped
1 tomato, chopped
1 cup chopped romaine lettuce
1 tablespoon extra-virgin olive oil

½ tablespoon red wine vinegar
1 teaspoon Dijon mustard
1 tablespoon crumbled feta cheese
Sea salt and freshly ground pepper, to taste
1 whole-wheat pita

1. Combine all the ingredients, except for the pita, in a large bowl. Toss to mix well. Stuff the pita with the salad, then serve immediately. **Per Serving** calories: 137 | fat: 8.1g | protein: 3.1g | carbs: 14.3g | fiber: 2.4g | sodium: 166mg

Artichoke and Cucumber Hoagies

Prep time: 10 minutes | Cook time: 15 minutes | Makes 1

1 (12-ounce / 340-g) whole grain baguette, sliced in half horizontally
1 cup frozen and thawed artichoke hearts, roughly chopped
1 cucumber, sliced
2 tomatoes, sliced
1 red bell pepper, sliced

⅓ cup Kalamata olives, pitted and chopped
¼ small red onion, thinly sliced
Sea salt and ground black pepper, to taste
2 tablespoons pesto
Balsamic vinegar, to taste

1. range the baguette halves on a clean work surface, then cut off the top third from each half. Scoop some insides of the bottom half out and reserve as breadcrumbs.
2. Toast the baguette in a baking pan in the oven for 1 minute to brown lightly. Put the artichokes, cucumber, tomatoes, bell pepper, olives, and onion in a large bowl. Sprinkle with salt and ground black pepper. Toss to combine well.
3. Spread the bottom half of the baguette with the vegetable mixture and drizzle with balsamic vinegar, then smear the cut side of the baguette top with pesto. Assemble the two baguette halves. Wrap the hoagies in parchment paper and let sit for at least an hour before serving.

Per Serving (1 hoagies) calories: 1263 | fat: 37.7g | protein: 56.3g | carbs: 180.1g | fiber: 37.8g | sodium: 2137mg

Brown Rice and Black Bean Burgers

Prep time: 20 minutes | Cook time: 40 minutes | Makes 8 burgers

1 cup cooked brown rice
1 (15-ounce / 425-g) can black beans, drained and rinsed
1 tablespoon olive oil
2 tablespoons taco or Harissa seasoning
½ yellow onion, finely diced
1 beet, peeled and grated
1 carrot, peeled and grated
2 tablespoons no-salt-added tomato paste

2 tablespoons apple cider vinegar
3 garlic cloves, minced
¼ teaspoon sea salt
Ground black pepper, to taste
8 whole-wheat hamburger buns
Toppings:
16 lettuce leaves, rinsed well
8 tomato slices, rinsed well
Whole-grain mustard, to taste

1. Line a baking sheet with parchment paper. Put the brown rice and black beans in a food processor and pulse until mix well. Pour the mixture in a large bowl and set aside. Heat the olive oil in a nonstick skillet over medium heat until shimmering. Add the taco seasoning and stir for 1 minute or until fragrant. Add the onion, beet, and carrot and sauté for 5 minutes or until the onion is translucent and beet and carrot are tender. Pour in the tomato paste and vinegar, then add the garlic and cook for 3 minutes or until the sauce is thickened. Sprinkle with salt and ground black pepper. Transfer the vegetable mixture to the bowl of rice mixture, then stir to mix well until smooth. Divide and shape the mixture into 8 patties, then arrange the patties on the baking sheet and refrigerate for at least 1 hour. Preheat the oven to 400ºF (205ºC).
2. Remove the baking sheet from the refrigerator and allow to sit under room temperature for 10 minutes.
3. Bake in the preheated oven for 40 minutes or until golden brown on both sides. Flip the patties halfway through the cooking time. Remove the patties from the oven and allow to cool for 10 minutes. Assemble the buns with patties, lettuce, and tomato slices. Top the filling with mustard and serve immediately.
4. **Per Serving (1 burger)** calories: 544 | fat: 20.0g | protein: 15.8g | carbs: 76.0g | fiber: 10.6g | sodium: 446mg

Classic Socca

Prep time: 10 minutes | Cook time: 10 minutes | Serves 4

1½ cups chickpea flour	½ teaspoon ground black pepper
½ teaspoon ground turmeric	
½ teaspoon sea salt	2 tablespoons plus 2 teaspoons extra-virgin olive oil
	1½ cups water

1. Combine the chickpea flour, turmeric, salt, and black pepper in a bowl. Stir to mix well, then gently mix in 2 tablespoons of olive oil and water. Stir to mix until smooth.
2. Heat 2 teaspoons of olive oil in an 8-inch nonstick skillet over medium- high heat until shimmering. Add half cup of the mixture into the skillet and swirl the skillet so the mixture coat the bottom evenly. Cook for 5 minutes or until lightly browned and crispy. Flip the socca halfway through the cooking time. Repeat with the remaining mixture. Slice and serve warm. **Per Serving** calories: 207 | fat: 10.2g | protein: 7.9g | carbs: 20.7g | fiber: 3.9g | sodium: 315mg

Alfalfa Sprout and Nut Rolls

Prep time: 40 minutes | Cook time: 0 minutes | Makes 16 bite-size pieces

1 cup alfalfa sprouts	Zest and juice of 1 lemon
2 tablespoons Brazil nuts	Pinch cayenne pepper
½ cup chopped fresh cilantro	Sea salt and freshly ground black pepper, to taste
2 tablespoons flaked coconut	1 tablespoon melted coconut oil
1 garlic clove, minced	2 tablespoons water
2 tablespoons ground flaxseeds	2 whole-grain wraps

1. Combine all ingredients, except for the wraps, in a food processor, then pulse to combine well until smooth.
2. Unfold the wraps on a clean work surface, then spread the mixture over the wraps.
3. Roll the wraps up and refrigerate for 30 minutes until set.
4. Remove the rolls from the refrigerator and slice into 16 bite-sized pieces, if desired, and serve.

Per Serving (1 piece)

calories: 67 | fat: 7.1g | protein: 2.2g | carbs: 2.9g | fiber: 1.0g | sodium: 61mg

Mini Pork and Cucumber Lettuce Wraps

Prep time: 20 minutes | Cook time: 0 minutes | Makes 12 wraps

8 ounces (227 g) cooked ground pork	Juice of 1 lemon
1 cucumber, diced	1 tablespoon extra-virgin olive oil
1 tomato, diced	
1 red onion, sliced	Sea salt and freshly ground pepper, to taste
1 ounce (28 g) low-fat feta cheese, crumbled	12 small, intact iceberg lettuce leaves

1. Combine the ground pork, cucumber, tomato, and onion in a large bowl, then scatter with feta cheese.
2. Drizzle with lemon juice and olive oil, and sprinkle with salt and pepper. Toss to mix well.
3. Unfold the small lettuce leaves on a large plate or several small plates, then divide and top with the pork mixture.
4. Wrap and serve immediately.

Per Serving (1 warp)

calories: 78 | fat: 5.6g | protein: 5.5g | carbs: 1.4g | fiber: 0.3g | sodium: 50mg

Mushroom and Caramelized Onion Musakhan

Prep time: 20 minutes | Cook time: 1 hour 5 minutes | Serves 4

2 tablespoons sumac, plus more for sprinkling	3 medium white onions, coarsely chopped
1 teaspoon ground allspice	¼ cup water
½ teaspoon ground cardamom	Kosher salt, to taste
½ teaspoon ground cumin	1 whole-wheat Turkish flatbread
3 tablespoons extra-virgin olive oil, divided	¼ cup pine nuts
2 pounds (907 g) portobello mushroom caps, gills removed, caps halved and sliced ½ inch thick	1 lemon, wedged

1. Preheat the oven to 350°F (180°C).
2. Combine 2 tablespoons of sumac, allspice, cardamom, and cumin in a small bowl. Stir to mix well.
3. Heat 2 tablespoons of olive oil in an oven-proof skillet over medium-high heat until shimmering.
4. Add the mushroom to the skillet and sprinkle with half of sumac mixture. Sauté for 8 minutes or until the mushrooms are tender. You may need to work in batches to avoid overcrowding. Transfer the mushrooms to a plate and set side.
5. Heat 1 tablespoon of olive oil in the skillet over medium-high heat until shimmering.
6. Add the onion and sauté for 20 minutes or until caramelized. Sprinkle with remaining sumac mixture, then cook for 1 more minute.
7. Pour in the water and sprinkle with salt. Bring to a simmer.
8. Turn off the heat and put the mushroom back to the skillet.
9. Place the skillet in the preheated oven and bake for 30 minutes.
10. Remove the skillet from the oven and let the mushroom sit for 10 minutes until cooled down.
11. Heat the Turkish flatbread in a baking dish in the oven for 5 minutes or until warmed through.
12. Arrange the bread on a large plate and top with mushrooms, onions, and roasted pine nuts. Squeeze the lemon wedges over and sprinkle with more sumac. Serve immediately.

Per Serving

calories: 336 | fat: 18.7g | protein: 11.5g | carbs: 34.3g | fiber: 6.9g | sodium: 369mg

Red Pepper Coques with Pine Nuts

Prep time: 1 day 40 minutes | Cook time: 45 minutes | Makes 4 coques

Dough:
3 cups almond flour
½ teaspoon instant or rapid-rise yeast
2 teaspoons raw honey
1⅓ cups ice water
3 tablespoons extra-virgin olive oil
1½ teaspoons sea salt

Red Pepper Topping:
4 tablespoons extra-virgin olive oil, divided
2 cups jarred roasted red peppers, patted dry and sliced thinly

2 large onions, halved and sliced thin
3 garlic cloves, minced
¼ teaspoon red pepper flakes
2 bay leaves
3 tablespoons maple syrup
1½ teaspoons sea salt
3 tablespoons red whine vinegar

For Garnish:
¼ cup pine nuts (optional)
1 tablespoon minced fresh parsley

Make the Dough
1. Combine the flour, yeast, and honey in a food processor, pulse to combine well. Gently add water while pulsing. Let the dough sit for 10 minutes.
2. Mix the olive oil and salt in the dough and knead the dough until smooth. Wrap in plastic and refrigerate for at least 1 day.

Make the Topping
3. Heat 1 tablespoon of olive oil in a nonstick skillet over medium heat until shimmering.
4. Add the red peppers, onions, garlic, red pepper flakes, bay leaves, maple syrup, and salt. Sauté for 20 minutes or until the onion is caramelized.
5. Turn off the heat and discard the bay leaves. Remove the onion from the skillet and baste with wine vinegar. Let them sit until ready to use.

Make the Coques
6. Preheat the oven to 500°F (260°C). Grease two baking sheets with 1 tablespoon of olive oil.
7. Divide the dough ball into four balls, then press and shape them into equal-sized oval. Arrange the ovals on the baking sheets and pierce each dough about 12 times.
8. Rub the ovals with 2 tablespoons of olive oil and bake for 7 minutes or until puffed. Flip the ovals halfway through the cooking time.
9. Spread the ovals with the topping and pine nuts, then bake for an additional 15 minutes or until well browned.
10. Remove the coques from the oven and spread with parsley. Allow to cool for 10 minutes before serving.

Per Serving (1 coque)
calories: 658 | fat: 23.1g | protein: 3.4g | carbs: 112.0g | fiber: 6.2g | sodium: 1757mg

Ritzy Garden Burgers

Prep time: 1 hour 30 minutes | Cook time: 30 minutes | Serves 6

1 tablespoon avocado oil
1 yellow onion, diced
½ cup shredded carrots
4 garlic cloves, halved
1 (15 ounces / 425 g) can black beans, rinsed and drained
1 cup gluten-free rolled oats
¼ cup oil-packed sun-dried tomatoes, drained and chopped
½ cup sunflower seeds, toasted
1 teaspoon chili powder
1 teaspoon paprika
1 teaspoon ground cumin
½ cup fresh parsley, stems removed

¼ teaspoon ground red pepper flakes
¾ teaspoon sea salt
¼ teaspoon ground black pepper
¼ cup olive oil

For Serving:
6 whole-wheat buns, split in half and toasted
2 ripe avocados, sliced
1 cup kaiware sprouts or mung bean sprouts
1 ripe tomato, sliced

1. Line a baking sheet with parchment paper.
2. Heat 1 tablespoon of avocado oil in a nonstick skillet over medium heat.
3. Add the onion and carrots and sauté for 10 minutes or until the onion is caramelized.
4. Add the garlic and sauté for 30 seconds or until fragrant.
5. Transfer them into a food processor, then add the remaining ingredients, except for the olive oil. Pulse until chopped fine and the mixture holds together. Make sure not to purée the mixture.
6. Divide and form the mixture into six 4-inch diameter and ½-inch thick patties.
7. Arrange the patties on the baking sheet and wrap the sheet in plastic. Put the baking sheet in the refrigerator and freeze for at least an hour until firm.
8. Remove the baking sheet from the refrigerator, let them sit under room temperature for 10 minutes.
9. Heat the olive oil in a nonstick skillet over medium-high heat until shimmering.
10. Fry the patties in the skillet for 15 minutes or until lightly browned and crispy. Flip the patties halfway through the cooking time. You may need to work in batches to avoid overcrowding.
11. Assemble the buns with patties, avocados, sprouts, and tomato slices to make the burgers.

Per Serving
calories: 613 | fat: 23.1g | protein: 26.2g | carbs: 88.3g | fiber: 22.9g | sodium: 456mg

Roasted Tomato Panini

Prep time: 15 minutes | Cook time: 3 hours 6 minutes | Serves 2

2 teaspoons olive oil	Sea salt and freshly ground pepper, to taste
4 Roma tomatoes, halved	4 slices whole-grain bread
4 cloves garlic	4 basil leaves
1 tablespoon Italian seasoning	2 slices fresh Mozzarella cheese

1. Preheat the oven to 250°F (121°C). Grease a baking pan with olive oil.
2. Place the tomatoes and garlic in the baking pan, then sprinkle with Italian seasoning, salt, and ground pepper. Toss to coat well.
3. Roast in the preheated oven for 3 hours or until the tomatoes are lightly wilted.
4. Preheat the panini press.
5. Make the panini: Place two slices of bread on a clean work surface, then top them with wilted tomatoes. Sprinkle with basil and spread with Mozzarella cheese. Top them with remaining two slices of bread.
6. Cook the panini for 6 minutes or until lightly browned and the cheese melts. Flip the panini halfway through the cooking. Serve immediately.

Per Serving

calories: 323 | fat: 12.0g | protein: 17.4g | carbs: 37.5g | fiber: 7.5g | sodium: 603mg

Samosas in Potatoes

Prep time: 20 minutes | Cook time: 30 minutes | Makes 8

4 small potatoes	Sea salt and freshly ground black pepper, to taste
1 teaspoon coconut oil	¼ cup frozen peas, thawed
1 small onion, finely chopped	2 carrots, grated
1 small piece ginger, minced	¼ cup chopped fresh cilantro
2 garlic cloves, minced	
2 to 3 teaspoons curry powder	

1. Preheat the oven to 350°F (180°C).
2. Poke small holes into potatoes with a fork, then wrap with aluminum foil.
3. Bake in the preheated oven for 30 minutes until tender.
4. Meanwhile, heat the coconut oil in a nonstick skillet over medium-high heat until melted.
5. Add the onion and sauté for 5 minutes or until translucent.
6. Add the ginger and garlic to the skillet and sauté for 3 minutes or until fragrant.
7. Add the curry powder, salt, and ground black pepper, then stir to coat the onion. Remove them from the heat.
8. When the cooking of potatoes is complete, remove the potatoes from the foil and slice in half.
9. Hollow to potato halves with a spoon, then combine the potato fresh with sautéed onion, peas, carrots, and cilantro in a large bowl. Stir to mix well.
10. Spoon the mixture back to the tomato skins and serve immediately.

Per Serving (1 samosa)

calories: 131 | fat: 13.9g | protein: 3.2g | carbs: 8.8g | fiber: 3.0g | sodium: 111mg

Spicy Black Bean and Poblano Dippers

Prep time: 20 minutes | Cook time: 21 minutes | Serves 8

2 tablespoons avocado oil, plus more for brushing the dippers	1 yellow onion, quartered
	2 garlic cloves
	1 teaspoon chili powder
1 (15 ounces / 425 g) can black beans, drained and rinsed	1 teaspoon ground cumin
	1 teaspoon sea salt
	24 organic corn tortillas
1 poblano, deseeded and quartered	
1 jalapeño, halved and deseeded	
½ cup fresh cilantro, leaves and tender stems	

1. Preheat the oven to 400°F (205°C). Line a baking sheet with parchment paper and grease with avocado oil.
2. Combine the remaining ingredients, except for the tortillas, in a food processor, then pulse until chopped finely and the mixture holds together. Make sure not to purée the mixture.
3. Warm the tortillas on the baking sheet in the preheated oven for 1 minute or until softened.
4. Add a tablespoon of the mixture in the middle of each tortilla. Fold one side of the tortillas over the mixture and tuck to roll them up tightly to make the dippers.
5. Arrange the dippers on the baking sheet and brush them with avocado oil.
1. Bake in the oven for 20 minutes or until well browned. Flip the dippers halfway through the cooking time.
6. Serve immediately.

Per Serving

calories: 388 | fat: 6.5g | protein: 16.2g | carbs: 69.6g | fiber: 13.5g | sodium: 340mg

Spicy Tofu Tacos with Cherry Tomato Salsa

Prep time: 20 minutes | Cook time: 11 minutes | Makes 4 tacos

Cherry Tomato Salsa:
¼ cup sliced cherry tomatoes
½ jalapeño, deseeded and sliced
Juice of 1 lime
1 garlic clove, minced
Sea salt and freshly ground black pepper, to taste
2 teaspoons extra-virgin olive oil

Spicy Tofu Taco Filling:
4 tablespoons water, divided
½ cup canned black beans, rinsed and drained
2 teaspoons fresh chopped chives, divided
¾ teaspoon ground cumin, divided
¾ teaspoon smoked paprika, divided
Dash cayenne pepper (optional)
¼ teaspoon sea salt
¼ teaspoon freshly ground black pepper
1 teaspoon extra-virgin olive oil
6 ounces (170 g) firm tofu, drained, rinsed, and pressed
4 corn tortillas
¼ avocado, sliced
¼ cup fresh cilantro

Make the Cherry Tomato Salsa
1. Combine the ingredients for the salsa in a small bowl. Stir to mix well. Set aside until ready to use.

Make the Spicy Tofu Taco Filling
2. Add 2 tablespoons of water into a saucepan, then add the black beans and sprinkle with 1 teaspoon of chives, ½ teaspoon of cumin, ¼ teaspoon of smoked paprika, and cayenne. Stir to mix well.
3. Cook for 5 minutes over medium heat until heated through, then mash the black beans with the back of a spoon. Turn off the heat and set aside.
4. Add remaining water into a bowl, then add the remaining chives, cumin, and paprika. Sprinkle with cayenne, salt, and black pepper. Stir to mix well. Set aside.
5. Heat the olive oil in a nonstick skillet over medium heat until shimmering.
6. Add the tofu and drizzle with taco sauce, then sauté for 5 minutes or until the seasoning is absorbed. Remove the tofu from the skillet and set aside.
7. Warm the tortillas in the skillet for 1 minutes or until heated through.
8. Transfer the tortillas onto a large plate and top with tofu, mashed black beans, avocado, cilantro, then drizzle the tomato salsa over. Serve immediately.

Per Serving (1 taco)
calories: 240 | fat: 9.0g | protein: 11.6g | carbs: 31.6g | fiber: 6.7g | sodium: 195mg

Super Cheeses and Mushroom Tart

Prep time: 30 minutes | Cook time: 1 hour 30 minutes | Serves 4 to 6

Crust:
1¾ cups almond flour
1 tablespoon raw honey
¾ teaspoon sea salt
¼ cup extra-virgin olive oil
⅓ cup water

Filling:
2 tablespoons extra-virgin olive oil, divided
1 pound (454 g) white mushrooms, trimmed and sliced thinly
Sea salt, to taste
1 garlic clove, minced
2 teaspoons minced fresh thyme
¼ cup shredded Mozzarella cheese
½ cup grated Parmesan cheese
4 ounces (113 g) part-skim ricotta cheese
Ground black pepper, to taste
2 tablespoons ground basil

Make the Crust
1. Preheat the oven to 350°F (180°C).
2. Combine the flour, honey, salt and olive oil in a large bowl. Stir to mix well. Gently mix in the water until a smooth dough forms.
3. Drop walnut-size clumps from the dough in the single layer on a tart pan. Press the clumps to coat the bottom of the pan.
4. Bake the crust in the preheated oven for 50 minutes or until firm and browned. Rotate the pan halfway through.

Make the Filling
5. While baking the crust, heat 1 tablespoon of olive oil in a nonstick skillet over medium-high heat until shimmering.
6. Add the mushrooms and sprinkle with ½ teaspoon of salt. Sauté for 15 minutes or until tender.
7. Add the garlic and thyme and sauté for 30 seconds or until fragrant.

Make the Tart
8. Meanwhile, combine the cheeses, salt, ground black pepper, and 1 tablespoon of olive oil in a bowl. Stir to mix well.
9. Spread the cheese mixture over the crust, then top with the mushroom mixture.
10. Bake in the oven for 20 minutes or until the cheeses are frothy and the tart is heated through. Rotate the pan halfway through the baking time.
11. Remove the tart from the oven. Allow to cool for at least 10 minutes, then sprinkle with basil. Slice to serve.

Per Serving
calories: 530 | fat: 26.6g | protein: 11.7g | carbs: 63.5g | fiber: 4.6g | sodium: 785mg

Mediterranean Greek Salad Wraps

Prep time: 15 minutes | Cook time: 0 minutes | Serves 4

1½ cups seedless cucumber, peeled and chopped
1 cup chopped tomato
½ cup finely chopped fresh mint
¼ cup diced red onion
1 (2.25-ounce / 64-g) can sliced black olives, drained
2 tablespoons extra-virgin olive oil
1 tablespoon red wine vinegar
¼ teaspoon kosher salt
¼ teaspoon freshly ground black pepper
½ cup crumbled goat cheese
4 whole-wheat flatbread wraps or soft whole-wheat tortillas

1. In a large bowl, stir together the cucumber, tomato, mint, onion and olives.
2. In a small bowl, whisk together the oil, vinegar, salt, and pepper. Spread the dressing over the salad. Toss gently to combine.
3. On a clean work surface, lay the wraps. Divide the goat cheese evenly among the wraps. Scoop a quarter of the salad filling down the center of each wrap.
4. Fold up each wrap: Start by folding up the bottom, then fold one side over and fold the other side over the top. Repeat with the remaining wraps.
5. Serve immediately.

Per Serving

calories: 225 | fat: 12.0g | protein: 12.0g | carbs: 18.0g | fiber: 4.0g | sodium: 349mg

Salmon Salad Wraps

Prep time: 10 minutes | Cook time: 0 minutes | Serves 6

1 pound (454 g) salmon fillets, cooked and flaked
½ cup diced carrots
½ cup diced celery
3 tablespoons diced red onion
3 tablespoons chopped fresh dill
2 tablespoons capers
1½ tablespoons extra-virgin olive oil
1 tablespoon aged balsamic vinegar
¼ teaspoon kosher or sea salt
½ teaspoon freshly ground black pepper
4 whole-wheat flatbread wraps or soft whole-wheat tortillas

1. In a large bowl, stir together all the ingredients, except for the wraps.
2. On a clean work surface, lay the wraps. Divide the salmon mixture evenly among the wraps. Fold up the bottom of the wraps, then roll up the wrap.
3. Serve immediately.

Per Serving

calories: 194 | fat: 8.0g | protein: 18.0g | carbs: 13.0g | fiber: 3.0g | sodium: 536mg

Baked Parmesan Chicken Wraps

Prep time: 10 minutes | Cook time: 18 minutes | Serves 6

1 pound (454 g) boneless, skinless chicken breasts
1 large egg
¼ cup unsweetened almond milk
⅔ cup whole-wheat bread crumbs
½ cup grated Parmesan cheese
¾ teaspoon garlic powder, divided
1 cup canned low-sodium or no-salt-added crushed tomatoes
1 teaspoon dried oregano
6 (8-inch) whole-wheat tortillas, or whole-grain spinach wraps
1 cup fresh Mozzarella cheese, sliced
1½ cups loosely packed fresh flat-leaf (Italian) parsley, chopped
Cooking spray

1. Preheat the oven to 425ºF (220ºC). Line a large, rimmed baking sheet with aluminum foil. Place a wire rack on the aluminum foil, and spritz the rack with nonstick cooking spray. Set aside.
2. Place the chicken breasts into a large plastic bag. With a rolling pin, pound the chicken so it is evenly flattened, about ¼ inch thick. Slice the chicken into six portions.
3. In a bowl, whisk together the egg and milk. In another bowl, stir together the bread crumbs, Parmesan cheese and ½ teaspoon of the garlic powder.
4. Dredge each chicken breast portion into the egg mixture, and then into the Parmesan crumb mixture, pressing the crumbs into the chicken so they stick. Arrange the chicken on the prepared wire rack.
5. Bake in the preheated oven for 15 to 18 minutes, or until the internal temperature of the chicken reads 165ºF (74ºC) on a meat thermometer and any juices run clear.
6. Transfer the chicken to a cutting board, and cut each portion diagonally into ½-inch pieces.
7. In a small, microwave-safe bowl, stir together the tomatoes, oregano, and the remaining ¼ teaspoon of the garlic powder. Cover the bowl with a paper towel and microwave for about 1 minute on high, until very hot. Set aside.
8. Wrap the tortillas in a damp paper towel and microwave for 30 to 45 seconds on high, or until warmed through.
9. Assemble the wraps: Divide the chicken slices evenly among the six tortillas and top with the sliced Mozzarella cheese. Spread 1 tablespoon of the warm tomato sauce over the cheese on each tortilla, and top each with about ¼ cup of the parsley.
10. Wrap the tortilla: Fold up the bottom of the tortilla, then fold one side over and fold the other side over the top.
11. Serve the wraps warm with the remaining sauce for dipping.

Per Serving

calories: 358 | fat: 12.0g | protein: 21.0g | carbs: 41.0g | fiber: 7.0g | sodium: 755mg

Eggplant, Spinach, and Feta Sandwiches

Prep time: 10 minutes | Cook time: 6 to 8 minutes | Serves 2

1 medium eggplant, sliced into ½-inch-thick slices	5 to 6 tablespoons hummus
2 tablespoons olive oil	4 slices whole-wheat bread, toasted
Sea salt and freshly ground pepper, to taste	1 cup baby spinach leaves
	2 ounces (57 g) feta cheese, softened

1. Preheat the grill to medium-high heat.
2. Salt both sides of the sliced eggplant, and let sit for 20 minutes to draw out the bitter juices.
3. Rinse the eggplant and pat dry with a paper towel.
4. Brush the eggplant slices with olive oil and season with sea salt and freshly ground pepper to taste.
5. Grill the eggplant until lightly charred on both sides but still slightly firm in the middle, about 3 to 4 minutes per side.
6. Spread the hummus on the bread slices and top with the spinach leaves, feta cheese, and grilled eggplant. Top with the other slice of bread and serve immediately.

Per Serving

calories: 493 | fat: 25.3g | protein: 17.1g | carbs: 50.9g | fiber: 14.7g | sodium: 789mg

Grilled Caesar Salad Sandwiches

Prep time: 5 minutes | Cook time: 5 minutes | Serves 2

¾ cup olive oil, divided	¼ teaspoon Worcestershire sauce
2 romaine lettuce hearts, left intact	Sea salt and freshly ground pepper, to taste
3 to 4 anchovy fillets	2 slices whole-wheat bread, toasted
Juice of 1 lemon	
2 to 3 cloves garlic, peeled	Freshly grated Parmesan cheese, for serving
1 teaspoon Dijon mustard	

1. Preheat the grill to medium-high heat and oil the grates.
2. On a cutting board, drizzle the lettuce with 1 to 2 tablespoons of olive oil and place on the grates.
3. Grill for 5 minutes, turning until lettuce is slightly charred on all sides. Let lettuce cool enough to handle.
4. In a food processor, combine the remaining olive oil with the anchovies, lemon juice, garlic, mustard, and Worcestershire sauce.
5. Pulse the ingredients until you have a smooth emulsion. Season with sea salt and freshly ground pepper to taste. Chop the lettuce in half and place on the bread.
6. Drizzle with the dressing and serve with a sprinkle of Parmesan cheese.

Per Serving

calories: 949 | fat: 85.6g | protein: 12.9g | carbs: 34.1g | fiber: 13.9g | sodium: 786mg

Green Veggie Sandwiches

Prep time: 20 minutes | Cook time: 0 minutes | Serves 2

Spread:	**Sandwiches:**
1 (15-ounce / 425-g) can cannellini beans, drained and rinsed	4 whole-grain bread slices, toasted
⅓ cup packed fresh basil leaves	8 English cucumber slices
⅓ cup packed fresh parsley	1 large beefsteak tomato, cut into slices
⅓ cup chopped fresh chives	1 large avocado, halved, pitted, and cut into slices
2 garlic cloves, chopped	1 small yellow bell pepper, cut into slices
Zest and juice of ½ lemon	2 handfuls broccoli sprouts
1 tablespoon apple cider vinegar	2 handfuls fresh spinach

Make the Spread

1. In a food processor, combine the cannellini beans, basil, parsley, chives, garlic, lemon zest and juice, and vinegar. Pulse a few times, scrape down the sides, and purée until smooth. You may need to scrape down the sides again to incorporate all the basil and parsley. Refrigerate for at least 1 hour to allow the flavors to blend.
1. Assemble the Sandwiches
2. Build your sandwiches by spreading several tablespoons of spread on each slice of bread. Layer two slices of bread with the cucumber, tomato, avocado, bell pepper, broccoli sprouts, and spinach. Top with the remaining bread slices and press down lightly.
3. Serve immediately.

Per Serving

calories: 617 | fat: 21.1g | protein: 28.1g | carbs: 86.1g | fiber: 25.6g | sodium: 593mg

Pizza Pockets

Prep time: 10 minutes | Cook time: 0 minutes | Serves 2

½ cup tomato sauce	2 canned artichoke hearts, drained and chopped
½ teaspoon oregano	
½ teaspoon garlic powder	2 ounces (57 g) pepperoni, chopped
½ cup chopped black olives	½ cup shredded Mozzarella cheese
	1 whole-wheat pita, halved

1. In a medium bowl, stir together the tomato sauce, oregano, and garlic powder.
2. Add the olives, artichoke hearts, pepperoni, and cheese. Stir to mix.
3. Spoon the mixture into the pita halves and serve.

Per Serving

calories: 375 | fat: 23.5g | protein: 17.1g | carbs: 27.1g | fiber: 6.1g | sodium: 1080mg

Mushroom-Pesto Baked Pizza

Prep time: 5 minutes | Cook time: 15 minutes | Serves 2

1 teaspoon extra-virgin olive oil

½ cup sliced mushrooms

½ red onion, sliced

Salt and freshly ground black pepper

¼ cup store-bought pesto sauce

2 whole-wheat flatbreads

¼ cup shredded Mozzarella cheese

1. Preheat the oven to 350ºF (180ºC). In a small skillet, heat the oil over medium heat. Add the mushrooms and onion, and season with salt and pepper. Sauté for 3 to 5 minutes until the onion and mushrooms begin to soften. Spread 2 tablespoons of pesto on each flatbread. Divide the mushroom-onion mixture between the two flatbreads. Top each with 2 tablespoons of cheese. Place the flatbreads on a baking sheet and bake for 10 to 12 minutes until the cheese is melted and bubbly. Serve warm.

Per Serving calories: 348 | fat: 23.5g | protein: 14.2g | carbs: 28.1g | fiber: 7.1g | sodium: 792mg

Tuna and Hummus Wraps

Prep time: 10 minutes | Cook time: 0 minutes | Serves 2

Hummus:

1 cup from 1 (15-ounce / 425-g) can low-sodium chickpeas, drained and rinsed

2 tablespoons tahini

1 tablespoon extra-virgin olive oil

1 garlic clove

Juice of ½ lemon

¼ teaspoon salt

2 tablespoons water

Wraps:

4 large lettuce leaves

1 (5-ounce / 142-g) can chunk light tuna packed in water, drained

1 red bell pepper, seeded and cut into strips

1 cucumber, sliced

Make the Hummus

1. In a blender jar, combine the chickpeas, tahini, olive oil, garlic, lemon juice, salt, and water. Process until smooth. Taste and adjust with additional lemon juice or salt, as needed.

Make the Wraps

2. On each lettuce leaf, spread 1 tablespoon of hummus, and divide the tuna among the leaves. Top each with several strips of red pepper and cucumber slices.

3. Roll up the lettuce leaves, folding in the two shorter sides and rolling away from you, like a burrito. Serve immediately.

Per Serving calories: 192 | fat: 5.1g | protein: 26.1g | carbs: 15.1g | fiber: 4.1g | sodium: 352mg

Chickpea Lettuce Wraps

Prep time: 15 minutes | Cook time: 0 minutes | Serves 2

1 (15-ounce / 425-g) can chickpeas, drained and rinsed well

1 celery stalk, diced

½ shallot, minced

1 green apple, cored and diced

3 tablespoons tahini (sesame paste)

2 teaspoons freshly squeezed lemon juice

1 teaspoon raw honey

1 teaspoon Dijon mustard

Dash salt

Filtered water, to thin

4 romaine lettuce leaves

1. In a medium bowl, stir together the chickpeas, celery, shallot, apple, tahini, lemon juice, honey, mustard, and salt. If needed, add some water to thin the mixture.

2. Place the romaine lettuce leaves on a plate. Fill each with the chickpea filling, using it all. Wrap the leaves around the filling. Serve immediately.

Per Serving calories: 397 | fat: 15.1g | protein: 15.1g | carbs: 53.1g | fiber: 15.3g | sodium: 409mg

Turkish Eggplant and Tomatoes Pide with Mint

Prep time: 1 day 40 minutes | Cook time: 20 minutes | Makes 6 pides

Dough:

3 cups almond flour

2 teaspoons raw honey

½ teaspoon instant or rapid-rise yeast

1⅓ cups ice water

1 tablespoon extra-virgin olive oil

1½ teaspoons sea salt

Eggplant and Tomato Toppings:

28 ounces (794 g) whole tomatoes, peeled and puréed

5 tablespoons extra-virgin olive oil, divided

1 pound (454 g) eggplant, cut into ½-inch pieces

½ red bell pepper, chopped

Sea salt and ground black pepper, to taste

3 garlic cloves, minced

¼ teaspoon red pepper flakes

½ teaspoon smoked paprika

6 tablespoons minced fresh mint, divided

1½ cups crumbled feta cheese

Make the Dough

1. Combine the flour, yeast, and honey in a food processor, pulse to combine well. Gently add water while pulsing. Let the dough sit for 10 minutes.

2. Mix the olive oil and salt in the dough and knead the dough until smooth. Wrap in plastic and refrigerate for at least 1 day.

Make the Toppings

3. Heat 2 tablespoons of olive oil in a nonstick skillet over medium-high heat until shimmering.

4. Add the bell pepper, eggplant, and ½ teaspoon of salt. Sauté for 6 minutes or until the eggplant is lightly browned.

5. Add the red pepper flakes, paprika, and garlic. Sauté for 1 minute or until fragrant. Pour in the puréed tomatoes. Bring to a simmer, then cook for 10 minutes or until the mixture is thickened into about 3½ cups. Turn off the heat and mix in 4 tablespoons of mint, salt, and ground black pepper. Set them aside until ready to use.

Make the Turkish Pide

6. Preheat the oven to 500ºF (260ºC). Line three baking sheets with parchment papers.

7. On a clean work surface, divide and shape the dough into six 14 by 5- inch ovals. Transfer the dough to the baking sheets. Brush them with 3 tablespoons of olive oil and spread the eggplant mixture and feta cheese on top.

8. Bake in the preheated oven for 12 minutes or until golden brown. Rotate the pide halfway through the baking time.

9. Remove the pide from the oven and spread with remaining mint and serve immediately.

Per Serving (1 pide) calories: 500 | fat: 22.1g | protein: 8.0g | carbs: 69.7g | fiber: 5.8g | sodium: 1001mg

Veg Mix and Blackeye Pea Burritos

Prep time: 15 minutes | Cook time: 40 minutes | Makes 6 burritos

1 teaspoon olive oil	1 (14-ounce / 397-g) can
1 red onion, diced	blackeye peas
2 garlic cloves, minced	2 teaspoons chili powder
1 zucchini, chopped	Sea salt, to taste
1 tomato, diced	6 whole-grain tortillas
1 bell pepper, any color, deseeded and diced	

1. Preheat the oven to 325°F (160°C).
2. Heat the olive oil in a nonstick skillet over medium heat or until shimmering.
3. Add the onion and sauté for 5 minutes or until translucent.
4. Add the garlic and sauté for 30 seconds or until fragrant.
5. Add the zucchini and sauté for 5 minutes or until tender.
6. Add the tomato and bell pepper and sauté for 2 minutes or until soft.
7. Fold in the black peas and sprinkle them with chili powder and salt. Stir to mix well.
8. Place the tortillas on a clean work surface, then top them with sautéed vegetables mix.
9. Fold one ends of tortillas over the vegetable mix, then tuck and roll them into burritos.
10. Arrange the burritos in a baking dish, seam side down, then pour the juice remains in the skillet over the burritos.
11. Bake in the preheated oven for 25 minutes or until golden brown.
12. Serve immediately.

Per Serving

calories: 335 | fat: 16.2g | protein: 12.1g | carbs: 8.3g | fiber: 8.0g | sodium: 214mg

Tuna and Olive Salad Sandwiches

Prep time: 10 minutes | Cook time: 0 minutes | Serves 4

3 tablespoons freshly squeezed lemon juice	2 (5-ounce / 142-g) cans tuna, drained
2 tablespoons extra-virgin olive oil	1 (2.25-ounce / 64-g) can sliced olives, any green or
1 garlic clove, minced	black variety
½ teaspoon freshly ground black pepper	½ cup chopped fresh fennel, including fronds
	8 slices whole-grain crusty bread

1. In a medium bowl, whisk together the lemon juice, oil, garlic, and pepper. Add the tuna, olives and fennel to the bowl. Using a fork, separate the tuna into chunks and stir to incorporate all the ingredients.
2. Divide the tuna salad equally among 4 slices of bread. Top each with the remaining bread slices.
3. Let the sandwiches sit for at least 5 minutes so the zesty filling can soak into the bread before serving.

Per Serving

calories: 952 | fat: 17.0g | protein: 165.0g | carbs: 37.0g | fiber: 7.0g | sodium: 2572mg

Open-Faced Margherita Sandwiches

Prep time: 10 minutes | Cook time: 5 minutes | Serves 4

2 (6- to 7-inch) whole-wheat submarine or hoagie rolls, sliced open horizontally	¼ teaspoon dried oregano
	1 cup fresh Mozzarella, sliced
1 tablespoon extra-virgin olive oil	¼ cup lightly packed fresh basil leaves, torn into small
1 garlic clove, halved	pieces
1 large ripe tomato, cut into 8 slices	¼ teaspoon freshly ground black pepper

1. Preheat the broiler to High with the rack 4 inches under the heating element. Put the sliced bread on a large, rimmed baking sheet and broil for 1 minute, or until the bread is just lightly toasted. Remove from the oven.
2. Brush each piece of the toasted bread with the oil, and rub a garlic half over each piece. Put the toasted bread back on the baking sheet. Evenly divide the tomato slices on each piece. Sprinkle with the oregano and top with the cheese.
3. Place the baking sheet under the broiler. Set the timer for 1½ minutes, but check after 1 minute. When the cheese is melted and the edges are just starting to get dark brown, remove the sandwiches from the oven. Top each sandwich with the fresh basil and pepper before serving.

Per Serving calories: 93 | fat: 2.0g | protein: 10.0g | carbs: 8.0g | fiber: 2.0g | sodium: 313mg

Roasted Vegetable Panini

Prep time: 10 minutes | Cook time: 15 minutes | Serves 4

2 tablespoons extra-virgin olive oil, divided
1½ cups diced broccoli
1 cup diced zucchini
¼ cup diced onion
¼ teaspoon dried oregano
⅛ teaspoon kosher or sea salt
⅛ teaspoon freshly ground black pepper
1 (12-ounce / 340-g) jar roasted red peppers, drained and finely chopped
2 tablespoons grated Parmesan or Asiago cheese
1 cup fresh Mozzarella (about 4 ounces / 113 g), sliced
1 (2-foot-long) whole-grain Italian loaf, cut into 4 equal lengths Cooking spray

1. Place a large, rimmed baking sheet in the oven. Preheat the oven to 450°F (235°C) with the baking sheet inside.
2. In a large bowl, stir together 1 tablespoon of the oil, broccoli, zucchini, onion, oregano, salt and pepper.
3. Remove the baking sheet from the oven and spritz the baking sheet with cooking spray. Spread the vegetable mixture on the baking sheet and roast for 5 minutes, stirring once halfway through cooking. Remove the baking sheet from the oven. Stir in the red peppers and Parmesan cheese. In a large skillet over medium-high heat, heat the remaining 1 tablespoon of the oil.
4. Cut open each section of bread horizontally, but don't cut all the way through. Fill each with the vegetable mix (about ½ cup), and layer 1 ounce (28 g) of sliced Mozzarella cheese on top. Close the sandwiches, and place two of them on the skillet. Place a heavy object on top and grill for 2½ minutes. Flip the sandwiches and grill for another 2½ minutes. Repeat the grilling process with the remaining two sandwiches. Serve hot.

Per Serving calories: 116 | fat: 4.0g | protein: 12.0g | carbs: 9.0g | fiber: 3.0g | sodium: 569mg

White Pizzas with Arugula and Spinach

Prep time: 10 minutes | Cook time: 20 minutes | Serves 4

1 pound (454 g) refrigerated fresh pizza dough
2 tablespoons extra-virgin olive oil, divided
½ cup thinly sliced onion
2 garlic cloves, minced
3 cups baby spinach
3 cups arugula
1 tablespoon water
¼ teaspoon freshly ground black pepper
1 tablespoon freshly squeezed lemon juice
½ cup shredded Parmesan cheese
½ cup crumbled goat cheese Cooking spray

1. Preheat the oven to 500°F (260°C). Spritz a large, rimmed baking sheet with cooking spray.
2. Take the pizza dough out of the refrigerator.
3. Heat 1 tablespoon of the oil in a large skillet over medium heat. Add the onion to the skillet and cook for 4 minutes, stirring constantly. Add the garlic and cook for 1 minute, stirring constantly.
4. Stir in the spinach, arugula, water and pepper. Cook for about 2 minutes, stirring constantly, or until all the greens are coated with oil and they start to cook down. Remove the skillet from the heat and drizzle with the lemon juice.

5. On a lightly floured work surface, form the pizza dough into a 12-inch circle or a 10-by-12-inch rectangle, using a rolling pin or by stretching with your hands.
6. Place the dough on the prepared baking sheet. Brush the dough with the remaining 1 tablespoon of the oil. Spread the cooked greens on top of the dough to within ½ inch of the edge. Top with the Parmesan cheese and goat cheese.
7. Bake in the preheated oven for 10 to 12 minutes, or until the crust starts to brown around the edges.
8. Remove from the oven and transfer the pizza to a cutting board. Cut into eight pieces before serving.

Per Serving
calories: 521 | fat: 31.0g | protein: 23.0g | carbs: 38.0g | fiber: 4.0g | sodium: 1073mg

Za'atar Pizza

Prep time: 10 minutes | Cook time: 1o to 12 minutes | Serves 4 to 6

1 sheet puff pastry
¼ cup extra-virgin olive oil
⅓ cup za'atar seasoning

1. Preheat the oven to 350°F (180°C). Line a baking sheet with parchment paper.
2. Place the puff pastry on the prepared baking sheet. Cut the pastry into desired slices.
3. Brush the pastry with the olive oil. Sprinkle with the za'atar seasoning.
4. Put the pastry in the oven and bake for 10 to 12 minutes, or until edges are lightly browned and puffed up.
5. Serve warm.

Per Serving
calories: 374 | fat: 30.0g | protein: 3.0g | carbs: 20.0g | fiber: 1.0g | sodium: 166mg

Zucchini Hummus Wraps

Prep time: 15 minutes | Cook time: 6 minutes | Serves 2

1 zucchini, ends removed, thinly sliced lengthwise
½ teaspoon dried oregano
¼ teaspoon freshly ground black pepper
¼ teaspoon garlic powder
¼ cup hummus
2 whole wheat tortillas
2 Roma tomatoes, cut lengthwise into slices
1 cup chopped kale
2 tablespoons chopped red onion
½ teaspoon ground cumin

1. In a skillet over medium heat, add the zucchini slices and cook for 3 minutes per side. Sprinkle with the oregano, pepper, and garlic powder and remove from the heat.
2. Spread 2 tablespoons of hummus on each tortilla. Lay half the zucchini in the center of each tortilla. Top with tomato slices, kale, red onion, and ¼ teaspoon of cumin. Wrap tightly and serve.

Per Serving
calories: 248 | fat: 8.1g | protein: 9.1g | carbs: 37.1g | fiber: 8.1g | sodium: mg

Chapter 5

Beans, Grains, and Pastas

Baked Rolled Oat with Pears and Pecans

Prep time: 15 minutes | Cook time: 30 minutes | Serves 6

2 tablespoons coconut oil, melted, plus more for greasing the pan
3 ripe pears, cored and diced
2 cups unsweetened almond milk
1 tablespoon pure vanilla extract
¼ cup pure maple syrup
2 cups gluten-free rolled oats
½ cup raisins
¾ cup chopped pecans
¼ teaspoon ground nutmeg
1 teaspoon ground cinnamon
½ teaspoon ground ginger
¼ teaspoon sea salt

1. Preheat the oven to 350°F (180°C). Grease a baking dish with melted coconut oil, then spread the pears in a single layer on the baking dish evenly.
2. Combine the almond milk, vanilla extract, maple syrup, and coconut oil in a bowl. Stir to mix well.
3. Combine the remaining ingredients in a separate large bowl. Stir to mix well. Fold the almond milk mixture in the bowl, then pour the mixture over the pears.
4. Place the baking dish in the preheated oven and bake for 30 minutes or until lightly browned and set.
5. Serve immediately.

Per Serving
calories: 479 | fat: 34.9g | protein: 8.8g | carbs: 50.1g | fiber: 10.8g | sodium: 113mg

Brown Rice Pilaf with Pistachios and Raisins

Prep time: 5 minutes | Cook time: 15 minutes | Serves 6

1 tablespoon extra-virgin olive oil
1 cup chopped onion
½ cup shredded carrot
½ teaspoon ground cinnamon
1 teaspoon ground cumin
2 cups brown rice
1¾ cups pure orange juice
¼ cup water
½ cup shelled pistachios
1 cup golden raisins
½ cup chopped fresh chives

1. Heat the olive oil in a saucepan over medium-high heat until shimmering.
2. Add the onion and sauté for 5 minutes or until translucent.
3. Add the carrots, cinnamon, and cumin, then sauté for 1 minutes or until aromatic.
4. Pour int the brown rice, orange juice, and water. Bring to a boil. Reduce the heat to medium-low and simmer for 7 minutes or until the liquid is almost absorbed.
5. Transfer the rice mixture in a large serving bowl, then spread with pistachios, raisins, and chives. Serve immediately.

Per Serving
calories: 264 | fat: 7.1g | protein: 5.2g | carbs: 48.9g | fiber: 4.0g | sodium: 86mg

Cherry, Apricot, and Pecan Brown Rice Bowl

Prep time: 15 minutes | Cook time: 1 hour 1 minutes | Serves 2

2 tablespoons olive oil
2 green onions, sliced
½ cup brown rice
1 cup low -sodium chicken stock
2 tablespoons dried cherries
4 dried apricots, chopped
2 tablespoons pecans, toasted and chopped
Sea salt and freshly ground pepper, to taste

1. Heat the olive oil in a medium saucepan over medium-high heat until shimmering.
2. Add the green onions and sauté for 1 minutes or until fragrant.
3. Add the rice. Stir to mix well, then pour in the chicken stock.
4. Bring to a boil. Reduce the heat to low. Cover and simmer for 50 minutes or until the brown rice is soft.
5. Add the cherries, apricots, and pecans, and simmer for 10 more minutes or until the fruits are tender.
6. Pour them in a large serving bowl. Fluff with a fork. Sprinkle with sea salt and freshly ground pepper. Serve immediately.

Per Serving
calories: 451 | fat: 25.9g | protein: 8.2g | carbs: 50.4g | fiber: 4.6g | sodium: 122mg

Curry Apple Couscous with Leeks and Pecans

Prep time: 10 minutes | Cook time: 8 minutes | Serves 4

2 teaspoons extra-virgin olive oil
2 leeks, white parts only, sliced
1 apple, diced
2 cups cooked couscous
2 tablespoons curry powder
½ cup chopped pecans

1. Heat the olive oil in a skillet over medium heat until shimmering.
2. Add the leeks and sauté for 5 minutes or until soft.
3. Add the diced apple and cook for 3 more minutes until tender.
4. Add the couscous and curry powder. Stir to combine.
5. Transfer them in a large serving bowl, then mix in the pecans and serve.

Per Serving
calories: 254 | fat: 11.9g | protein: 5.4g | carbs: 34.3g | fiber: 5.9g | sodium: 15mg

Lebanese Flavor Broken Thin Noodles

Prep time: 10 minutes | Cook time: 25 minutes | Serves 6

1 tablespoon extra-virgin olive oil
1 (3-ounce / 85-g) cup vermicelli, broken into 1- to 1½-inch pieces
3 cups shredded cabbage
1 cup brown rice
3 cups low-sodium vegetable soup
½ cup water
2 garlic cloves, mashed
¼ teaspoon sea salt
⅛ teaspoon crushed red pepper flakes
½ cup coarsely chopped cilantro
Fresh lemon slices, for serving

1. Heat the olive oil in a saucepan over medium-high heat until shimmering.
2. Add the vermicelli and sauté for 3 minutes or until toasted.
3. Add the cabbage and sauté for 4 minutes or until tender.
4. Pour in the brown rice, vegetable soup, and water. Add the garlic and sprinkle with salt and red pepper flakes.
5. Bring to a boil over high heat. Reduce the heat to medium low. Put the lid on and simmer for another 10 minutes.
6. Turn off the heat, then let sit for 5 minutes without opening the lid.
7. Pour them on a large serving platter and spread with cilantro. Squeeze the lemon slices over and serve warm.

Per Serving

calories: 127 | fat: 3.1g | protein: 4.2g | carbs: 22.9g | fiber: 3.0g | sodium: 224mg

Lemony Farro and Avocado Bowl

Prep time: 5 minutes | Cook time: 25 minutes | Serves 4

1 tablespoon plus 2 teaspoons extra-virgin olive oil, divided
½ medium onion, chopped
1 carrot, shredded
2 garlic cloves, minced
1 (6-ounce / 170-g) cup pearled farro
2 cups low-sodium vegetable soup
2 avocados, peeled, pitted, and sliced
Zest and juice of 1 small lemon
¼ teaspoon sea salt

1. Heat 1 tablespoon of olive oil in a saucepan over medium-high heat until shimmering.
2. Add the onion and sauté for 5 minutes or until translucent.
3. Add the carrot and garlic and sauté for 1 minute or until fragrant.
4. Add the farro and pour in the vegetable soup. Bring to a boil over high heat. Reduce the heat to low. Put the lid on and simmer for 20 minutes or until the farro is al dente.
5. Transfer the farro in a large serving bowl, then fold in the avocado slices. Sprinkle with lemon zest and salt, then drizzle with lemon juice and 2 teaspoons of olive oil.
6. Stir to mix well and serve immediately.

Per Serving calories: 210 | fat: 11.1g | protein: 4.2g | carbs: 27.9g | fiber: 7.0g | sodium: 152mg

Rice and Blueberry Stuffed Sweet Potatoes

Prep time: 15 minutes | Cook time: 20 minutes | Serves 4

2 cups cooked wild rice
½ cup dried blueberries
½ cup chopped hazelnuts
½ cup shredded Swiss chard
1 teaspoon chopped fresh thyme
1 scallion, white and green parts, peeled and thinly sliced
Sea salt and freshly ground black pepper, to taste
4 sweet potatoes, baked in the skin until tender

1. Preheat the oven to 400ºF (205ºC).
2. Combine all the ingredients, except for the sweet potatoes, in a large bowl. Stir to mix well.
3. Cut the top third of the sweet potato off length wire, then scoop most of the sweet potato flesh out.
4. Fill the potato with the wild rice mixture, then set the sweet potato on a greased baking sheet.
5. Bake in the preheated oven for 20 minutes or until the sweet potato skin is lightly charred.
6. Serve immediately.

Per Serving

calories: 393 | fat: 7.1g | protein: 10.2g | carbs: 76.9g | fiber: 10.0g | sodium: 93mg

Slow Cooked Turkey and Brown Rice

Prep time: 20 minutes | Cook time: 3 hours 10 minutes | Serves 6

1 tablespoon extra-virgin olive oil
1½ pounds (680 g) ground turkey
2 tablespoons chopped fresh sage, divided
2 tablespoons chopped fresh thyme, divided
1 teaspoon sea salt
½ teaspoon ground black pepper
2 cups brown rice
1 (14-ounce / 397-g) can stewed tomatoes, with the juice
¼ cup pitted and sliced Kalamata olives
3 medium zucchini, sliced thinly
¼ cup chopped fresh flat-leaf parsley
1 medium yellow onion, chopped
1 tablespoon plus 1 teaspoon balsamic vinegar
2 cups low-sodium chicken stock
2 garlic cloves, minced
½ cup grated Parmesan cheese, for serving

1. Heat the olive oil in a nonstick skillet over medium-high heat until shimmering.
2. Add the ground turkey and sprinkle with 1 tablespoon of sage, 1 tablespoon of thyme, salt and ground black pepper.
3. Sauté for 10 minutes or until the ground turkey is lightly browned.
4. Pour them in the slow cooker, then pour in the remaining ingredients, except for the Parmesan. Stir to mix well.
5. Put the lid on and cook on high for 3 hours or until the rice and vegetables are tender.
6. Pour them in a large serving bowl, then spread with Parmesan cheese before serving.

Per Serving

calories: 499 | fat: 16.4g | protein: 32.4g | carbs: 56.5g | fiber: 4.7g | sodium: 758mg

Papaya, Jicama, and Peas Rice Bowl

Prep time: 20 minutes | Cook time: 45 minutes | Serves 4

Sauce:
Juice of ¼ lemon
2 teaspoons chopped fresh basil
1 tablespoon raw honey
1 tablespoon extra-virgin olive oil
Sea salt, to taste

Rice:
1½ cups wild rice
2 papayas, peeled, seeded, and diced
1 jicama, peeled and shredded
1 cup snow peas, julienned
2 cups shredded cabbage
1 scallion, white and green parts, chopped

1. Combine the ingredients for the sauce in a bowl. Stir to mix well. Set aside until ready to use.
2. Pour the wild rice in a saucepan, then pour in enough water to cover. Bring to a boil.
3. Reduce the heat to low, then simmer for 45 minutes or until the wild rice is soft and plump. Drain and transfer to a large serving bowl.
4. Top the rice with papayas, jicama, peas, cabbage, and scallion. Pour the sauce over and stir to mix well before serving.

Per Serving

calories: 446 | fat: 7.9g | protein: 13.1g | carbs: 85.8g | fiber: 16.0g | sodium: 70mg

Black Bean Chili with Mangoes

Prep time: 10 minutes | Cook time: 10 minutes | Serves 4

2 tablespoons coconut oil
1 onion, chopped
2 (15-ounce / 425-g) cans black beans, drained and rinsed
1 tablespoon chili powder
1 teaspoon sea salt
¼ teaspoon freshly ground black pepper
1 cup water
2 ripe mangoes, sliced thinly
¼ cup chopped fresh cilantro, divided
¼ cup sliced scallions, divided

1. Heat the coconut oil in a pot over high heat until melted.
2. Put the onion in the pot and sauté for 5 minutes or until translucent. Add the black beans to the pot. Sprinkle with chili powder, salt, and ground black pepper. Pour in the water. Stir to mix well.
3. Bring to a boil. Reduce the heat to low, then simmering for 5 minutes or until the beans are tender.
4. Turn off the heat and mix in the mangoes, then garnish with scallions and cilantro before serving.

Per Serving

calories: 430 | fat: 9.1g | protein: 20.2g | carbs: 71.9g | fiber: 22.0g | sodium: 608mg

Israeli Style Eggplant and Chickpea Salad

Prep time: 5 minutes | Cook time: 20 minutes | Serves 6

2 tablespoons freshly squeezed lemon juice
1 teaspoon ground cumin
¼ teaspoon sea salt
2 tablespoons olive oil, divided
1 (1-pound / 454-g) medium globe eggplant, stem removed, cut into flat cubes (about ½ inch thick)
2 tablespoons balsamic vinegar
1 (15-ounce / 425-g) can chickpeas, drained and rinsed
¼ cup chopped mint leaves
1 cup sliced sweet onion
1 garlic clove, finely minced
1 tablespoon sesame seeds, toasted

1. Preheat the oven to 550ºF (288ºC) or the highest level of your oven or broiler. Grease a baking sheet with 1 tablespoon of olive oil.
2. Combine the balsamic vinegar, lemon juice, cumin, salt, and 1 tablespoon of olive oil in a small bowl. Stir to mix well.
3. Arrange the eggplant cubes on the baking sheet, then brush with 2 tablespoons of the balsamic vinegar mixture on both sides.
4. Broil in the preheated oven for 8 minutes or until lightly browned. Flip the cubes halfway through the cooking time.
5. Meanwhile, combine the chickpeas, mint, onion, garlic, and sesame seeds in a large serving bowl. Drizzle with remaining balsamic vinegar mixture. Stir to mix well.
6. Remove the eggplant from the oven. Allow to cool for 5 minutes, then slice them into ½-inch strips on a clean work surface.
7. Add the eggplant strips in the serving bowl, then toss to combine well before serving.

Per Serving

calories: 125 | fat: 2.9g | protein: 5.2g | carbs: 20.9g | fiber: 6.0g | sodium: 222mg

Italian Sautéd Cannellini Beans

Prep time: 10 minutes | Cook time: 15 minutes | Serves 6

2 teaspoons extra-virgin olive oil
½ cup minced onion
¼ cup red wine vinegar
1 (12-ounce / 340-g) can no-salt-added tomato paste
2 tablespoons raw honey
½ cup water
¼ teaspoon ground cinnamon

1. 2 (15-ounce / 425-g) cans cannellini beans
1. Heat the olive oil in a saucepan over medium heat until shimmering.
2. Add the onion and sauté for 5 minutes or until translucent.
3. Pour in the red wine vinegar, tomato paste, honey, and water. Sprinkle with cinnamon. Stir to mix well.
4. Reduce the heat to low, then pour all the beans into the saucepan. Cook for 10 more minutes. Stir constantly.
5. Serve immediately.

Per Serving

calories: 435 | fat: 2.1g | protein: 26.2g | carbs: 80.3g | fiber: 24.0g | sodium: 72mg

Lentil and Vegetable Curry Stew

Prep time: 20 minutes | Cook time: 4 hours 7 minutes | Serves 8

1 tablespoon coconut oil	2 carrots, peeled and diced
1 yellow onion, diced	8 cups low-sodium vegetable soup, divided
¼ cup yellow Thai curry paste	1 bunch kale, stems removed and roughly chopped
2 cups unsweetened coconut milk	
2 cups dry red lentils, rinsed well and drained	Sea salt, to taste
3 cups bite-sized cauliflower florets	½ cup fresh cilantro, chopped
2 golden potatoes, cut into chunks	Pinch crushed red pepper flakes

1. Heat the coconut oil in a nonstick skillet over medium-high heat until melted. Add the onion and sauté for 5 minutes or until translucent. Pour in the curry paste and sauté for another 2 minutes, then fold in the coconut milk and stir to combine well. Bring to a simmer and turn off the heat.
2. Put the lentils, cauliflower, potatoes, and carrot in the slow cooker. Pour in 6 cups of vegetable soup and the curry mixture. Stir to combine well.
3. Cover and cook on high for 4 hours or until the lentils and vegetables are soft. Stir periodically.
4. During the last 30 minutes, fold the kale in the slow cooker and pour in the remaining vegetable soup. Sprinkle with salt. Pour the stew in a large serving bowl and spread the cilantro and red pepper flakes on top before serving hot.

Per Serving calories: 530 | fat: 19.2g | protein: 20.3g | carbs: 75.2g | fiber: 15.5g | sodium: 562mg

Chickpea, Vegetable, and Fruit Stew

Prep time: 20 minutes | Cook time: 6 hours 4 minutes | Serves 6

1 large bell pepper, any color, chopped	1 teaspoon grated fresh ginger
6 ounces (170 g) green beans, trimmed and cut into bite-size pieces	2 garlic cloves, minced
	1¾ cups low-sodium vegetable soup
3 cups canned chickpeas, rinsed and drained	1 teaspoon ground cumin
1 (15-ounce / 425-g) can diced tomatoes, with the juice	1 tablespoon ground coriander
	¼ teaspoon ground red pepper flakes
1 large carrot, cut into ¼-inch rounds	Sea salt and ground black pepper, to taste
2 large potatoes, peeled and cubed	8 ounces (227 g) fresh baby spinach
1 large yellow onion, chopped	¼ cup diced dried figs
	¼ cup diced dried apricots
	1 cup plain Greek yogurt

1. Place the bell peppers, green beans, chicken peas, tomatoes and juice, carrot, potatoes, onion, ginger, and garlic in the slow cooker. Pour in the vegetable soup and sprinkle with cumin, coriander, red pepper flakes, salt, and ground black pepper. Stir to mix well.
2. Put the slow cooker lid on and cook on high for 6 hours or until the vegetables are soft. Stir periodically.
3. Open the lid and fold in the spinach, figs, apricots, and yogurt. Stir to mix well.
4. Cook for 4 minutes or until the spinach is wilted. Pour them in a large serving bowl. Allow to cool for at least 20 minutes, then serve warm.

Per Serving
calories: 611 | fat: 9.0g | protein: 30.7g | carbs: 107.4g | fiber: 20.8g | sodium: 344mg

Quinoa and Chickpea Vegetable Bowls

Prep time: 20 minutes | Cook time: 15 minutes | Serves 4

1 cup red dry quinoa, rinsed and drained	**Mango Sauce:**
	1 mango, diced
2 cups low-sodium vegetable soup	¼ cup fresh lime juice
	½ teaspoon ground turmeric
2 cups fresh spinach	1 teaspoon finely minced fresh ginger
2 cups finely shredded red cabbage	
	¼ teaspoon sea salt
1 (15-ounce / 425-g) can chickpeas, drained and rinsed	Pinch of ground red pepper
	1 teaspoon pure maple syrup
1 ripe avocado, thinly sliced	2 tablespoons extra-virgin olive oil
1 cup shredded carrots	
1 red bell pepper, thinly sliced	
4 tablespoons Mango Sauce	
½ cup fresh cilantro, chopped	

1. Pour the quinoa and vegetable soup in a saucepan. Bring to a boil. Reduce the heat to low. Cover and cook for 15 minutes or until tender. Fluffy with a fork.
2. Meanwhile, combine the ingredients for the mango sauce in a food processor. Pulse until smooth.
3. Divide the quinoa, spinach, and cabbage into 4 serving bowls, then top with chickpeas, avocado, carrots, and bell pepper. Dress them with the mango sauce and spread with cilantro. Serve immediately.

Per Serving calories: 366 | fat: 11.1g | protein: 15.5g | carbs: 55.6g | fiber: 17.7g | sodium: 746mg

Ritzy Veggie Chili

Prep time: 15 minutes | Cook time: 5 hours | Serves 4

1 (28-ounce / 794-g) can chopped tomatoes, with the juice
1 (15-ounce / 425-g) can black beans, drained and rinsed
1 (15-ounce / 425-g) can redly beans, drained and rinsed
1 medium green bell pepper, chopped
1 yellow onion, chopped
1 tablespoon onion powder
1 teaspoon paprika
1 teaspoon cayenne pepper
1 teaspoon garlic powder
½ teaspoon sea salt
½ teaspoon ground black pepper
1 tablespoon olive oil
1 large hass avocado, pitted, peeled, and chopped, for garnish

1. Combine all the ingredients, except for the avocado, in the slow cooker. Stir to mix well.
2. Put the slow cooker lid on and cook on high for 5 hours or until the vegetables are tender and the mixture has a thick consistency.
3. Pour the chili in a large serving bowl. Allow to cool for 30 minutes, then spread with chopped avocado and serve.

Per Serving calories: 633 | fat: 16.3g | protein: 31.7g | carbs: 97.0g | fiber: 28.9g | sodium: 792mg

Spicy Italian Bean Balls with Marinara

Prep time: 20 minutes | Cook time: 30 minutes | Serves 2 to 4

Bean Balls:
1 tablespoon extra-virgin olive oil
½ yellow onion, minced
1 teaspoon fennel seeds
2 teaspoons dried oregano
½ teaspoon crushed red pepper flakes
1 teaspoon garlic powder
1 (15-ounce / 425-g) can white beans (cannellini or navy), drained and rinsed
½ cup whole-grain bread crumbs
Sea salt and ground black pepper, to taste
Marinara:
1 tablespoon extra-virgin olive oil
3 garlic cloves, minced
Handful basil leaves
1 (28-ounce / 794-g) can chopped tomatoes with juice reserved
Sea salt, to taste

Make the Bean Balls
1. Preheat the oven to 350°F (180°C). Line a baking sheet with parchment paper.
2. Heat the olive oil in a nonstick skillet over medium heat until shimmering.
3. Add the onion and sauté for 5 minutes or until translucent.
4. Sprinkle with fennel seeds, oregano, red pepper flakes, and garlic powder, then cook for 1 minute or until aromatic.
5. Pour the sautéed mixture in a food processor and add the beans and bread crumbs. Sprinkle with salt and ground black pepper, then pulse to combine well and the mixture holds together.
6. Shape the mixture into balls with a 2-ounce (57-g) cookie scoop, then arrange the balls on the baking sheet.
7. Bake in the preheated oven for 30 minutes or until lightly browned. Flip the balls halfway through the cooking time.

Make the Marinara
8. While baking the bean balls, heat the olive oil in a saucepan over medium-high heat until shimmering.

9. Add the garlic and basil and sauté for 2 minutes or until fragrant. Fold in the tomatoes and juice. Bring to a boil. Reduce the heat to low. Put the lid on and simmer for 15 minutes. Sprinkle with salt. Transfer the bean balls on a large plate and baste with marinara before serving.

Per Serving calories: 351 | fat: 16.4g | protein: 11.5g | carbs: 42.9g | fiber: 10.3g | sodium: 377mg

Wild Rice, Celery, and Cauliflower Pilaf

Prep time: 10 minutes | Cook time: 45 minutes | Serves 4

1 tablespoon olive oil, plus more for greasing the baking dish
1 cup wild rice
2 cups low-sodium chicken broth
1 sweet onion, chopped
2 stalks celery, chopped
1 teaspoon minced garlic
2 carrots, peeled, halved lengthwise, and sliced
½ cauliflower head, cut into small florets
1 teaspoon chopped fresh thyme
Sea salt, to taste

1. Preheat the oven to 350°F (180°C). Line a baking sheet with parchment paper and grease with olive oil.
2. Put the wild rice in a saucepan, then pour in the chicken broth. Bring to a boil. Reduce the heat to low and simmer for 30 minutes or until the rice is plump.
3. Meanwhile, heat the remaining olive oil in an oven-proof skillet over medium-high heat until shimmering.
4. Add the onion, celery, and garlic to the skillet and sauté for 3 minutes or until the onion is translucent.
5. Add the carrots and cauliflower to the skillet and sauté for 5 minutes. Turn off the heat and set aside.
6. Pour the cooked rice in the skillet with the vegetables. Sprinkle with thyme and salt.
7. Set the skillet in the preheated oven and bake for 15 minutes or until the vegetables are soft. Serve immediately.

Per Serving calories: 214 | fat: 3.9g | protein: 7.2g | carbs: 37.9g | fiber: 5.0g | sodium: 122mg

Walnut and Ricotta Spaghetti

Prep time: 15 minutes | Cook time: 10 minutes | Serves 6

1 pound (454 g) cooked whole-wheat spaghetti
2 tablespoons extra-virgin olive oil
4 cloves garlic, minced
¾ cup walnuts, toasted and finely chopped
2 tablespoons ricotta cheese
¼ cup flat-leaf parsley, chopped
½ cup grated Parmesan cheese
Sea salt and freshly ground pepper, to taste

1. Reserve a cup of spaghetti water while cooking the spaghetti.
2. Heat the olive oil in a nonstick skillet over medium-low heat or until shimmering.
3. Add the garlic and sauté for a minute or until fragrant.
4. Pour the spaghetti water into the skillet and cook for 8 more minutes.
5. Turn off the heat and mix in the walnuts and ricotta cheese.
6. Put the cooked spaghetti on a large serving plate, then pour the walnut sauce over. Spread with parsley and Parmesan, then sprinkle with salt and ground pepper. Toss to serve.

Per Serving
calories: 264 | fat: 16.8g | protein: 8.6g | carbs: 22.8g | fiber: 4.0g | sodium: 336mg

Butternut Squash, Spinach, and Cheeses Lasagna

Prep time: 30 minutes | Cook time: 3 hours 45 minutes | Serves 4 to 6

2 tablespoons extra-virgin olive oil, divided	½ cup unsweetened almond milk
1 butternut squash, halved lengthwise and deseeded	5 layers whole-wheat lasagna noodles (about 12 ounces / 340 g in total)
½ teaspoon sage	
½ teaspoon sea salt	4 ounces (113 g) fresh spinach leaves, divided
¼ teaspoon ground black pepper	½ cup shredded part skim Mozzarella, for garnish
¼ cup grated Parmesan cheese	
2 cups ricotta cheese	

1. Preheat the oven to 400ºF (205ºC). Line a baking sheet with parchment paper. Brush 1 tablespoon of olive oil on the cut side of the butternut squash, then place the squash on the baking sheet. Bake in the preheated oven for 45 minutes or until the squash is tender. Allow to cool until you can handle it, then scoop the flesh out and put the flesh in a food processor to purée. Combine the puréed butternut squash flesh with sage, salt, and ground black pepper in a large bowl. Stir to mix well.
2. Combine the cheeses and milk in a separate bowl, then sprinkle with salt and pepper, to taste.
3. Grease the slow cooker with 1 tablespoon of olive oil, then add a layer of lasagna noodles to coat the bottom of the slow cooker. Spread half of the squash mixture on top of the noodles, then top the squash mixture with another layer of lasagna noodles. Spread half of the spinach over the noodles, then top the spinach with half of cheese mixture. Repeat with remaining 3 layers of lasagna noodles, squash mixture, spinach, and cheese mixture. Top the cheese mixture with Mozzarella, then put the lid on and cook on low for 3 hours or until the lasagna noodles are al dente. Serve immediately.

Per Serving calories: 657 | fat: 37.1g | protein: 30.9g | carbs: 57.2g | fiber: 8.3g | sodium: 918mg

Minestrone Chickpeas and Macaroni Casserole

Prep time: 20 minutes | Cook time: 7 hours 20 minutes | Serves 5

1 (15-ounce / 425-g) can chickpeas, drained and rinsed	1 teaspoon dried oregano
	2 teaspoons maple syrup
1 (28-ounce / 794-g) can diced tomatoes, with the juice	½ teaspoon sea salt
	¼ teaspoon ground black pepper
1 (6-ounce / 170-g) can no-salt-added tomato paste	½ pound (227-g) fresh green beans, trimmed and cut into bite-size pieces
3 medium carrots, sliced	
3 cloves garlic, minced	1 cup macaroni pasta
1 medium yellow onion, chopped	2 ounces (57 g) Parmesan cheese, grated
1 cup low-sodium vegetable soup	
½ teaspoon dried rosemary	

1. Except for the green beans, pasta, and Parmesan cheese, combine all the ingredients in the slow cooker and stir to mix well. Put the slow cooker lid on and cook on low for 7 hours. Fold in the pasta and green beans. Put the lid on and cook on high for 20 minutes or until the vegetable are soft and the pasta is al dente.
2. Pour them in a large serving bowl and spread with Parmesan cheese before serving.

Per Serving calories: 349 | fat: 6.7g | protein: 16.5g | carbs: 59.9g | fiber: 12.9g | sodium: 937mg

Garlic and Parsley Chickpeas

Prep time: 10 minutes | Cook time: 18 to 20 minutes | Serves 4 to 6

¼ cup extra-virgin olive oil, divided	Black pepper, to taste
	2 (15-ounce / 425-g) cans chickpeas, rinsed
4 garlic cloves, sliced thinly	
⅛ teaspoon red pepper flakes	1 cup vegetable broth
	2 tablespoons minced fresh parsley
1 onion, chopped finely	
¼ teaspoon salt, plus more to taste	2 teaspoons lemon juice

1. Add 3 tablespoons of the olive oil, garlic, and pepper flakes to a skillet over medium heat. Cook for about 3 minutes, stirring constantly, or until the garlic turns golden but not brown. Stir in the onion and ¼ teaspoon salt and cook for 5 to 7 minutes, or until softened and lightly browned.
2. Add the chickpeas and broth to the skillet and bring to a simmer. Reduce the heat to medium-low, cover, and cook for about 7 minutes, or until the chickpeas are cooked through and flavors meld. Uncover, increase the heat to high and continue to cook for about 3 minutes more, or until nearly all liquid has evaporated.
3. Turn off the heat, stir in the parsley and lemon juice. Season to taste with salt and pepper and drizzle with remaining 1 tablespoon of the olive oil. Serve warm.

Per Serving calories: 220 | fat: 11.4g | protein: 6.5g | carbs: 24.6g | fiber: 6.0g | sodium: 467mg

Black-Eyed Peas Salad with Walnuts

Prep time: 10 minutes | Cook time: 0 minutes | Serves 4 to 6

3 tablespoons extra-virgin olive oil	2 (15-ounce / 425-g) cans black-eyed peas, rinsed
3 tablespoons dukkah, divided	½ cup pomegranate seeds
	½ cup minced fresh parsley
2 tablespoons lemon juice	½ cup walnuts, toasted and chopped
2 tablespoons pomegranate molasses	
	4 scallions, sliced thinly
¼ teaspoon salt, or more to taste	
⅛ teaspoon pepper, or more to taste	

1. In a large bowl, whisk together the olive oil, 2 tablespoons of the dukkah, lemon juice, pomegranate molasses, salt and pepper. Stir in the remaining ingredients. Season with salt and pepper. Sprinkle with the remaining 1 tablespoon of the dukkah before serving.

Per Serving calories: 155 | fat: 11.5g | protein: 2.0g | carbs: 12.5g | fiber: 2.1g | sodium: 105mg

Mashed Beans with Cumin

Prep time: 10 minutes | Cook time: 10 to 12 minutes | Serves 4 to 6

1 tablespoon extra-virgin olive oil, plus extra for serving

4 garlic cloves, minced

1 teaspoon ground cumin

2 (15-ounce / 425-g) cans fava beans

3 tablespoons tahini

2 tablespoons lemon juice, plus lemon wedges for serving

Salt and pepper, to taste

1 tomato, cored and cut into ½-inch pieces

1 small onion, chopped finely

2 hard-cooked large eggs, chopped

2 tablespoons minced fresh parsley

1. Add the olive oil, garlic and cumin to a medium saucepan over medium heat. Cook for about 2 minutes, or until fragrant. Stir in the beans with their liquid and tahini. Bring to a simmer and cook for 8 to 10 minutes, or until the liquid thickens slightly.
2. Turn off the heat, mash the beans to a coarse consistency with a potato masher. Stir in the lemon juice and 1 teaspoon pepper. Season with salt and pepper.
3. Transfer the mashed beans to a serving dish. Top with the tomato, onion, eggs and parsley. Drizzle with the extra olive oil. Serve with the lemon wedges.

Per Serving

calories: 125 | fat: 8.6g | protein: 4.9g | carbs: 9.1g | fiber: 2.9g | sodium: 131mg

Turkish Canned Pinto Bean Salad

Prep time: 10 minutes | Cook time: 3 minutes | Serves 4 to 6

¼ cup extra-virgin olive oil, divided

3 garlic cloves, lightly crushed and peeled

2 (15-ounce / 425-g) cans pinto beans, rinsed 2 cups plus

1 tablespoon water

Salt and pepper, to taste

¼ cup tahini

3 tablespoons lemon juice

1 tablespoon ground dried Aleppo pepper, plus extra for serving

8 ounces (227 g) cherry tomatoes, halved

¼ red onion, sliced thinly

½ cup fresh parsley leaves

2 hard-cooked large eggs, quartered

1 tablespoon toasted sesame seeds

1. Add 1 tablespoon of the olive oil and garlic to a medium saucepan over medium heat. Cook for about 3 minutes, stirring constantly, or until the garlic turns golden but not brown.
2. Add the beans, 2 cups of the water and 1 teaspoon salt and bring to a simmer. Remove from the heat, cover and let sit for 20 minutes. Drain the beans and discard the garlic.
3. In a large bowl, whisk together the remaining 3 tablespoons of the oil, tahini, lemon juice, Aleppo, the remaining 1 tablespoon of the water and ¼ teaspoon salt. Stir in the beans, tomatoes, onion and parsley. Season with salt and pepper to taste.
4. Transfer to a serving platter and top with the eggs. Sprinkle with the sesame seeds and extra Aleppo before serving.

Per Serving calories: 402 | fat: 18.9g | protein: 16.2g | carbs: 44.4g | fiber: 11.2g | sodium: 456mg

Fava and Garbanzo Bean Ful

Prep time: 10 minutes | Cook time: 10 minutes | Serves 6

1 (15-ounce / 425-g) can fava beans, rinsed and drained

1 (1-pound / 454-g) can garbanzo beans, rinsed and drained

3 cups water

½ cup lemon juice

3 cloves garlic, peeled and minced

1 teaspoon salt

3 tablespoons extra-virgin olive oil

1. In a pot over medium heat, cook the beans and water for 10 minutes.
2. Drain the beans and transfer to a bowl. Reserve 1 cup of the liquid from the cooked beans.
3. Add the reserved liquid, lemon juice, minced garlic and salt to the bowl with the beans. Mix to combine well. Using a potato masher, mash up about half the beans in the bowl.
4. Give the mixture one more stir to make sure the beans are evenly mixed.
5. Drizzle with the olive oil and serve.

Per Serving

calories: 199 | fat: 9.0g | protein: 10.0g | carbs: 25.0g | fiber: 9.0g | sodium: 395mg

Triple-Green Pasta with Cheese

Prep time: 5 minutes | Cook time: 14 to 16 minutes | Serves 4

8 ounces (227 g) uncooked penne

1 tablespoon extra-virgin olive oil

2 garlic cloves, minced

¼ teaspoon crushed red pepper

2 cups chopped fresh flat-leaf parsley, including stems

5 cups loosely packed baby spinach

¼ teaspoon ground nutmeg

¼ teaspoon kosher salt

¼ teaspoon freshly ground black pepper

⅓ cup Castelvetrano olives, pitted and sliced

⅓ cup grated Parmesan cheese

1. In a large stockpot of salted water, cook the pasta for about 8 to 10 minutes. Drain the pasta and reserve ¼ cup of the cooking liquid.
2. Meanwhile, heat the olive oil in a large skillet over medium heat. Add the garlic and red pepper and cook for 30 seconds, stirring constantly.
3. Add the parsley and cook for 1 minute, stirring constantly. Add the spinach, nutmeg, salt, and pepper, and cook for 3 minutes, stirring occasionally, or until the spinach is wilted.
4. Add the cooked pasta and the reserved ¼ cup cooking liquid to the skillet. Stir in the olives and cook for about 2 minutes, or until most of the pasta water has been absorbed.
5. Remove from the heat and stir in the cheese before serving.

Per Serving

calories: 262 | fat: 4.0g | protein: 15.0g | carbs: 51.0g | fiber: 13.0g | sodium: 1180mg

Caprese Pasta with Roasted Asparagus

Prep time: 5 minutes | Cook time: 25 minutes | Serves 6

8 ounces (227 g) uncooked small pasta, like orecchiette (little ears) or farfalle (bow ties)

1½ pounds (680 g) fresh asparagus, ends trimmed and stalks chopped into 1- inch pieces

1½ cups grape tomatoes, halved

2 tablespoons extra-virgin olive oil

¼ teaspoon kosher salt

¼ teaspoon freshly ground black pepper

2 cups fresh Mozzarella, drained and cut into bite-size pieces (about 8 ounces / 227 g)

⅓ cup torn fresh basil leaves

2 tablespoons balsamic vinegar

1. Preheat the oven to 400°F (205°C).
2. In a large stockpot of salted water, cook the pasta for about 8 to 10 minutes. Drain and reserve about ¼ cup of the cooking liquid.
3. Meanwhile, in a large bowl, toss together the asparagus, tomatoes, oil, salt and pepper. Spread the mixture onto a large, rimmed baking sheet and bake in the oven for 15 minutes, stirring twice during cooking.
4. Remove the vegetables from the oven and add the cooked pasta to the baking sheet. Mix with a few tablespoons of cooking liquid to help the sauce become smoother and the saucy vegetables stick to the pasta.
5. Gently mix in the Mozzarella and basil. Drizzle with the balsamic vinegar. Serve from the baking sheet or pour the pasta into a large bowl.

Per Serving

calories: 147 | fat: 3.0g | protein: 16.0g | carbs: 17.0g | fiber: 5.0g | sodium: 420mg

Garlic Shrimp Fettuccine

Prep time: 10 minutes | Cook time: 15 minutes | Serves 4 to 6

8 ounces (227 g) fettuccine pasta

¼ cup extra-virgin olive oil

3 tablespoons garlic, minced

1 pound (454 g) large shrimp, peeled and deveined

⅓ cup lemon juice

1 tablespoon lemon zest

½ teaspoon salt

½ teaspoon freshly ground black pepper

1. Bring a large pot of salted water to a boil. Add the fettuccine and cook for 8 minutes. Reserve ½ cup of the cooking liquid and drain the pasta.
2. In a large saucepan over medium heat, heat the olive oil. Add the garlic and sauté for 1 minute.
3. Add the shrimp to the saucepan and cook each side for 3 minutes. Remove the shrimp from the pan and set aside.
4. Add the remaining ingredients to the saucepan. Stir in the cooking liquid. Add the pasta and toss together to evenly coat the pasta.
5. Transfer the pasta to a serving dish and serve topped with the cooked shrimp.

Per Serving

calories: 615 | fat: 17.0g | protein: 33.0g | carbs: 89.0g | fiber: 4.0g | sodium: 407mg

Pesto Pasta

Prep time: 10 minutes | Cook time: 8 minutes | Serves 4 to 6

1 pound (454 g) spaghetti

4 cups fresh basil leaves, stems removed

3 cloves garlic

1 teaspoon salt

½ teaspoon freshly ground black pepper

½ cup toasted pine nuts

¼ cup lemon juice

½ cup grated Parmesan cheese

1 cup extra-virgin olive oil

1. Bring a large pot of salted water to a boil. Add the spaghetti to the pot and cook for 8 minutes.
2. In a food processor, place the remaining ingredients, except for the olive oil, and pulse.
3. While the processor is running, slowly drizzle the olive oil through the top opening. Process until all the olive oil has been added.
4. Reserve ½ cup of the cooking liquid. Drain the pasta and put it into a large bowl. Add the pesto and cooking liquid to the bowl of pasta and toss everything together.
5. Serve immediately.

Per Serving

calories: 1067 | fat: 72.0g | protein: 23.0g | carbs: 91..0g | fiber: 6.0g | sodium: 817mg

Spaghetti with Pine Nuts and Cheese

Prep time: 10 minutes | Cook time: 11 minutes | Serves 4 to 6

8 ounces (227 g) spaghetti

4 tablespoons almond butter

1 teaspoon freshly ground black pepper

½ cup pine nuts

1 cup fresh grated Parmesan cheese, divided

1. Bring a large pot of salted water to a boil. Add the pasta and cook for 8 minutes.
2. In a large saucepan over medium heat, combine the butter, black pepper, and pine nuts. Cook for 2 to 3 minutes, or until the pine nuts are lightly toasted.
3. Reserve ½ cup of the pasta water. Drain the pasta and place it into the pan with the pine nuts.
4. Add ¾ cup of the Parmesan cheese and the reserved pasta water to the pasta and toss everything together to evenly coat the pasta.
5. Transfer the pasta to a serving dish and top with the remaining ¼ cup of the Parmesan cheese. Serve immediately.

Per Serving

calories: 542 | fat: 32.0g | protein: 20.0g | carbs: 46.0g | fiber: 2.0g | sodium: 552mg

Creamy Garlic Parmesan Chicken Pasta

Prep time: 5 minutes | Cook time: 15 minutes | Serves 4

3 tablespoons extra-virgin olive oil
2 boneless, skinless chicken breasts, cut into thin strips
1 large onion, thinly sliced
3 tablespoons garlic, minced
1½ teaspoons salt
1 pound (454 g) fettuccine pasta
1 cup heavy whipping cream
¾ cup freshly grated Parmesan cheese, divided
½ teaspoon freshly ground black pepper

1. In a large skillet over medium heat, heat the olive oil. Add the chicken and cook for 3 minutes.
2. Add the onion, garlic and salt to the skillet. Cook for 7 minutes, stirring occasionally.
3. Meanwhile, bring a large pot of salted water to a boil and add the pasta, then cook for 7 minutes.
4. While the pasta is cooking, add the heavy cream, ½ cup of the Parmesan cheese and black pepper to the chicken. Simmer for 3 minutes.
5. Reserve ½ cup of the pasta water. Drain the pasta and add it to the chicken cream sauce.
6. Add the reserved pasta water to the pasta and toss together. Simmer for 2 minutes. Top with the remaining ¼ cup of the Parmesan cheese and serve warm.

Per Serving

calories: 879 | fat: 42.0g | protein: 35.0g | carbs: 90.0g | fiber: 5.0g | sodium: 1336mg

Bulgur Pilaf with Garbanzo

Prep time: 5 minutes | Cook time: 20 minutes | Serves 4 to 6

3 tablespoons extra-virgin olive oil
1 large onion, chopped
1 (1-pound / 454-g) can garbanzo beans, rinsed and drained
2 cups bulgur wheat, rinsed and drained
1½ teaspoons salt
½ teaspoon cinnamon
4 cups water

1. In a large pot over medium heat, heat the olive oil. Add the onion and cook for 5 minutes.
2. Add the garbanzo beans and cook for an additional 5 minutes.
3. Stir in the remaining ingredients.
4. Reduce the heat to low. Cover and cook for 10 minutes.
5. When done, fluff the pilaf with a fork. Cover and let sit for another 5 minutes before serving.

Per Serving

calories: 462 | fat: 13.0g | protein: 15.0g | carbs: 76.0g | fiber: 19.0g | sodium: 890mg

Pearl Barley Risotto with Parmesan Cheese

Prep time: 5 minutes | Cook time: 20 minutes | Serves 6

4 cups low-sodium or no-salt-added vegetable broth
1 tablespoon extra-virgin olive oil
1 cup chopped yellow onion
2 cups uncooked pearl barley
½ cup dry white wine
1 cup freshly grated Parmesan cheese, divided
¼ teaspoon kosher or sea salt
¼ teaspoon freshly ground black pepper
Fresh chopped chives and lemon wedges, for serving (optional)

1. Pour the broth into a medium saucepan and bring to a simmer.
2. Heat the olive oil in a large stockpot over medium-high heat. Add the onion and cook for about 4 minutes, stirring occasionally.
3. Add the barley and cook for 2 minutes, stirring, or until the barley is toasted. Pour in the wine and cook for about 1 minute, or until most of the liquid evaporates. Add 1 cup of the warm broth into the pot and cook, stirring, for about 2 minutes, or until most of the liquid is absorbed.
4. Add the remaining broth, 1 cup at a time, cooking until each cup is absorbed (about 2 minutes each time) before adding the next. The last addition of broth will take a bit longer to absorb, about 4 minutes.
5. Remove the pot from the heat, and stir in ½ cup of the cheese, and the salt and pepper.
6. Serve with the remaining ½ cup of the cheese on the side, along with the chives and lemon wedges (if desired).

Per Serving calories: 421 | fat: 11.0g | protein: 15.0g | carbs: 67.0g | fiber: 11.0g | sodium: 641mg

Israeli Couscous with Asparagus

Prep time: 5 minutes | Cook time: 25 minutes | Serves 6

1½ pounds (680 g) asparagus spears, ends trimmed and stalks chopped into 1-inch pieces
1 garlic clove, minced
1 tablespoon extra-virgin olive oil
¼ teaspoon freshly ground black pepper
1¾ cups water
1 (8-ounce / 227-g) box uncooked whole-wheat or regular Israeli couscous (about 1⅓ cups)
¼ teaspoon kosher salt
1 cup garlic-and-herb goat cheese, at room temperature

1. Preheat the oven to 425ºF (220ºC).
2. In a large bowl, stir together the asparagus, garlic, oil, and pepper. Spread the asparagus on a large, rimmed baking sheet and roast for 10 minutes, stirring a few times. Remove the pan from the oven, and spoon the asparagus into a large serving bowl. Set aside.
3. While the asparagus is roasting, bring the water to a boil in a medium saucepan. Add the couscous and season with salt, stirring well.
4. Reduce the heat to medium-low. Cover and cook for 12 minutes, or until the water is absorbed.
5. Pour the hot couscous into the bowl with the asparagus. Add the goat cheese and mix thoroughly until completely melted. Serve immediately.

Per Serving calories: 103 | fat: 2.0g | protein: 6.0g | carbs: 18.0g | fiber: 5.0g | sodium: 343mg

Freekeh Pilaf with Dates and Pistachios

Prep time: 10 minutes | Cook time: 10 minutes | Serves 4 to 6

2 tablespoons extra-virgin olive oil, plus extra for drizzling
1 shallot, minced
1½ teaspoons grated fresh ginger
¼ teaspoon ground coriander
¼ teaspoon ground cumin
Salt and pepper, to taste
1¾ cups water
1½ cups cracked freekeh, rinsed
3 ounces (85 g) pitted dates, chopped
¼ cup shelled pistachios, toasted and coarsely chopped
1½ tablespoons lemon juice
¼ cup chopped fresh mint

1. Set the Instant Pot to Sauté mode and heat the olive oil until shimmering. Add the shallot, ginger, coriander, cumin, salt, and pepper to the pot and cook for about 2 minutes, or until the shallot is softened. Stir in the water and freekeh.
2. Secure the lid. Select the Manual mode and set the cooking time for 4 minutes at High Pressure. Once cooking is complete, do a quick pressure release. Carefully open the lid. Add the dates, pistachios and lemon juice and gently fluff the freekeh with a fork to combine. Season to taste with salt and pepper.
3. Transfer to a serving dish and sprinkle with the mint. Serve drizzled with extra olive oil.

Per Serving calories: 280 | fat: 8.0g | protein: 8.0g | carbs: 46.0g | fiber: 9.0g | sodium: 200mg

Quinoa with Baby Potatoes and Broccoli

Prep time: 5 minutes | Cook time: 10 minutes | Serves 4

2 tablespoons olive oil
1 cup baby potatoes, cut in half
1 cup broccoli florets
2 cups cooked quinoa
Zest of 1 lemon
Sea salt and freshly ground pepper, to taste

1. Heat the olive oil in a large skillet over medium heat until shimmering. Add the potatoes and cook for about 6 to 7 minutes, or until softened and golden brown. Add the broccoli and cook for about 3 minutes, or until tender.
2. Remove from the heat and add the quinoa and lemon zest. Season with salt and pepper to taste, then serve.

Per Serving calories: 205 | fat: 8.6g | protein: 5.1g | carbs: 27.3g | fiber: 3.7g | sodium: 158mg

Black-Eyed Pea and Vegetable Stew

Prep time: 15 minutes | Cook time: 40 minutes | Serves 2

½ cup black-eyed peas, soaked in water overnight
3 cups water, plus more as needed
1 large carrot, peeled and cut into ½-inch pieces (about ¾ cup)
1 large beet, peeled and cut into ½-inch pieces (about ¾ cup)
¼ teaspoon turmeric
¼ teaspoon cayenne pepper
¼ teaspoon ground cumin seeds, toasted
¼ cup finely chopped parsley
¼ teaspoon salt (optional)
½ teaspoon fresh lime juice

1. Pour the black-eyed peas and water into a large pot, then cook over medium heat for 25 minutes. Add the carrot and beet to the pot and cook for 10 minutes more, adding more water as needed.
2. Add the turmeric, cayenne pepper, cumin, and parsley to the pot and cook for another 6 minutes, or until the vegetables are softened.
3. Stir the mixture periodically. Season with salt, if desired.
4. Serve drizzled with the fresh lime juice.

Per Serving

calories: 89 | fat: 0.7g | protein: 4.1g | carbs: 16.6g | fiber: 4.5g | sodium: 367mg

Chickpea Salad with Tomatoes and Basil

Prep time: 5 minutes | Cook time: 45 minutes | Serves 2

1 cup dried chickpeas, rinsed
1 quart water, or enough to cover the chickpeas by 3 to 4 inches
1½ cups halved grape tomatoes
1 cup chopped fresh basil leaves
2 to 3 tablespoons balsamic vinegar
½ teaspoon garlic powder
½ teaspoon salt, or more to taste

1. In your Instant Pot, combine the chickpeas and water.
2. Secure the lid. Select the Manual mode and set the cooking time for 45 minutes at High Pressure.
3. Once cooking is complete, do a natural pressure release for 20 minutes, then release any remaining pressure. Carefully open the lid and drain the chickpeas. Refrigerate to cool (unless you want to serve this warm, which is good, too).
4. While the chickpeas cool, in a large bowl, stir together the basil, tomatoes, vinegar, garlic powder, and salt. Add the beans, stir to combine, and serve.

Per Serving

calories: 395 | fat: 6.0g | protein: 19.8g | carbs: 67.1g | fiber: 19.0g | sodium: 612mg

Mediterranean Lentils

Prep time: 7 minutes | Cook time: 24 minutes | Serves 2

1 tablespoon olive oil
1 small sweet or yellow onion, diced
1 garlic clove, diced
1 teaspoon dried oregano
½ teaspoon ground cumin
½ teaspoon dried parsley
½ teaspoon salt, plus more as needed
¼ teaspoon freshly ground black pepper, plus more as needed
1 tomato, diced
1 cup brown or green lentils
2½ cups vegetable stock
1 bay leaf

1. Set your Instant Pot to Sauté and heat the olive oil until it shimmers. Add the onion and cook for 3 to 4 minutes until soft. Turn off the Instant Pot and add the garlic, oregano, cumin, parsley, salt, and pepper. Cook until fragrant, about 1 minute.
2. Stir in the tomato, lentils, stock, and bay leaf.
3. Lock the lid. Select the Manual mode and set the cooking time for 18 minutes at High Pressure.
4. When the timer beeps, perform a natural pressure release for 10 minutes, then release any remaining pressure. Carefully open the lid. Remove and discard the bay leaf. Taste and season with more salt and pepper, as needed. If there's too much liquid remaining, select Sauté and cook until it evaporates. Serve warm.

Per Serving calories: 426 | fat: 8.1g | protein: 26.2g | carbs: 63.8g | fiber: 31.0g | sodium: 591mg

Mediterranean-Style Beans and Greens

Prep time: 10 minutes | Cook time: 15 minutes | Serves 2

1 (14.5-ounce / 411-g) can diced tomatoes with juice

1 (15-ounce / 425-g) can cannellini beans, drained and rinsed

2 tablespoons chopped green olives, plus 1 or 2 sliced for garnish

¼ cup vegetable broth, plus more as needed

1 teaspoon extra-virgin olive oil

2 cloves garlic, minced

4 cups arugula

¼ cup freshly squeezed lemon juice

1. In a medium saucepan, bring the tomatoes, beans, and chopped olives to a low boil, adding just enough broth to make the ingredients saucy (you may need more than ¼ cup if your canned tomatoes don't have a lot of juice). Reduce heat to low and simmer for about 5 minutes.
2. Meanwhile, in a large skillet, heat the olive oil over medium-high heat. When the oil is hot and starts to shimmer, add garlic and sauté just until it starts to turn slightly tan, about 30 seconds. Add the arugula and lemon juice, stirring to coat leaves with the olive oil and juice. Cover, reduce the heat to low, and simmer for 3 to 5 minutes. Serve the beans over the greens and garnish with olive slices.

Per Serving calories: 262 | fat: 5.9g | protein: 13.2g | carbs: 40.4g | fiber: 9.8g | sodium: 897mg

Rich Cauliflower Alfredo

Prep time: 35 minutes | Cook time: 30 minutes | Serves 4

Cauliflower Alfredo Sauce:

1 tablespoon avocado oil

½ yellow onion, diced

2 cups cauliflower florets

2 garlic cloves, minced

1½ teaspoons miso

1 teaspoon Dijon mustard

Pinch of ground nutmeg

½ cup unsweetened almond milk

1½ tablespoons fresh lemon juice

2 tablespoons nutritional yeast

Sea salt and ground black pepper, to taste

Fettuccine:

1 tablespoon avocado oil

½ yellow onion, diced

1 cup broccoli florets

1 zucchini, halved lengthwise and cut into ¼-inch-thick half-moons

Sea salt and ground black pepper, to taste

½ cup sun-dried tomatoes, drained if packed in oil

8 ounces (227 g) cooked whole-wheat fettuccine

½ cup fresh basil, cut into ribbons

Make the Sauce

1. Heat the avocado oil in a nonstick skillet over medium-high heat until shimmering.
2. Add half of the onion to the skillet and sauté for 5 minutes or until translucent. Add the cauliflower and garlic to the skillet. Reduce the heat to low and cook for 8 minutes or until the cauliflower is tender.
3. Pour them in a food processor, add the remaining ingredients for the sauce and pulse to combine well. Set aside.

Make the Fettuccine

4. Heat the avocado oil in a nonstick skillet over medium-high heat. Add the remaining half of onion and sauté for 5 minutes or until translucent.

5. Add the broccoli and zucchini. Sprinkle with salt and ground black pepper, then sauté for 5 minutes or until tender.
6. Add the sun-dried tomatoes, reserved sauce, and fettuccine. Sauté for 3 minutes or until well-coated and heated through. Serve the fettuccine on a large plate and spread with basil before serving.

Per Serving calories: 288 | fat: 15.9g | protein: 10.1g | carbs: 32.5g | fiber: 8.1g | sodium: 185mg

Butternut Squash and Zucchini with Penne

Prep time: 15 minutes | Cook time: 30 minutes | Serves 6

1 large zucchini, diced

1 large butternut squash, peeled and diced

1 large yellow onion, chopped

2 tablespoons extra-virgin olive oil

1 teaspoon paprika

½ teaspoon garlic powder

½ teaspoon sea salt

½ teaspoon freshly ground black pepper

1 pound (454 g) whole-grain penne

½ cup dry white wine

2 tablespoons grated Parmesan cheese

1. Preheat the oven to 400°F (205°C). Line a baking sheet with aluminum foil. Combine the zucchini, butternut squash, and onion in a large bowl. Drizzle with olive oil and sprinkle with paprika, garlic powder, salt, and ground black pepper. Toss to coat well.
2. Spread the vegetables in the single layer on the baking sheet, then roast in the preheated oven for 25 minutes or until the vegetables are tender.
3. Meanwhile, bring a pot of water to a boil, then add the penne and cook for 14 minutes or until al dente. Drain the penne through a colander.
4. Transfer ½ cup of roasted vegetables in a food processor, then pour in the dry white wine. Pulse until smooth.
5. Pour the puréed vegetables in a nonstick skillet and cook with penne over medium-high heat for a few minutes to heat through. Transfer the penne with the purée on a large serving plate, then spread the remaining roasted vegetables and Parmesan on top before serving.

Per Serving calories: 340 | fat: 6.2g | protein: 8.0g | carbs: 66.8g | fiber: 9.1g | sodium: 297mg

Small Pasta and Beans Pot

Prep time: 20 minutes | Cook time: 15 minutes | Serves 2 to 4

1 pound (454 g) small whole wheat pasta

1 (14.5-ounce / 411-g) can diced tomatoes, juice reserved

1 (15-ounce / 425-g) can cannellini beans, drained and rinsed

2 tablespoons no-salt-added tomato paste

1 red or yellow bell pepper, chopped

1 yellow onion, chopped

1 tablespoon Italian seasoning mix

3 garlic cloves, minced

¼ teaspoon crushed red pepper flakes, optional

1 tablespoon extra-virgin olive oil

5 cups water

1 bunch kale, stemmed and chopped

½ cup pitted Kalamata olives, chopped

1 cup sliced basil

1. Except for the kale, olives, and basil, combine all the ingredients in a pot. Stir to mix well. Bring to a boil over high heat. Stir constantly. Reduce the heat to medium high and add the kale.
2. Cook for 10 minutes or until the pasta is al dente. Stir constantly. Transfer all of them on a large plate and serve with olives and basil on top.

Per Serving calories: 357 | fat: 7.6g | protein: 18.2g | carbs: 64.5g | fiber: 10.1g | sodium: 454mg

Swoodles with Almond Butter Sauce

Prep time: 20 minutes | Cook time: 20 minutes | Serves 4

Sauce:

1 garlic clove

1-inch piece fresh ginger, peeled and sliced

¼ cup chopped yellow onion

¾ cup almond butter

1 tablespoon tamari

1 tablespoon raw honey

1 teaspoon paprika

1 tablespoon fresh lemon juice

⅛ teaspoon ground red pepper

Sea salt and ground black pepper, to taste

¼ cup water

Swoodles:

2 large sweet potatoes, spiralized

2 tablespoons coconut oil, melted

Sea salt and ground black pepper, to taste

For Serving:

½ cup fresh parsley, chopped

½ cup thinly sliced scallions

Make the Sauce

1. Put the garlic, ginger, and onion in a food processor, then pulse to combine well.
2. Add the almond butter, tamari, honey, paprika, lemon juice, ground red pepper, salt, and black pepper to the food processor. Pulse to combine well.
3. Pour in the water during the pulsing until the mixture is thick and smooth.

Make the Swoodles

4. Preheat the oven to 425ºF (220ºC). Line a baking sheet with parchment paper. Put the spiralized sweet potato in a bowl, then drizzle with olive oil. Toss to coat well. Transfer them on the baking sheet. Sprinkle with salt and pepper.
5. Bake in the preheated oven for 20 minutes or until lightly browned and al dente.

6. Check the doneness during the baking and remove any well-cooked swoodles.
7. Transfer the swoodles on a large plate and spread with sauce, parsley, and scallions. Toss to serve.

Per Serving calories: 441 | fat: 33.6g | protein: 12.0g | carbs: 29.6g | fiber: 7.8g | sodium: 479mg

Tomato Sauce and Basil Pesto Fettuccine

Prep time: 15 minutes | Cook time: 15 minutes | Serves 4

4 Roma tomatoes, diced

2 teaspoons no-salt-added tomato paste

1 tablespoon chopped fresh oregano

2 garlic cloves, minced

1 cup low-sodium vegetable soup

½ teaspoon sea salt

1 packed cup fresh basil leaves

¼ cup pine nuts

¼ cup grated Parmesan cheese

2 tablespoons extra-virgin olive oil

1 pound (454 g) cooked whole-grain fettuccine

1. Put the tomatoes, tomato paste, oregano, garlic, vegetable soup, and salt in a skillet. Stir to mix well.
2. Cook over medium heat for 10 minutes or until lightly thickened. Put the remaining ingredients, except for the fettuccine, in a food processor and pulse to combine until smooth.
3. Pour the puréed basil mixture into the tomato mixture, then add the fettuccine. Cook for a few minutes or until heated through and the fettuccine is well coated.
4. Serve immediately.

Per Serving calories: 389 | fat: 22.7g | protein: 9.7g | carbs: 40.2g | fiber: 4.8g | sodium: 616mg

Broccoli and Carrot Pasta Salad

Prep time: 5 minutes | Cook time: 10 minutes | Serves 2

8 ounces (227 g) whole-wheat pasta

2 cups broccoli florets

1 cup peeled and shredded carrots

¼ cup plain Greek yogurt

Juice of 1 lemon

1 teaspoon red pepper flakes

Sea salt and freshly ground pepper, to taste

1. Bring a large pot of lightly salted water to a boil. Add the pasta to the boiling water and cook until al dente, about 8 to 10 minutes. Drain the pasta and let rest for a few minutes.
2. When cooled, combine the pasta with the veggies, yogurt, lemon juice, and red pepper flakes in a large bowl, and stir thoroughly to combine.
3. Taste and season to taste with salt and pepper. Serve immediately.

Per Serving

calories: 428 | fat: 2.9g | protein: 15.9g | carbs: 84.6g | fiber: 11.7g | sodium: 642mg

Bean and Veggie Pasta

Prep time: 10 minutes | Cook time: 15 minutes | Serves 2

16 ounces (454 g) small whole wheat pasta, such as penne, farfalle, or macaroni
5 cups water
1 (15-ounce / 425-g) can cannellini beans, drained and rinsed
1 (14.5-ounce / 411-g) can diced (with juice) or crushed tomatoes
1 yellow onion, chopped
1 red or yellow bell pepper, chopped
2 tablespoons tomato paste
1 tablespoon olive oil
3 garlic cloves, minced
¼ teaspoon crushed red pepper (optional)
1 bunch kale, stemmed and chopped
1 cup sliced basil
½ cup pitted Kalamata olives, chopped

1. Add the pasta, water, beans, tomatoes (with juice if using diced), onion, bell pepper, tomato paste, oil, garlic, and crushed red pepper (if desired), to a large stockpot. Bring to a boil over high heat, stirring often.
2. Reduce the heat to medium-high, add the kale, and cook, continuing to stir often, until the pasta is al dente, about 10 minutes.
3. Remove from the heat and let sit for 5 minutes. Garnish with the basil and olives and serve.

Per Serving

calories: 565 | fat: 17.7g | protein: 18.0g | carbs: 85.5g | fiber: 16.5g | sodium: 540mg

Roasted Ratatouille Pasta

Prep time: 10 minutes | Cook time: 30 minutes | Serves 2

1 small eggplant (about 8 ounces / 227 g)
1 small zucchini
1 portobello mushroom
1 Roma tomato, halved
½ medium sweet red pepper, seeded
½ teaspoon salt, plus additional for the pasta water
1 teaspoon Italian herb seasoning
1 tablespoon olive oil
2 cups farfalle pasta (about 8 ounces / 227 g)
2 tablespoons minced sun-dried tomatoes in olive oil with herbs
2 tablespoons prepared pesto

1. Slice the ends off the eggplant and zucchini. Cut them lengthwise into ½- inch slices. Place the eggplant, zucchini, mushroom, tomato, and red pepper in a large bowl and sprinkle with ½ teaspoon of salt. Using your hands, toss the vegetables well so that they're covered evenly with the salt. Let them rest for about 10 minutes.
2. While the vegetables are resting, preheat the oven to 400°F (205°C). Line a baking sheet with parchment paper.
3. When the oven is hot, drain off any liquid from the vegetables and pat them dry with a paper towel. Add the Italian herb seasoning and olive oil to the vegetables and toss well to coat both sides.
4. Lay the vegetables out in a single layer on the baking sheet. Roast them for 15 to 20 minutes, flipping them over after about 10 minutes or once they start to brown on the underside. When the vegetables are charred in spots, remove them from the oven.
5. While the vegetables are roasting, fill a large saucepan with water. Add salt and cook the pasta until al dente, about 8 to 10 minutes. Drain the pasta, reserving ½ cup of the pasta water. When cool enough to handle, cut the vegetables into large chunks (about 2 inches) and add them to the hot pasta. Stir in the sun-dried tomatoes and pesto and toss everything well. Serve immediately.

Per Serving calories: 613 | fat: 16.0g | protein: 23.1g | carbs: 108.5g | fiber: 23.0g | sodium: 775mg

Lentil and Mushroom Pasta

Prep time: 10 minutes | Cook time: 50 minutes | Serves 2

2 tablespoons olive oil
1 large yellow onion, finely diced
2 portobello mushrooms, trimmed and chopped finely
2 tablespoons tomato paste
3 garlic cloves, chopped
1 teaspoon oregano
2½ cups water
1 cup brown lentils
1 (28-ounce / 794-g) can diced tomatoes with basil (with juice if diced)
1 tablespoon balsamic vinegar
Salt and black pepper, to taste
Chopped basil, for garnish
8 ounces (227 g) pasta of choice, cooked

1. Place a large stockpot over medium heat and add the olive oil. Once the oil is hot, add the onion and mushrooms. Cover and cook until both are soft, about 5 minutes. Add the tomato paste, garlic, and oregano and cook 2 minutes, stirring constantly. Stir in the water and lentils. Bring to a boil, then reduce the heat to medium-low and cook covered for 5 minutes. Add the tomatoes (and juice if using diced) and vinegar. Reduce the heat to low and cook until the lentils are tender, about 30 minutes.
2. Remove from the heat and season with salt and pepper to taste. Garnish with the basil and serve over the cooked pasta.

Per Serving

calories: 463 | fat: 15.9g | protein: 12.5g | carbs: 70.8g | fiber: 16.9g | sodium: 155mg

Tomato Basil Pasta

Prep time: 3 minutes | Cook time: 2 minutes | Serves 2

2 cups dried campanelle or similar pasta	1 or 2 pinches red pepper flakes
1¾ cups vegetable stock	½ teaspoon garlic powder
½ teaspoon salt, plus more as needed	½ teaspoon dried oregano
2 tomatoes, cut into large dices	10 to 12 fresh sweet basil leaves
	Freshly ground black pepper, to taste

1. In your Instant Pot, stir together the pasta, stock, and salt. Scatter the tomatoes on top (do not stir).
2. Secure the lid. Select the Manual mode and set the cooking time for 2 minutes at High Pressure.
3. Once cooking is complete, do a quick pressure release. Carefully open the lid.
4. Stir in the red pepper flakes, oregano, and garlic powder. If there's more than a few tablespoons of liquid in the bottom, select Sauté and cook for 2 to 3 minutes until it evaporates.
5. When ready to serve, chiffonade the basil and stir it in. Taste and season with more salt and pepper, as needed. Serve warm.

Per Serving

calories: 415 | fat: 2.0g | protein: 15.2g | carbs: 84.2g | fiber: 5.0g | sodium: 485mg

Lentil Risotto

Prep time: 10 minutes | Cook time: 20 minutes | Serves 2

½ tablespoon olive oil	1 sprig parsley, chopped
½ medium onion, chopped	½ cup Arborio (short-grain Italian) rice
½ cup dry lentils, soaked overnight	1 garlic clove, lightly mashed
½ celery stalk, chopped	2 cups vegetable stock

1. Press the Sauté button to heat your Instant Pot.
2. Add the oil and onion to the Instant Pot and sauté for 5 minutes.
3. Add the remaining ingredients to the Instant Pot, stirring well.
4. Secure the lid. Select the Manual mode and set the cooking time for 15 minutes at High Pressure.
5. Once cooking is complete, do a natural pressure release for 20 minutes, then release any remaining pressure. Carefully open the lid.
6. Stir and serve hot.

Per Serving

calories: 261 | fat: 3.6g | protein: 10.6g | carbs: 47.1g | fiber: 8.4g | sodium: 247mg

Bulgur Pilaf with Kale and Tomatoes

Prep time: 10 minutes | Cook time: 10 minutes | Serves 2

2 tablespoons olive oil,	Juice of 1 lemon
2 cloves garlic, minced	2 cups cooked bulgur wheat
1 bunch kale, trimmed and cut into bite-sized pieces	1 pint cherry tomatoes, halved
	Sea salt and freshly ground pepper, to taste

1. Heat the olive oil in a large skillet over medium heat. Add the garlic and sauté for 1 minute.
2. Add the kale leaves and stir to coat. Cook for 5 minutes until leaves are cooked through and thoroughly wilted.
3. Add the lemon juice, bulgur and tomatoes. Season with sea salt and freshly ground pepper to taste, then serve.

Per Serving

calories: 300 | fat: 14.0g | protein: 6.2g | carbs: 37.8g | fiber: 8.7g | sodium: 595mg

Cranberry and Almond Quinoa

Prep time: 5 minutes | Cook time: 10 minutes | Serves 2

2 cups water	½ cup slivered almonds
1 cup quinoa, rinsed	1 cup dried cranberries
¼ cup salted sunflower seeds	

1. Combine water and quinoa in the Instant Pot.
2. Secure the lid. Select the Manual mode and set the cooking time for 10 minutes at High Pressure.
3. Once cooking is complete, do a quick pressure release. Carefully open the lid.
4. Add sunflower seeds, almonds, and dried cranberries and gently mix until well combined.
5. Serve hot.

Per Serving

calories: 445 | fat: 14.8g | protein: 15.1g | carbs: 64.1g | fiber: 10.2g | sodium: 113mg

Pork and Spinach Spaghetti

Prep time: 15 minutes | Cook time: 16 minutes | Serves 4

2 tablespoons olive oil	1 tablespoon dried oregano
½ cup onion, chopped	1 teaspoon Italian seasoning
1 garlic clove, minced	1 fresh jalapeño chile, stemmed, seeded, and minced
1 pound (454 g) ground pork	
2 cups water	
1 (14-ounce / 397-g) can diced tomatoes, drained	1 teaspoon salt
½ cup sun-dried tomatoes	8 ounces (227 g) dried spaghetti, halved
	1 cup spinach

1. Warm oil onSauté. Add onion and garlic and cook for 2 minutes until softened. Stir in pork and cook for 5 minutes. Stir in jalapeño, water, sun- dried tomatoes, Italian seasoning, oregano, diced tomatoes, and salt with the chicken; mix spaghetti and press to submerge into the sauce.
2. Seal the lid and cook on High Pressure for 9 minutes. Release the pressure quickly. Stir in spinach, close lid again, and simmer on Keep Warm for 5 minutes until spinach is wilted.

Per Serving

calories: 621 | fat: 32.2g | protein: 29.1g | carbs: 53.9g | fiber: 5.9g | sodium: 738mg

Gouda Beef and Spinach Fettuccine

Prep time: 10 minutes | Cook time: 15 minutes | Serves 6

10 ounces (283 g) ground beef	2 cups tomatoes, diced
1 pound (454 g) fettuccine pasta	1 tablespoon olive oil
1 cup gouda cheese, shredded	1 teaspoon salt
1 cup fresh spinach, torn	½ teaspoon ground black pepper
1 medium onion, chopped	

1. Heat the olive oil on Sauté mode in the Instant Pot. Stir-fry the beef and onion for 5 minutes. Add the pasta. Pour water enough to cover and season with salt and pepper. Cook on High Pressure for 5 minutes. Do a quick release. Press Sauté and stir in the tomato and spinach; cook for 5 minutes. Top with Gouda to serve.

Per Serving calories: 493 | fat: 17.7g | protein: 20.6g | carbs: 64.3g | fiber: 9.5g | sodium: 561mg

Rigatoni and Zucchini Minestrone

Prep time: 20 minutes | Cook time: 7 minutes | Serves 4

3 tablespoons olive oil	1 cup chopped zucchini
1 onion, diced	1 bay leaf
1 celery stalk, diced	1 teaspoon mixed herbs
1 large carrot, peeled and diced	¼ teaspoon cayenne pepper
14 ounces (397 g) canned chopped tomatoes	½ teaspoon salt
	¼ cup shredded Pecorino Romano cheese
4 ounces (113 g) rigatoni	1 garlic clove, minced
3 cups water	⅓ cup olive oil-based pesto

1. Heat oil on Sauté and cook onion, celery, garlic, and carrot for 3 minutes, stirring occasionally until the vegetables are softened. Stir in rigatoni, tomatoes, water, zucchini, bay leaf, herbs, cayenne, and salt. Seal the lid and cook on High for 4 minutes. Do a natural pressure release for 5 minutes. Adjust the taste of the soup with salt and black pepper, and remove the bay leaf. Ladle the soup into serving bowls and drizzle the pesto over. Serve with the garlic toasts.

Per Serving calories: 278 | fat: 23.4g | protein: 6.7g | carbs: 12.2g | fiber: 3.5g | sodium: 793mg

Asparagus and Broccoli Primavera Farfalle

Prep time: 15 minutes | Cook time: 12 minutes | Serves 4

1 bunch asparagus, trimmed, cut into 1-inch pieces	3 garlic cloves, minced
2 cups broccoli florets	2½ cups vegetable stock
3 tablespoons olive oil	½ cup heavy cream
3 teaspoons salt	1 cup small tomatoes, halved
10 ounces (283 g) egg noodles	¼ cup chopped basil
	½ cup grated Parmesan cheese

1. Pour 2 cups of water, add the noodles, 2 tablespoons of olive oil, garlic and salt. Place a trivet over the water. Combine asparagus, broccoli, remaining olive oil and salt in a bowl. Place the vegetables on the trivet. Seal the lid and cook on Steam for 12 minutes on High. Do a quick release. Remove the vegetables to a plate. Stir the heavy cream and tomatoes in the pasta. Press Sauté and simmer the cream until desired consistency.

2. Gently mix in the asparagus and broccoli. Garnish with basil and Parmesan, to serve.

Per Serving calories: 544 | fat: 23.8g | protein: 18.5g | carbs: 66.1g | fiber: 6.0g | sodium: 2354mg

Super Cheesy Tagliatelle

Prep time: 10 minutes | Cook time: 20 minutes | Serves 6

¼ cup goat cheese, chevre	2 tablespoons olive oil
¼ cup grated Pecorino cheese	1 tablespoon Italian Seasoning mix
½ cup grated Parmesan	1 cup vegetable broth
1 cup heavy cream	1 pound (454 g) tagliatelle
½ cup grated Gouda	

1. In a bowl, mix goat cheese, pecorino, Parmesan, and heavy cream. Stir in Italian seasoning. Transfer to your instant pot. Stir in the broth and olive oil.
2. Seal the lid and cook on High Pressure for 4 minutes. Do a quick release.
1. Meanwhile, drop the tagliatelle in boiling water and cook for 6 minutes.
2. Remove the instant pot's lid and stir in the tagliatelle. Top with grated gouda and let simmer for about 10 minutes on Sauté mode.

Per Serving

calories: 511 | fat: 22.0g | protein: 14.5g | carbs: 65.7g | fiber: 9.0g | sodium: 548mg

Chickpea Curry

Prep time: 10 minutes | Cook time: 24 minutes | Serves 4

½ cup raw chickpeas	1 cup fresh tomato purée
1½ tablespoons cooking oil	½ green chili, finely chopped
½ cup chopped onions	¼ teaspoon turmeric
1 bay leaf	½ teaspoon coriander powder
½ tablespoon grated garlic	
¼ tablespoon grated ginger	1 teaspoon chili powder
¾ cup water	1 cup chopped baby spinach
	Salt, to taste
	Boiled white rice, for serving

1. Add the oil and onions to the Instant Pot. Sauté for 5 minutes.
2. Stir in ginger, garlic paste, green chili and bay leaf. Cook for 1 minute, then add all the spices.
3. Add the chickpeas, tomato purée and the water to the pot.
4. Cover and secure the lid. Turn its pressure release handle to the sealing position.
5. Cook on the Manual function with High Pressure for 15 minutes.
6. After the beep, do a Natural release for 20 minutes.
7. Stir in spinach and cook for 3 minutes on the Sauté setting.
8. Serve hot with boiled white rice.

Per Serving

calories: 176 | fat: 6.8g | protein: 6.7g | carbs: 24.1g | fiber: 5.1g | sodium: 185mg

Cumin Quinoa Pilaf

Prep time: 5 minutes | Cook time: 5 minutes | Serves 2

2 tablespoons extra virgin olive oil	2 teaspoons ground cumin
2 cloves garlic, minced	2 teaspoons turmeric
3 cups water	Salt, to taste
2 cups quinoa, rinsed	1 handful parsley, chopped

1. Press the Sauté button to heat your Instant Pot.
2. Once hot, add the oil and garlic to the pot, stir and cook for 1 minute. Add water, quinoa, cumin, turmeric, and salt, stirring well. Lock the lid. Select the Manual mode and set the cooking time for 1 minute at High Pressure.
3. When the timer beeps, perform a natural pressure release for 10 minutes, then release any remaining pressure. Carefully remove the lid.
4. Fluff the quinoa with a fork. Season with more salt, if needed.
5. Sprinkle the chopped parsley on top and serve.

Per Serving

calories: 384 | fat: 12.3g | protein: 12.8g | carbs: 57.4g | fiber: 6.9g | sodium: 448mg

Mint Brown Rice

Prep time: 5 minutes | Cook time: 22 minutes | Serves 2

2 cloves garlic, minced	1 cup short- or long-grain brown rice
¼ cup chopped fresh mint, plus more for garnish	1½ cups water or low-sodium vegetable broth
1 tablespoon chopped dried chives	½ to 1 teaspoon sea salt

1. Place the garlic, mint, chives, rice, and water in the Instant Pot. Stir to combine.
2. Secure the lid. Select the Manual mode and set the cooking time for 22 minutes at High Pressure.
3. Once cooking is complete, do a natural pressure release for 10 minutes, then release any remaining pressure. Carefully open the lid.
4. Add salt to taste and serve garnished with more mint.

Per Serving

calories: 514 | fat: 6.6g | protein: 20.7g | carbs: 80.4g | fiber: 3.3g | sodium: 786mg

Rice and Sweet Potato Pilaf

Prep time: 15 minutes | Cook time: 10 minutes | Serves 4 to 6

2 tablespoons extra-virgin olive oil	12 ounces (340 g) sweet potato, peeled, quartered lengthwise, and sliced ½ inch thick
1 onion, chopped fine	
½ teaspoon table salt	½ preserved lemon, pulp and white pith removed, rind rinsed and minced (2 tablespoons)
2 garlic cloves, minced	
1½ teaspoons ground turmeric	
1 teaspoon ground coriander	
⅛ teaspoon cayenne pepper	½ cup shelled pistachios, toasted and chopped
2 cups chicken broth	
1½ cups long-grain white rice, rinsed	¼ cup fresh cilantro leaves
	¼ cup pomegranate seeds

1. Using highest Sauté function, heat oil in Instant Pot until shimmering. Add onion and salt and cook until onion is softened, about 5 minutes.
2. Stir in garlic, turmeric, coriander, and cayenne and cook until fragrant, about 30 seconds. Stir in broth, rice, and sweet potato. Lock lid in place and close pressure release valve. Select Manual function and cook for 4 minutes. Turn off Instant Pot and quick release pressure. Carefully remove lid, allowing steam to escape away from you.
3. Add preserved lemon and gently fluff rice with fork to combine. Lay clean dish towel over pot, replace lid, and let sit for 5 minutes. Season with salt and pepper to taste. Transfer to serving dish and sprinkle with pistachios, cilantro, and pomegranate seeds. Serve.

Per Serving

calories: 698 | fat: 22.8g | protein: 36.8g | carbs: 85.5g | fiber: 5.9g | sodium: 802mg

Shrimp and Asparagus Risotto

Prep time: 15 minutes | Cook time: 58 minutes | Serves 4

1 tablespoon olive oil	1¼ cups chicken broth
1 pound (454 g) asparagus, trimmed and roughly chopped	¾ cup milk
	1 tablespoon coconut oil
1 cup spinach, chopped	16 shrimp, cleaned and deveined
1½ cups mushrooms, chopped	Salt and ground black pepper, to taste
1 cup rice, rinsed and drained	¾ cup Parmesan cheese, shredded

1. Warm the oil on Sauté. Add spinach, mushrooms and asparagus and Sauté for 10 minutes until cooked through. Press Cancel. Add rice, milk and chicken broth to the pot as you stir. Seal the lid, press Multigrain and cook for 40 minutes on High Pressure. Do a quick release, open the lid and put the rice on a serving plate.
2. Take back the empty pot to the pressure cooker, add coconut oil and press Sauté. Add shrimp and cook each side for 4 minutes until cooked through and turns pink. Set shrimp over rice, add pepper and salt for seasoning. Serve topped with shredded Parmesan cheese.

Per Serving calories: 385 | fat: 14.3g | protein: 16.5g | carbs: 48.4g | fiber: 4.1g | sodium: 771mg

Pancetta with Garbanzo Beans

Prep time: 10 minutes | Cook time: 38 minutes | Serves 6

3 strips pancetta	½ cup ketchup
1 onion, diced	¼ cup sugar
15 ounces (425 g) canned garbanzo beans	1 teaspoon ground mustard powder
2 cups water	1 teaspoon salt
1 cup apple cider	1 teaspoon black pepper
2 garlic cloves, minced	Fresh parsley, for garnish

1. Cook pancetta for 5 minutes, until crispy, on Sauté mode. Add onion and garlic, and cook for 3 minutes until soft. Mix in garbanzo beans, ketchup, sugar, salt, apple cider, mustard powder, water, and pepper.
2. Seal the lid, press Bean/Chili and cook on High Pressure for 30 minutes. Release pressure naturally for 10 minutes. Serve in bowls garnished with parsley.

Per Serving

calories: 163 | fat: 5.7g | protein: 5.4g | carbs: 22.1g | fiber: 3.7g | sodium: 705mg

67

Brown Rice Stuffed Portobello Mushrooms

Prep time: 15 minutes | Cook time: 10 minutes | Serves 4

4 large portobello mushrooms, stems and gills removed	1 green bell pepper, seeded and diced
2 tablespoons olive oil	½ cup feta cheese, crumbled
½ cup brown rice, cooked	Juice of 1 lemon
1 tomato, seed removed and chopped	½ teaspoon salt
¼ cup black olives, pitted and chopped	½ teaspoon ground black pepper
	Minced fresh cilantro, for garnish
	1 cup vegetable broth

1. Brush the mushrooms with olive oil.
2. Arrange the mushrooms in a single layer in an oiled baking pan. In a bowl, mix the rice, tomato, olives, bell pepper, feta cheese, lemon juice, salt, and black pepper.
3. Spoon the rice mixture into the mushrooms. Pour in the broth, seal the lid and cook on High Pressure for 10 minutes. Do a quick release. Garnish with fresh cilantro and serve immediately.

Per Serving

calories: 190 | fat: 12.5g | protein: 5.9g | carbs: 15.2g | fiber: 2.6g | sodium: 682mg

Spinach and Ricotta Stuffed Pasta Shells

Prep time: 15 minutes | Cook time: 35 minutes | Serves 6

2 cups onion, chopped	1½ cups feta cheese, crumbled
1 cup carrot, chopped	2 cups spinach, chopped
3 garlic cloves, minced	¾ cup grated Pecorino Romano cheese
3½ tablespoons olive oil,	2 tablespoons chopped fresh chives
1 (28-ounce / 794-g) canned tomatoes, crushed	1 tablespoon chopped fresh dill
12 ounces (340 g) conchiglie pasta	Salt and ground black pepper to taste
1 tablespoon olive oil	1 cup shredded Cheddar cheese
2 cups ricotta cheese, crumbled	

1. Warm olive oil on Sauté. Add onion, carrot, and garlic, and cook for 5 minutes until tender. Stir in tomatoes and cook for another 10 minutes.
2. Remove to a bowl and set aside.
3. Wipe the pot with a damp cloth, add pasta and cover with enough water. Seal the lid and cook for 5 minutes on High Pressure. Do a quick release and drain the pasta. Lightly Grease olive oil to a baking sheet.
4. In a bowl, combine feta and ricotta cheese.
5. Add spinach, Pecorino Romano cheese, dill, and chives, and stir well. Adjust the seasonings. Using a spoon, fill the shells with the mixture.
6. Spread 4 cups tomato sauce on the baking sheet. Place the stuffed shells over with seam-sides down and sprinkle Cheddar cheese atop. Use aluminum foil to the cover the baking dish.
7. Pour 1 cup of water in the pot of the Pressure cooker and insert the trivet. Lower the baking dish onto the trivet. Seal the lid, and cook for 15 minutes on High Pressure.
8. Do a quick pressure release. Take away the foil. Place the stuffed shells to serving plates and top with tomato sauce before serving.

Per Serving

calories: 730 | fat: 41.5g | protein: 30.0g | carbs: 62.7g | fiber: 10.6g | sodium: 966mg

Chili Halloumi Cheese with Rice

Prep time: 10 minutes | Cook time: 8 minutes | Serves 6

2 cups water	1 teaspoon fresh minced garlic
2 tablespoons brown sugar	20 ounces (567 g) Halloumi cheese, cubed
2 tablespoons rice vinegar	1 cup rice
1 tablespoon sweet chili sauce	¼ cup chopped fresh chives, for garnish
1 tablespoon olive oil	

1. Heat the oil on Sauté and fry the halloumi for 5 minutes until golden brown. Set aside.
2. To the pot, add water, garlic, olive oil, vinegar, sugar, soy sauce, and chili sauce and mix well until smooth. Stir in rice noodles. Seal the lid and cook on High Pressure for 3 minutes. Release the pressure quickly. Split the rice between bowls. Top with fried halloumi and sprinkle with fresh chives before serving.

Per Serving

calories: 534 | fat: 34.3g | protein: 24.9g | carbs: 30.1g | fiber: 1.0g | sodium: 652mg

Grana Padano Risotto

Prep time: 10 minutes | Cook time: 23 minutes | Serves 6

1 tablespoon olive oil	1 teaspoon salt
1 white onion, chopped	½ teaspoon ground white pepper
2 cups Carnaroli rice, rinsed	2 tablespoons Grana padano cheese, grated
¼ cup dry white wine	¼ tablespoon Grana padano cheese, flakes
4 cups chicken stock	

1. Warm oil on Sauté. Stir-fry onion for 3 minutes until soft and translucent. Add rice and cook for 5 minutes stirring occasionally.
2. Pour wine into the pot to deglaze, scrape away any browned bits of food from the pan.
3. Stir in stock, pepper, and salt to the pot. Seal the lid, press Rice and cook on High Pressure for 15 minutes. Release the pressure quickly.
4. Sprinkle with grated Parmesan cheese and stir well. Top with flaked cheese for garnish before serving.

Per Serving

calories: 307 | fat: 6.0g | protein: 8.2g | carbs: 53.2g | fiber: 2.1g | sodium: 945mg

Turkey and Bell Pepper Tortiglioni

Prep time: 20 minutes | Cook time: 10 minutes | Serves 6

2 teaspoons chili powder	1 cup salsa
1 teaspoon salt	1 pound (454 g) tortiglioni
1 teaspoon cumin	1 red bell pepper, chopped diagonally
1 teaspoon onion powder	
1 teaspoon garlic powder	1 yellow bell pepper, chopped diagonally
½ teaspoon thyme	
1½ pounds (680 g) turkey breast, cut into strips	1 green bell pepper, chopped diagonally
1 tablespoon olive oil	1 cup shredded Gouda cheese
1 red onion, cut into wedges	
4 garlic cloves, minced	½ cup sour cream
3 cups chicken broth	½ cup chopped parsley

1. In a bowl, mix chili powder, cumin, garlic powder, onion powder, salt, and oregano. Reserve 1 teaspoon of seasoning. Coat turkey with the remaining seasoning.
2. Warm oil on Sauté. Add turkey strips and sauté for 4 to 5 minutes until browned. Place the turkey in a bowl. Sauté the onion and garlic for 1 minute in the cooker until soft. Press Cancel. Mix in salsa, broth, and scrape the bottom of any brown bits. Into the broth mixture, stir in tortiglioni pasta and cover with bell peppers and chicken.
3. Seal the lid and cook for 5 minutes on High Pressure. Do a quick Pressure release.
4. Open the lid and sprinkle with shredded gouda cheese and reserved seasoning, and stir well. Divide into plates and top with sour cream. Add parsley for garnishing and serve.

Per Serving calories: 646 | fat: 21.7g | protein: 41.1g | carbs: 72.9g | fiber: 11.1g | sodium: 1331mg

Carrot Risoni

Prep time: 5 minutes | Cook time: 11 minutes | Serves 6

1 cup orzo, rinsed	2 tablespoons olive oil
2 cups water	Salt, to taste
2 carrots, cut into sticks	Fresh cilantro, chopped, for garnish
1 large onion, chopped	

1. Heat oil on Sauté. Add onion and carrots and stir-fry for about 10 minutes until tender and crispy. Remove to a plate and set aside. Add water, salt and orzo in the instant pot.
2. Seal the lid and cook on High Pressure for 1 minute. Do a quick release. Fluff the cooked orzo with a fork. Transfer to a serving plate and top with the carrots and onion. Serve scattered with cilantro.

Per Serving
calories: 121 | fat: 4.9g | protein: 1.7g | carbs: 18.1g | fiber: 2.9g | sodium: 17mg

Roasted Butternut Squash and Rice

Prep time: 15 minutes | Cook time: 15 minutes | Serves 4

½ cup water	1 teaspoon freshly ground black pepper
2 cups vegetable broth	
1 small butternut squash, peeled and sliced	1 cup feta cheese, cubed
2 tablespoons olive oil, divided	1 tablespoon coconut aminos
1 teaspoon salt	2 teaspoons arrowroot starch
	1 cup jasmine rice, cooked

1. Pour the rice and broth in the pot and stir to combine. In a bowl, toss butternut squash with 1 tablespoon of olive oil and season with salt and black pepper.
2. In another bowl, mix the remaining olive oil, water and coconut aminos. Toss feta in the mixture, add the arrowroot starch, and toss again to combine well. Transfer to a greased baking dish.
3. Lay a trivet over the rice and place the baking dish on the trivet. Seal the lid and cook on High for 15 minutes. Do a quick pressure release. Fluff the rice with a fork and serve with squash and feta.

Per Serving
calories: 258 | fat: 14.9g | protein: 7.8g | carbs: 23.2g | fiber: 1.2g | sodium: 1180mg

Pesto Arborio Rice and Veggie Bowls

Prep time: 10 minutes | Cook time: 1 minute | Serves 2

1 cup arborio rice, rinsed and drained	1 bunch baby carrots, peeled
	¼ cabbage, chopped
2 cups vegetable broth	2 eggs
Salt and black pepper to taste	¼ cup pesto sauce
1 potato, peeled, cubed	Lemon wedges, for serving
1 head broccoli, cut into small florets	

1. In the pot, mix broth, pepper, rice and salt. Set trivet to the inner pot on top of rice and add a steamer basket to the top of the trivet. Mix carrots, potato, eggs and broccoli in the steamer basket. Add pepper and salt for seasoning.
2. Seal the lid and cook for 1 minute on High Pressure. Quick release the pressure. Take away the trivet and steamer basket from the pot.
3. Set the eggs in a bowl of ice water. Then peel and halve the eggs. Use a fork to fluff rice.
4. Adjust the seasonings. In two bowls, equally divide rice, broccoli, eggs, carrots, sweet potatoes, and a dollop of pesto. Serve alongside a lemon wedge.

Per Serving calories: 858 | fat: 24.4g | protein: 26.4g | carbs: 136.2g | fiber: 14.1g | sodium: 985mg

Rice and Bean Stuffed Zucchini

Prep time: 10 minutes | Cook time: 15 minutes | Serves 4

2 small zucchinis, halved lengthwise	½ cup chopped toasted cashew nuts
½ cup cooked rice	½ cup grated Parmesan cheese
½ cup canned white beans, drained and rinsed	
	1 tablespoon olive oil
½ cup chopped tomatoes	½ teaspoon salt
	½ teaspoon freshly ground black pepper

1. Pour 1 cup of water in the instant pot and insert a trivet. Scoop out the pulp of zucchini and chop roughly.
2. In a bowl, mix the zucchini pulp, rice, tomatoes, cashew nuts, ¼ cup of Parmesan, olive oil, salt, and black pepper. Fill the zucchini boats with the mixture, and arrange the stuffed boats in a single layer on the trivet. Seal the lid and cook for 15 minutes on Steam on High. Do a quick release and serve.

Per Serving calories: 239 | fat: 14.7g | protein: 9.4g | carbs: 19.0g | fiber: 2.6g | sodium: 570mg

Chard and Mushroom Risotto

Prep time: 15 minutes | Cook time: 20 minutes | Serves 4

3 tablespoons olive oil	3 cups vegetable stock
1 onion, chopped	½ teaspoon salt
2 Swiss chard, stemmed and chopped	½ cup mushrooms
1 cup risotto rice	4 tablespoons pumpkin seeds, toasted
⅓ cup white wine	⅓ cup grated Pecorino Romano cheese

1. Heat oil on Sauté, and cook onion and mushrooms for 5 minutes, stirring, until tender. Add the rice and cook for a minute. Stir in wine and cook for 2 to 3 minutes until almost evaporated.
2. Pour in stock and season with salt. Seal the lid and cook on High Pressure for 10 minutes.
3. Do a quick release. Stir in chard until wilted, mix in cheese to melt, and serve scattered with pumpkin seeds.

Per Serving calories: 420 | fat: 17.7g | protein: 11.8g | carbs: 54.9g | fiber: 4.9g | sodium: 927mg

Cheesy Tomato Linguine

Prep time: 15 minutes | Cook time: 11 minutes | Serves 4

2 tablespoons olive oil	½ teaspoon ground black pepper
1 small onion, diced	¼ teaspoon red chili flakes
2 garlic cloves, minced	1 pound (454 g) Linguine noodles, halved
1 cup cherry tomatoes, halved	Fresh basil leaves for garnish
1½ cups vegetable stock	½ cup Parmigiano-Reggiano cheese, grated
¼ cup julienned basil leaves	
1 teaspoon salt	

1. Warm oil on Sauté. Add onion and Sauté for 2 minutes until soft. Mix garlic and tomatoes and sauté for 4 minutes. To the pot, add vegetable stock, salt, julienned basil, red chili flakes and pepper.
2. Add linguine to the tomato mixture until covered. Seal the lid and cook on High Pressure for 5 minutes.
3. Naturally release the pressure for 5 minutes. Stir the mixture to ensure it is broken down.
4. Divide into plates. Top with basil and Parmigiano-Reggiano cheese and serve.

Per Serving calories: 311 | fat: 11.3g | protein: 10.3g | carbs: 42.1g | fiber: 1.9g | sodium: 1210mg

Beef and Bean Stuffed Pasta Shells

Prep time: 15 minutes | Cook time: 17 minutes | Serves 4

2 tablespoons olive oil	10 ounces (283 g) red enchilada sauce
1 pound (454 g) ground beef	4 ounces (113 g) diced green chiles
1 pound (454 g) pasta shells	
2 cups water	1 cup shredded Mozzarella cheese
15 ounces (425 g) tomato sauce	
1 (15-ounce / 425-g) can black beans, drained and rinsed	Salt and ground black pepper to taste
	Additional cheese for topping
15 ounces (425 g) canned corn, drained (or 2 cups frozen corn)	Finely chopped parsley for garnish

1. Heat oil on Sauté. Add ground beef and cook for 7 minutes until it starts to brown.
2. Mix in pasta, tomato sauce, enchilada sauce, black beans, water, corn, and green chiles and stir to coat well. Add more water if desired.
3. Seal the lid and cook on High Pressure for 10 minutes. Do a quick Pressure release. Into the pasta mixture, mix in Mozzarella cheese until melted; add black pepper and salt. Garnish with parsley to serve.

Per Serving
calories: 1006 | fat: 30.0g | protein: 53.3g | carbs: 138.9g | fiber: 24.4g | sodium: 1139mg

Caprese Fusilli

Prep time: 15 minutes | Cook time: 7 minutes | Serves 3

1 tablespoon olive oil	1 cup tomatoes, halved
1 onion, thinly chopped	1 cup water
6 garlic cloves, minced	¼ cup basil leaves
1 teaspoon red pepper flakes	1 teaspoon salt
2½ cups dried fusilli	1 cup Ricotta cheese, crumbled
1 (15-ounce / 425-g) can tomato sauce	2 tablespoons chopped fresh basil

1. Warm oil on Sauté. Add red pepper flakes, garlic and onion and cook for 3 minutes until soft.
2. Mix in fusilli, tomatoes, half of the basil leaves, water, tomato sauce, and salt. Seal the lid, and cook on High Pressure for 4 minutes. Release the pressure quickly.
3. Transfer the pasta to a serving platter and top with the crumbled ricotta and remaining chopped basil.

Per Serving
calories: 589 | fat: 17.7g | protein: 19.5g | carbs: 92.8g | fiber: 13.8g | sodium: 879mg

Chicken and Spaghetti Ragù Bolognese

Prep time: 15 minutes | Cook time: 42 minutes | Serves 8

2 tablespoons olive oil	¼ teaspoon crushed red pepper flakes
6 ounces (170 g) bacon, cubed	1½ pounds (680 g) ground chicken
1 onion, minced	½ cup white wine
1 carrot, minced	1 cup milk
1 celery stalk, minced	1 cup chicken broth
2 garlic cloves, crushed	Salt, to taste
¼ cup tomato paste	1 pound (454 g) spaghetti

1. Warm oil on Sauté. Add bacon and fry for 5 minutes until crispy.
2. Add celery, carrot, garlic and onion and cook for 5 minutes until fragrant. Mix in red pepper flakes and tomato paste, and cook for 2 minutes. Break chicken into small pieces and place in the pot.
3. Cook for 10 minutes, as you stir, until browned. Pour in wine and simmer for 2 minutes. Add chicken broth and milk. Seal the lid and cook for 15 minutes on High Pressure. Release the pressure quickly.
4. Add the spaghetti and stir. Seal the lid, and cook on High Pressure for another 5 minutes.
5. Release the pressure quickly. Check the pasta for doneness. Taste, adjust the seasoning and serve hot.

Per Serving calories: 477 | fat: 20.6g | protein: 28.1g | carbs: 48.5g | fiber: 5.3g | sodium: 279mg

Parmesan Squash Linguine

Prep time: 15 minutes | Cook time: 5 minutes | Serves 4

1 cup flour
2 teaspoons salt
2 eggs
4 cups water
1 cup seasoned breadcrumbs
½ cup grated Parmesan cheese, plus more for garnish
1 yellow squash, peeled and sliced
1 pound (454 g) linguine
24 ounces (680 g) canned seasoned tomato sauce
2 tablespoons olive oil
1 cup shredded Mozzarella cheese
Minced fresh basil, for garnish

1. Break the linguine in half. Put it in the pot and add water and half of salt. Seal the lid and cook on High Pressure for 5 minutes. Combine the flour and 1 teaspoon of salt in a bowl. In another bowl, whisk the eggs and 2 tablespoons of water. In a third bowl, mix the breadcrumbs and Mozzarella cheese.
2. Coat each squash slices in the flour. Shake off excess flour, dip in the egg wash, and dredge in the bread crumbs. Set aside. Quickly release the pressure. Remove linguine to a serving bowl and mix in the tomato sauce and sprinkle with fresh basil. Heat oil on Sauté and fry breaded squash until crispy.
3. Serve the squash topped Mozzarella cheese with the linguine on side.

Per Serving

calories: 857 | fat: 17.0g | protein: 33.2g | carbs: 146.7g | fiber: 18.1g | sodium: 1856mg

Red Bean Curry

Prep time: 10 minutes | Cook time: 24 minutes | Serves 4

½ cup raw red beans
1½ tablespoons cooking oil
½ cup chopped onions
1 bay leaf
½ tablespoon grated garlic
¼ tablespoon grated ginger
¾ cup water
1 cup fresh tomato purée
½ green chili, finely chopped
¼ teaspoon turmeric
½ teaspoon coriander powder
1 teaspoon chili powder
1 cup chopped baby spinach
Salt, to taste
Boiled white rice or quinoa, for serve

1. Add the oil and onions to the Instant Pot. Sauté for 5 minutes.
2. Stir in ginger, garlic paste, green chili and bay leaf. Cook for 1 minute, then add all the spices.
3. Add the red beans, tomato purée and water to the pot.
4. Cover and secure the lid. Turn its pressure release handle to the sealing position.
5. Cook on the Manual function with High Pressure for 15 minutes.
6. After the beep, do a Natural release for 20 minutes.
7. Stir in spinach and cook for 3 minutes on the Sauté setting.
8. Serve hot with boiled white rice or quinoa.

Per Serving

calories: 159 | fat: 5.6g | protein: 6.8g | carbs: 22.5g | fiber: 5.5g | sodium: 182mg

Chapter 6

<u>Vegetable Mains</u>

<u>Stuffed Portobello Mushrooms with Spinach</u>

Prep time: 5 minutes | Cook time: 20 minutes | Serves 4

8 large portobello mushrooms, stems removed
3 teaspoons extra-virgin olive oil, divided
1 medium red bell pepper, diced
4 cups fresh spinach
¼ cup crumbled feta cheese

1. Preheat the oven to 450°F (235°C).
2. Using a spoon to scoop out the gills of the mushrooms and discard them. Brush the mushrooms with 2 teaspoons of olive oil.
3. Arrange the mushrooms (cap-side down) on a baking sheet. Roast in the preheated oven for 20 minutes.
4. Meantime, in a medium skillet, heat the remaining olive oil over medium heat until it shimmers.
5. Add the bell pepper and spinach and sauté for 8 to 10 minutes, stirring occasionally, or until the spinach is wilted.
6. Remove the mushrooms from the oven to a paper towel-lined plate. Using a spoon to stuff each mushroom with the bell pepper and spinach mixture. Scatter the feta cheese all over.
7. Serve immediately.

Per Serving (2 mushrooms)

calories: 115 | fat: 5.9g | protein: 7.2g | carbs: 11.5g | fiber: 4.0g | sodium: 125mg

<u>Chickpea Lettuce Wraps with Celery</u>

Prep time: 10 minutes | Cook time: 0 minutes | Serves 4

1 (15-ounce / 425-g) can low-sodium chickpeas, drained and rinsed
1 celery stalk, thinly sliced
2 tablespoons finely chopped red onion
2 tablespoons unsalted tahini
3 tablespoons honey mustard
1 tablespoon capers, undrained
12 butter lettuce leaves

1. In a bowl, mash the chickpeas with a potato masher or the back of a fork until mostly smooth.
2. Add the celery, red onion, tahini, honey mustard, and capers to the bowl and stir until well incorporated.
3. For each serving, place three overlapping lettuce leaves on a plate and top with ¼ of the mashed chickpea filling, then roll up. Repeat with the remaining lettuce leaves and chickpea mixture.

Per Serving

calories: 182 | fat: 7.1g | protein: 10.3g | carbs: 19.6g | fiber: 3.0g | sodium: 171mg

<u>Zoodles with Walnut Pesto</u>

Prep time: 10 minutes | Cook time: 10 minutes | Serves 4

4 medium zucchinis, spiralized
¼ cup extra-virgin olive oil, divided
1 teaspoon minced garlic, divided
½ teaspoon crushed red pepper
¼ teaspoon freshly ground black pepper, divided
¼ teaspoon kosher salt, divided
2 tablespoons grated Parmesan cheese, divided
1 cup packed fresh basil leaves
¾ cup walnut pieces, divided

1. In a large bowl, stir together the zoodles, 1 tablespoon of the olive oil, ½ teaspoon of the minced garlic, red pepper, ⅛ teaspoon of the black pepper and ⅛ teaspoon of the salt. Set aside.
2. Heat ½ tablespoon of the oil in a large skillet over medium-high heat. Add half of the zoodles to the skillet and cook for 5 minutes, stirring constantly. Transfer the cooked zoodles into a bowl. Repeat with another ½ tablespoon of the oil and the remaining zoodles. When done, add the cooked zoodles to the bowl.
3. Make the pesto: In a food processor, combine the remaining ½ teaspoon of the minced garlic, ⅛ teaspoon of the black pepper and ⅛ teaspoon of the salt, 1 tablespoon of the Parmesan, basil leaves and ¼ cup of the walnuts. Pulse until smooth and then slowly drizzle the remaining 2 tablespoons of the oil into the pesto. Pulse again until well combined.
4. Add the pesto to the zoodles along with the remaining 1 tablespoon of the Parmesan and the remaining ½ cup of the walnuts. Toss to coat well.
5. Serve immediately.

Per Serving

calories: 166 | fat: 16.0g | protein: 4.0g | carbs: 3.0g | fiber: 2.0g | sodium: 307mg

Cheesy Sweet Potato Burgers

Prep time: 10 minutes | Cook time: 19 to 20 minutes | Serves 4

1 large sweet potato (about 8 ounces / 227 g)	1 garlic clove
2 tablespoons extra-virgin olive oil, divided	1 cup old-fashioned rolled oats
1 cup chopped onion	1 tablespoon dried oregano
1 large egg	1 tablespoon balsamic vinegar
	¼ teaspoon kosher salt
	½ cup crumbled Gorgonzola cheese

1. Using a fork, pierce the sweet potato all over and microwave on high for 4 to 5 minutes, until softened in the center. Cool slightly before slicing in half.
2. Meanwhile, in a large skillet over medium-high heat, heat 1 tablespoon of the olive oil. Add the onion and sauté for 5 minutes.
3. Spoon the sweet potato flesh out of the skin and put the flesh in a food processor. Add the cooked onion, egg, garlic, oats, oregano, vinegar and salt. Pulse until smooth. Add the cheese and pulse four times to barely combine.
4. Form the mixture into four burgers. Place the burgers on a plate, and press to flatten each to about ¾-inch thick.
5. Wipe out the skillet with a paper towel. Heat the remaining 1 tablespoon of the oil over medium-high heat for about 2 minutes. Add the burgers to the hot oil, then reduce the heat to medium. Cook the burgers for 5 minutes per side.
6. Transfer the burgers to a plate and serve.

Per Serving

calories: 290 | fat: 12.0g | protein: 12.0g | carbs: 43.0g | fiber: 8.0g | sodium: 566mg

Eggplant and Zucchini Gratin

Prep time: 10 minutes | Cook time: 19 minutes | Serves 6

2 large zucchinis, finely chopped	¾ cup unsweetened almond milk
1 large eggplant, finely chopped	1 tablespoon all-purpose flour
¼ teaspoon kosher salt	⅓ cup plus 2 tablespoons grated Parmesan cheese, divided
¼ teaspoon freshly ground black pepper	
3 tablespoons extra-virgin olive oil, divided	1 cup chopped tomato
	1 cup diced fresh Mozzarella
	¼ cup fresh basil leaves

1. Preheat the oven to 425°F (220°C).
2. In a large bowl, toss together the zucchini, eggplant, salt and pepper.
3. In a large skillet over medium-high heat, heat 1 tablespoon of the oil. Add half of the veggie mixture to the skillet. Stir a few times, then cover and cook for about 4 minutes, stirring occasionally. Pour the cooked veggies into a baking dish. Place the skillet back on the heat, add 1 tablespoon of the oil and repeat with the remaining veggies. Add the veggies to the baking dish.
4. Meanwhile, heat the milk in the microwave for 1 minute. Set aside.
5. Place a medium saucepan over medium heat. Add the remaining 1 tablespoon of the oil and flour to the saucepan. Whisk together until well blended.
6. Slowly pour the warm milk into the saucepan, whisking the entire time. Continue to whisk frequently until the mixture thickens a bit. Add ⅓ cup of the Parmesan cheese and whisk until melted. Pour the cheese sauce over the vegetables in the baking dish and mix well.
7. Fold in the tomatoes and Mozzarella cheese. Roast in the oven for 10 minutes, or until the gratin is almost set and not runny.
8. Top with the fresh basil leaves and the remaining 2 tablespoons of the Parmesan cheese before serving.

Per Serving

calories: 122 | fat: 5.0g | protein: 10.0g | carbs: 11.0g | fiber: 4.0g | sodium: 364mg

Veggie-Stuffed Portabello Mushrooms

Prep time: 5 minutes | Cook time: 24 to 25 minutes | Serves 6

3 tablespoons extra-virgin olive oil, divided	¼ teaspoon kosher salt
1 cup diced onion	¼ teaspoon crushed red pepper
2 garlic cloves, minced	6 large portabello mushrooms, stems and gills removed
1 large zucchini, diced	
3 cups chopped mushrooms	
1 cup chopped tomato	Cooking spray
1 teaspoon dried oregano	4 ounces (113 g) fresh Mozzarella cheese, shredded

1. In a large skillet over medium heat, heat 2 tablespoons of the oil. Add the onion and sauté for 4 minutes. Stir in the garlic and sauté for 1 minute.
2. Stir in the zucchini, mushrooms, tomato, oregano, salt and red pepper. Cook for 10 minutes, stirring constantly. Remove from the heat.
3. Meanwhile, heat a grill pan over medium-high heat.
4. Brush the remaining 1 tablespoon of the oil over the portabello mushroom caps. Place the mushrooms, bottom-side down, on the grill pan. Cover with a sheet of aluminum foil sprayed with nonstick cooking spray. Cook for 5 minutes.
5. Flip the mushroom caps over, and spoon about ½ cup of the cooked vegetable mixture into each cap. Top each with about 2½ tablespoons of the Mozzarella.
6. Cover and grill for 4 to 5 minutes, or until the cheese is melted.
7. Using a spatula, transfer the portabello mushrooms to a plate. Let cool for about 5 minutes before serving.

Per Serving

calories: 111 | fat: 4.0g | protein: 11.0g | carbs: 11.0g | fiber: 4.0g | sodium: 314mg

Stir-Fried Eggplant

Prep time: 25 minutes | Cook time: 15 minutes | Serves 2

1 cup water, plus more as needed
½ cup chopped red onion
1 tablespoon finely chopped garlic
1 tablespoon dried Italian herb seasoning
1 teaspoon ground cumin
1 small eggplant (about 8 ounces / 227 g), peeled and cut into ½-inch cubes
1 medium carrot, sliced
2 cups green beans, cut into 1-inch pieces
2 ribs celery, sliced
1 cup corn kernels
2 tablespoons almond butter
2 medium tomatoes, chopped

1. Heat 1 tablespoon of water in a large soup pot over medium-high heat until it sputters.
2. Cook the onion for 2 minutes, adding a little more water as needed.
3. Add the garlic, Italian seasoning, cumin, and eggplant and stir-fry for 2 to 3 minutes, adding a little more water as needed.
4. Add the carrot, green beans, celery, corn kernels, and ½ cup of water and stir well. Reduce the heat to medium, cover, and cook for 8 to 10 minutes, stirring occasionally, or until the vegetables are tender.
5. Meanwhile, in a bowl, stir together the almond butter and ½ cup of water.
6. Remove the vegetables from the heat and stir in the almond butter mixture and chopped tomatoes. Cool for a few minutes before serving.

Per Serving

calories: 176 | fat: 5.5g | protein: 5.8g | carbs: 25.4g | fiber: 8.6g | sodium: 198mg

Honey-Glazed Baby Carrots

Prep time: 5 minutes | Cook time: 6 minutes | Serves 2

⅔ cup water
1½ pounds (680 g) baby carrots
4 tablespoons almond butter
½ cup honey
1 teaspoon dried thyme
1½ teaspoons dried dill Salt, to taste

1. Pour the water into the Instant Pot and add a steamer basket. Place the baby carrots in the basket.
2. Secure the lid. Select the Manual mode and set the cooking time for 4 minutes at High Pressure.
3. Once cooking is complete, do a quick pressure release. Carefully open the lid.
4. Transfer the carrots to a plate and set aside.
5. Pour the water out of the Instant Pot and dry it.
6. Press the Sauté button on the Instant Pot and heat the almond butter.
7. Stir in the honey, thyme, and dill.
8. Return the carrots to the Instant Pot and stir until well coated. Sauté for another 1 minute.
9. Taste and season with salt as needed. Serve warm.

Per Serving

calories: 575 | fat: 23.5g | protein: 2.8g | carbs: 90.6g | fiber: 10.3g | sodium: 547mg

Quick Steamed Broccoli

Prep time: 5 minutes | Cook time: 0 minutes | Serves 2

¼ cup water
3 cups broccoli florets
Salt and ground black pepper, to taste

1. Pour the water into the Instant Pot and insert a steamer basket. Place the broccoli florets in the basket.
2. Secure the lid. Select the Manual mode and set the cooking time for 0 minutes at High Pressure.
3. Once cooking is complete, do a quick pressure release. Carefully open the lid.
4. Transfer the broccoli florets to a bowl with cold water to keep bright green color.
5. Season the broccoli with salt and pepper to taste, then serve.

Per Serving

calories: 16 | fat: 0.2g | protein: 1.9g | carbs: 1.7g | fiber: 1.6g | sodium: 292mg

Garlic-Butter Asparagus with Parmesan

Prep time: 5 minutes | Cook time: 8 minutes | Serves 2

1 cup water
1 pound (454 g) asparagus, trimmed
2 cloves garlic, chopped
3 tablespoons almond butter
Salt and ground black pepper, to taste
3 tablespoons grated Parmesan cheese

1. Pour the water into the Instant Pot and insert a trivet.
2. Put the asparagus on a tin foil add the butter and garlic. Season to taste with salt and pepper.
3. Fold over the foil and seal the asparagus inside so the foil doesn't come open. Arrange the asparagus on the trivet.
4. Secure the lid. Select the Manual mode and set the cooking time for 8 minutes at High Pressure.
5. Once cooking is complete, do a quick pressure release. Carefully open the lid. Unwrap the foil packet and serve sprinkled with the Parmesan cheese.

Per Serving calories: 243 | fat: 15.7g | protein: 12.3g | carbs: 15.3g | fiber: 7.3g | sodium: 435mg

Ratatouille

Prep time: 10 minutes | Cook time: 6 minutes | Serves 4

2 large zucchinis, sliced
2 medium eggplants, sliced
4 medium tomatoes, sliced
2 small red onions, sliced
4 cloves garlic, chopped
2 tablespoons thyme leaves
2 teaspoons sea salt
1 teaspoon black pepper
2 tablespoons balsamic vinegar
4 tablespoons olive oil
2 cups water

1. Line a springform pan with foil and place the chopped garlic in the bottom.
2. Now arrange the vegetable slices, alternately, in circles.
3. Sprinkle the thyme, pepper and salt over the vegetables. Top with oil and vinegar.
4. Pour a cup of water into the instant pot and place the trivet inside. Secure the lid and cook on Manual function for 6 minutes at High Pressure.
5. Release the pressure naturally and remove the lid.
6. Remove the vegetables along with the tin foil.
7. Serve on a platter and enjoy.

Per Serving calories: 240 | fat: 14.3g | protein: 4.7g | carbs: 27.5g | fiber: 10.8g | sodium: 1181mg

Mushroom and Potato Teriyaki

Prep time: 10 minutes | Cook time: 18 minutes | Serves 4

¾ large yellow or white onion, chopped
1½ medium carrots, diced
1½ ribs celery, chopped
1 medium portabella mushroom, diced
¾ tablespoon garlic, chopped
2 cups water
1 pound (454 g) white potatoes, peeled and diced
¼ cup tomato paste
½ tablespoon sesame oil
2 teaspoons sesame seeds
½ tablespoon paprika
1 teaspoon fresh rosemary
¾ cups peas
¼ cup fresh parsley for garnishing, chopped

1. Add the oil, sesame seeds, and all the vegetables in the instant pot and Sauté for 5 minutes.
2. Stir in the remaining ingredients and secure the lid.
3. Cook on Manual function for 13 minutes at High Pressure.
4. After the beep, natural release the pressure and remove the lid.
5. Garnish with fresh parsley and serve hot.

Per Serving

calories: 160 | fat: 3.0g | protein: 4.7g | carbs: 30.6g | fiber: 5.5g | sodium: 52mg

Peanut and Coconut Stuffed Eggplants

Prep time: 15 minutes | Cook time: 9 minutes | Serves 4

1 tablespoon coriander seeds
½ teaspoon cumin seeds
½ teaspoon mustard seeds
2 to 3 tablespoons chickpea flour
2 tablespoons chopped peanuts
2 tablespoons coconut shreds
1-inch ginger, chopped
2 cloves garlic, chopped
1 hot green chili, chopped
½ teaspoon ground cardamom
A pinch of cinnamon
⅓ to ½ teaspoon cayenne
½ teaspoon turmeric
½ teaspoon raw sugar
½ to ¾ teaspoon salt
1 teaspoon lemon juice
Water as needed
4 baby eggplants
Fresh Cilantro for garnishing

1. Add the coriander, mustard seeds and cumin in the instant pot.
2. Roast on Sauté function for 2 minutes.
3. Add the chickpea flour, nuts and coconut shred to the pot, and roast for 2 minutes.
4. Blend this mixture in a blender, then transfer to a medium-sized bowl. Roughly blend the ginger, garlic, raw sugar, chili, and all the spices in a blender.
5. Add the water and lemon juice to make a paste. Combine it with the dry flour mixture.
6. Cut the eggplants from one side and stuff with the spice mixture. Add 1 cup of water to the instant pot and place the stuffed eggplants inside.
7. Sprinkle some salt on top and secure the lid.
8. Cook on Manual for 5 minutes at High Pressure, then quick release the steam. Remove the lid and garnish with fresh cilantro, then serve hot.

Per Serving calories: 207 | fat: 4.9g | protein: 7.9g | carbs: 39.6g | fiber: 18.3g | sodium: 315mg

Cauliflower with Sweet Potato

Prep time: 15 minutes | Cook time: 8 minutes | Serves 8

1 small onion
4 tomatoes
4 garlic cloves, chopped
2-inch ginger, chopped
2 teaspoons olive oil
1 teaspoon turmeric
2 teaspoons ground cumin
Salt, to taste
1 teaspoon paprika
2 medium sweet potatoes, cubed small
2 small cauliflowers, diced
2 tablespoons fresh cilantro for topping, chopped

1. Blend the tomatoes, garlic, ginger and onion in a blender.
2. Add the oil and cumin in the instant pot and Sauté for 1 minute.
3. Stir in the blended mixture and the remaining spices.
4. Add the sweet potatoes and cook for 5 minutes on Sauté
5. Add the cauliflower chunks and secure the lid.
6. Cook on Manual for 2 minutes at High Pressure.
7. Once done, Quick release the pressure and remove the lid.
8. Stir and serve with cilantro on top.

Per Serving

calories: 76 | fat: 1.6g | protein: 2.7g | carbs: 14.4g | fiber: 3.4g | sodium: 55mg

Potato Curry

Prep time: 10 minutes | Cook time: 30 minutes | Serves 2

2 large potatoes, peeled and diced
1 small onion, peeled and diced
8 ounces (227 g) fresh tomatoes
1 tablespoon olive oil
1 cup water
2 tablespoons garlic cloves, grated
½ tablespoon rosemary
½ tablespoon cayenne pepper
1½ tablespoons thyme
Salt and pepper, to taste

1. Pour a cup of water into the instant pot and place the steamer trivet inside.
2. Place the potatoes and half the garlic over the trivet and sprinkle some salt and pepper on top.
3. Secure the lid and cook on Steam function for 20 minutes.
4. After the beep, natural release the pressure and remove the lid.
5. Put the potatoes to one side and empty the pot.
6. Add the remaining ingredients to the cooker and Sauté for 10 minutes.
7. Use an immerse blender to purée the cooked mixture.
8. Stir in the steamed potatoes and serve hot.

Per Serving

calories: 398 | fat: 7.6g | protein: 9.6g | carbs: 76.2g | fiber: 10.9g | sodium: 111mg

Mushroom, Potato, and Green Bean Mix

Prep time: 10 minutes | Cook time: 18 minutes | Serves 3

1 tablespoon olive oil
½ carrot, peeled and minced
½ celery stalk, minced
½ small onion, minced
1 garlic clove, minced
½ teaspoon dried sage, crushed
½ teaspoon dried rosemary, crushed
4 ounces (113 g) fresh Portabella mushrooms, sliced
4 ounces (113 g) fresh white mushrooms, sliced
¼ cup red wine
1 Yukon Gold potato, peeled and diced
¾ cup fresh green beans, trimmed and chopped
1 cup tomatoes, chopped
½ cup tomato paste
½ tablespoon balsamic vinegar
3 cups water
Salt and freshly ground black pepper to taste
2 ounces (57 g) frozen peas
½ lemon juice
2 tablespoons fresh cilantro for garnishing, chopped

1. Put the oil, onion, tomatoes and celery into the instant pot and Sauté for 5 minutes. Stir in the herbs and garlic and cook for 1 minute. Add the mushrooms and sauté for 5 minutes. Stir in the wine and cook for a further 2 minutes.
2. Add the diced potatoes and mix. Cover the pot with a lid and let the potatoes cook for 2-3 minutes.
3. Now add the green beans, carrots, tomato paste, peas, salt, pepper, water and vinegar.
4. Secure the lid and cook on Manual function for 8 minutes at High Pressure with the pressure valve in the sealing position. Do a Quick release and open the pot, stir the veggies and then add lemon juice and cilantro, then serve with rice or any other of your choice.

Per Serving calories: 238 | fat: 5.4g | protein: 8.3g | carbs: 42.7g | fiber: 8.5g | sodium: 113mg

Mushroom Tacos

Prep time: 10 minutes | Cook time: 13 minutes | Serves 3

4 large guajillo chilies
2 teaspoons oil
2 bay leaves
2 large onions, sliced
2 garlic cloves
2 chipotle chillies in adobo sauce
2 teaspoons ground cumin
1 teaspoon dried oregano
1 teaspoon smoked hot paprika
½ teaspoon ground cinnamon, Salt, to taste
¾ cup vegetable broth
1 teaspoon apple cider vinegar
3 teaspoons lime juice
¼ teaspoon sugar
8 ounces (227 g) mushrooms chopped
Whole-wheat tacos, for serving

1. Put the oil, onion, garlic, salt and bay leaves into the instant pot and Sauté for 5 minutes.
2. Blend the half of this mixture, in a blender, with all the spices and chillies.
3. Add the mushrooms to the remaining onions and Sauté for 3 minutes. Pour the blended mixture into the pot and secure the lid. Cook on Manual function for 5 minutes at High Pressure. Once done, Quick release the pressure and remove the lid. Stir well and serve with tacos.

Per Serving calories: 138 | fat: 4.1g | protein: 5.7g | carbs: 23.8g | fiber: 4.8g | sodium: 208mg

Lentils and Eggplant Curry

Prep time: 10 minutes | Cook time: 22 minutes | Serves 4

¾ cup lentils, soaked and rinsed
1 teaspoon olive oil
½ onion, chopped
4 garlic cloves, chopped
1 teaspoon ginger, chopped
1 hot green chili, chopped
¼ teaspoon turmeric
½ teaspoon ground cumin
2 tomatoes, chopped
1 cup eggplant, chopped
1 cup sweet potatoes, cubed
¾ teaspoon salt
2 cups water
1 cup baby spinach leaves
Cayenne and lemon/lime to taste
Pepper flakes (garnish)

1. Add the oil, garlic, ginger, chili and salt into the instant pot and Sauté for 3 minutes.
2. Stir in the tomatoes and all the spices. Cook for 5 minutes.
3. Add all the remaining ingredients, except the spinach leaves and garnish.
4. Secure the lid and cook on Manual function for 12 minutes at High Pressure.
5. After the beep, release the pressure naturally and remove the lid.
6. Stir in the spinach leaves and let the pot simmer for 2 minutes on Sauté.
7. Garnish with the pepper flakes and serve warm.

Per Serving

calories: 88 | fat: 1.5g | protein: 3.4g | carbs: 17.4g | fiber: 3.3g | sodium: 470mg

Sweet Potato and Tomato Curry

Prep time: 5 minutes | Cook time: 8 minutes | Serves 8

2 large brown onions, finely diced
4 tablespoons olive oil
4 teaspoons salt
4 large garlic cloves, diced
1 red chili, sliced
4 tablespoons cilantro, chopped
4 teaspoons ground cumin
2 teaspoons ground coriander
2 teaspoons paprika
2 pounds (907 g) sweet potato, diced
4 cups chopped, tinned tomatoes
2 cups water
2 cups vegetable stock
Lemon juice and cilantro (garnish)

1. Put the oil and onions into the instant pot and Sauté for 5 minutes.
2. Stir in the remaining ingredients and secure the lid.
3. Cook on Manual function for 3 minutes at High Pressure.
4. Once done, Quick release the pressure and remove the lid.
5. Garnish with cilantro and lemon juice.
6. Serve.

Per Serving

calories: 224 | fat: 8.0g | protein: 4.6g | carbs: 35.9g | fiber: 7.5g | sodium: 1385mg

Anti-Inflammatory Cookbook for Beginners 2022

Veggie Chili

Prep time: 15 minutes | Cook time: 10 minutes | Serves 3

½ tablespoon olive oil
1 small yellow onion, chopped
4 garlic cloves, minced
¾ (15-ounce / 425-g) can diced tomatoes
1 ounce (28 g) sugar-free tomato paste
½ (4-ounce / 113-g) can green chilies with liquid
1 tablespoon Worcestershire sauce

2 tablespoons red chili powder
½ cup carrots, diced
½ cup scallions, chopped
½ cup green bell pepper, chopped
¼ cup peas
1 tablespoon ground cumin
½ tablespoon dried oregano, crushed
Salt and freshly ground black pepper to taste

1. Add the oil, onion, and garlic into the instant pot and Sauté for 5 minutes.
2. Stir in the remaining vegetables and stir-fry for 3 minutes.
3. Add the remaining ingredients and secure the lid.
4. Cook on Manual function for 2 minutes at High Pressure.
5. After the beep, natural release the pressure and remove the lid.
6. Stir well and serve warm.

Per Serving

calories: 106 | fat: 3.9g | protein: 3.4g | carbs: 18.0g | fiber: 6.2g | sodium: 492mg

Cabbage Stuffed Acorn Squash

Prep time: 15 minutes | Cook time: 23 minutes | Serves 4

½ tablespoon olive oil
2 medium Acorn squashes
¼ small yellow onion, chopped
1 jalapeño pepper, chopped
½ cup green onions, chopped
½ cup carrots, chopped
¼ cup cabbage, chopped
1 garlic clove, minced

½ (6-ounce / 170-g) can sugar-free tomato sauce
½ tablespoon chili powder
½ tablespoon ground cumin
Salt and freshly ground black pepper to taste
2 cups water
¼ cup Cheddar cheese, shredded

1. Pour the water into the instant pot and place the trivet inside.
2. Slice the squash into 2 halves and remove the seeds.
3. Place over the trivet, skin side down, and sprinkle some salt and pepper over it.
4. Secure the lid and cook on Manual for 15 minutes at High Pressure.
5. Release the pressure naturally and remove the lid. Empty the pot into a bowl.
6. Now add the oil, onion, and garlic in the instant pot and Sauté for 5 minutes.
7. Stir in the remaining vegetables and stir-fry for 3 minutes.
8. Add the remaining ingredients and secure the lid.
9. Cook on Manual function for 2 minutes at High Pressure.
10. After the beep, natural release the pressure and remove the lid.
11. Stuff the squashes with the prepared mixture and serve warm.

Per Serving

calories: 163 | fat: 5.1g | protein: 4.8g | carbs: 28.4g | fiber: 4.9g | sodium: 146mg

Creamy Potato Curry

Prep time: 10 minutes | Cook time: 18 minutes | Serves 4

¾ large yellow or white onion, chopped
1½ ribs celery, chopped
¼ cup carrots, diced
¼ cup green onions
½ cup coconut milk
¾ tablespoon garlic, chopped
1½ cups water
1 pound (454 g) white potatoes, peeled and diced

¼ cup heavy cream
¼ teaspoon thyme
¼ teaspoon rosemary
½ tablespoon black pepper
¾ cup peas Salt, to taste
2 tablespoons fresh cilantro for garnishing, chopped

1. Add the oil and all the vegetables in the instant pot and Sauté for 5 minutes.
2. Stir in the remaining ingredients and secure the lid.
3. Cook on Manual function for 13 minutes at High Pressure.
4. Once it beeps, natural release the pressure and remove the lid.
5. Garnish with fresh cilantro and serve hot.

Per Serving

calories: 210 | fat: 10.1g | protein: 4.1g | carbs: 27.6g | fiber: 4.7g | sodium: 74mg

Mushroom and Spinach Stuffed Peppers

Prep time: 15 minutes | Cook time: 8 minutes | Serves 7

7 mini sweet peppers
1 cup button mushrooms, minced
5 ounces (142 g) organic baby spinach
½ teaspoon fresh garlic

½ teaspoon coarse sea salt
¼ teaspoon cracked mixed pepper
2 tablespoons water
1 tablespoon olive oil
Organic Mozzarella cheese, diced

1. Put the sweet peppers and water in the instant pot and Sauté for 2 minutes.
2. Remove the peppers and put the olive oil into the pot.
3. Stir in the mushrooms, garlic, spices and spinach.
4. Cook on Sauté until the mixture is dry.
5. Stuff each sweet pepper with the cheese and spinach mixture.
6. Bake the stuffed peppers in an oven for 6 minutes at 400°F (205°C).
7. Once done, serve hot.

Per Serving

calories: 81 | fat: 2.4g | protein: 4.1g | carbs: 13.2g | fiber: 2.4g | sodium: 217mg

Black Bean and Corn Tortilla Bowls

Prep time: 10 minutes | Cook time: 8 minutes | Serves 4

1½ cups vegetable broth	2 small potatoes, cubed
½ cup tomatoes, undrained diced	½ cup bell pepper, chopped
1 small onion, diced	½ can black beans, drained and rinsed
2 garlic cloves, finely minced	1 cup frozen corn kernels
1 teaspoon chili powder	½ tablespoon lime juice
1 teaspoon cumin	2 tablespoons cilantro for topping, chopped
½ teaspoon paprika	Whole-wheat tortilla chips
½ teaspoon ground coriander	
Salt and pepper to taste	
½ cup carrots, diced	

1. Add the oil and all the vegetables into the instant pot and Sauté for 3 minutes.
2. Add all the spices, corn, lime juice, and broth, along with the beans, to the pot.
3. Seal the lid and cook on Manual setting at High Pressure for 5 minutes.
4. Once done, natural release the pressure when the timer goes off. Remove the lid.
5. To serve, put the prepared mixture into a bowl.
6. Top with tortilla chips and fresh cilantro. Serve.

Per Serving

calories: 183 | fat: 0.9g | protein: 7.1g | carbs: 39.8g | fiber: 8.3g | sodium: 387mg

Cauliflower and Broccoli Bowls

Prep time: 5 minutes | Cook time: 7 minutes | Serves 3

½ medium onion, diced	½ pound (227 g) broccoli florets
2 teaspoons olive oil	½ cup vegetable broth
1 garlic clove, minced	½ teaspoon paprika
½ cup tomato paste	¼ teaspoon dried thyme
½ pound (227 g) frozen cauliflower	2 pinches sea salt

1. Add the oil, onion and garlic into the instant pot and Sauté for 2 minutes.
2. Add the broth, tomato paste, cauliflower, broccoli, and all the spices, to the pot.
3. Secure the lid. Cook on the Manual setting at with pressure for 5 minutes.
4. After the beep, Quick release the pressure and remove the lid.
5. Stir well and serve hot.

Per Serving

calories: 109 | fat: 3.8g | protein: 6.1g | carbs: 16.7g | fiber: 6.1g | sodium: 265mg

Radish and Cabbage Congee

Prep time: 5 minutes | Cook time: 20 minutes | Serves 3

1 cup carrots, diced	1 tablespoon grated fresh ginger
½ cup radish, diced	4 cups cabbage, shredded
6 cups vegetable broth	Green onions for garnishing, chopped
Salt, to taste	
1½ cups short grain rice, rinsed	

1. Add all the ingredients, except the cabbage and green onions, into the instant pot.
2. Select the Porridge function and cook on the default time and settings.
3. After the beep, Quick release the pressure and remove the lid Stir in the shredded cabbage and cover with the lid.
4. Serve after 10 minutes with chopped green onions on top.

Per Serving calories: 438 | fat: 0.8g | protein: 8.7g | carbs: 98.4g | fiber: 6.7g | sodium: 1218mg

Potato and Broccoli Medley

Prep time: 10 minutes | Cook time: 20 minutes | Serves 3

1 tablespoon olive oil	1 pound (454 g) baby carrots, cut in half
½ white onion, diced	¼ cup vegetable broth
1½ cloves garlic, finely chopped	½ teaspoon Italian seasoning
1 pound (454 g) potatoes, cut into chunks	½ teaspoon Spike original seasoning
1 pound (454 g) broccoli florets, diced	Fresh parsley for garnishing

1. Put the oil and onion into the instant pot and Sauté for 5 minutes. Stir in the carrots, and garlic and stir-fry for 5 minutes. Add the remaining ingredients and secure the lid.
2. Cook on the Manual function for 10 minutes at High Pressure. After the beep, Quick release the pressure and remove the lid. Stir gently and garnish with fresh parsley, then serve.

Per Serving calories: 256 | fat: 5.6g | protein: 9.1g | carbs: 46.1g | fiber: 12.2g | sodium: 274mg

Mushroom and Potato Oat Burgers

Prep time: 20 minutes | Cook time: 21 minutes | Serves 5

½ cup minced onion	2 tablespoons chopped cilantro
1 teaspoon grated fresh ginger	1 tablespoon curry powder
½ cup minced mushrooms	1 cup quick oats
½ cup red lentils, rinsed	Brown rice flour, optional
¾ sweet potato, peeled and diced	5 tomato slices
1 cup vegetable stock	Lettuce leaves
2 tablespoons hemp seeds	5 whole-wheat buns
2 tablespoons chopped parsley	

1. Add the oil, ginger, mushrooms and onion into the instant pot and Sauté for 5 minutes.
2. Stir in the lentils, stock, and the sweet potatoes.
3. Secure the lid and cook on the Manual function for 6 minutes at High Pressure.
4. After the beep, natural release the pressure and remove the lid. Meanwhile, heat the oven to 375°F (190°C) and line a baking tray with parchment paper.
5. Mash the prepared lentil mixture with a potato masher.
6. Add the oats and the remaining spices. Put in some brown rice flour if the mixture is not thick enough.
7. Wet your hands and prepare 5 patties, using the mixture, and place them on the baking tray.
8. Bake the patties for 10 minutes in the preheated oven.
9. Slice the buns in half and stack each with a tomato slice, a vegetable patty and lettuce leaves. Serve and enjoy.

Per Serving calories: 266 | fat: 5.3g | protein: 14.5g | carbs: 48.7g | fiber: 9.6g | sodium: 276mg

Potato, Corn, and Spinach Medley

Prep time: 10 minutes | Cook time: 10 minutes | Serves 6

1 tablespoon olive oil	1 tablespoon fish sauce
3 scallions, chopped	2 tablespoons light soy sauce
½ cup onion, chopped	2 large cloves garlic, diced
2 large white potatoes, peeled and diced	⅓ teaspoon white pepper
1 tablespoon ginger, grated	1 teaspoon salt
3 cups frozen corn kernels	3-4 handfuls baby spinach leaves
1 cup vegetable stock	Juice of ½ lemon

1. Put the oil, ginger, garlic and onions in the instant pot and Sauté for 5 minutes. Add all the remaining ingredients except the spinach leaves and lime juice
2. Secure the lid and cook on the Manual setting for 5 minutes at High Pressure. After the beep, Quick release the pressure and remove the lid.
3. Add the spinach and cook for 3 minutes on Sauté
4. Drizzle the lime juice over the dish and serve hot.

Per Serving

calories: 217 | fat: 3.4g | protein: 6.5g | carbs: 44.5g | fiber: 6.3g | sodium: 892mg

Italian Zucchini Pomodoro

Prep time: 10 minutes | Cook time: 12 minutes | Serves 4

1 tablespoon avocado oil	½ cup water
1 large onion, peeled and diced	1 tablespoon Italian seasoning
3 cloves garlic, minced	1 teaspoon sea salt
1 (28-ounce / 794-g) can diced tomatoes, including juice	½ teaspoon ground black pepper
	2 medium zucchini, spiraled

1. Press Sauté button on the Instant Pot. Heat avocado oil. Add onions and stir-fry for 3 to 5 minutes until translucent. Add garlic and cook for an additional minute. Add tomatoes, water, Italian seasoning, salt, and pepper. Add zucchini and toss to combine. Lock lid.
2. Press the Manual button and adjust time to 1 minute. When timer beeps, let pressure release naturally for 5 minutes. Quick release any additional pressure until float valve drops and then unlock lid.
3. Transfer zucchini to four bowls. Press Sauté button, press Adjust button to change the temperature to Less, and simmer sauce in the Instant Pot unlidded for 5 minutes. Ladle over zucchini and serve immediately.

Per Serving calories: 92 | fat: 4.1g | protein: 2.5g | carbs: 13.1g | fiber: 5.1g | sodium: 980mg

Mushroom Swoodles

Prep time: 5 minutes | Cook time: 3 minutes | Serves 4

2 tablespoons coconut aminos	3 cloves garlic, minced
1 tablespoon white vinegar	1 large sweet potato, peeled and spiraled
2 teaspoons olive oil	1 pound (454 g) shiitake mushrooms, sliced
1 teaspoon sesame oil	1 cup vegetable broth
1 tablespoon honey	¼ cup chopped fresh parsley
¼ teaspoon red pepper flakes	

1. In a large bowl, whisk together coconut aminos, vinegar, olive oil, sesame oil, honey, red pepper flakes, and garlic.

2. Toss sweet potato and shiitake mushrooms in sauce. Refrigerate covered for 30 minutes.
3. Pour vegetable broth into Instant Pot. Add trivet. Lower steamer basket onto trivet and add the sweet potato mixture to the basket. Lock lid.
4. Press the Manual button and adjust time to 3 minutes. When timer beeps, let pressure release naturally for 5 minutes. Quick release any additional pressure until float valve drops and then unlock lid.
5. Remove basket from the Instant Pot and distribute sweet potatoes and mushrooms evenly among four bowls; pour liquid from the Instant Pot over bowls and garnish with chopped parsley.

Per Serving calories: 127 | fat: 4.0g | protein: 4.2g | carbs: 20.9g | fiber: 4.1g | sodium: 671mg

Rice, Corn, and Bean Stuffed Peppers

Prep time: 15 minutes | Cook time: 15 minutes | Serves 4

4 large bell peppers	¼ cup canned cannellini beans, rinsed and drained
2 cups cooked white rice	
1 medium onion, peeled and diced	¼ cup canned black beans, rinsed and drained
3 small Roma tomatoes, diced	1 teaspoon sea salt
	1 teaspoon garlic powder
¼ cup marinara sauce	½ cup vegetable broth
1 cup corn kernels (cut from the cob is preferred)	2 tablespoons grated Parmesan cheese
¼ cup sliced black olives	

1. Cut off the bell pepper tops as close to the tops as possible. Hollow out and discard seeds. Poke a few small holes in the bottom of the peppers to allow drippings to drain.
2. In a medium bowl, combine remaining ingredients except for broth and Parmesan cheese. Stuff equal amounts of mixture into each of the bell peppers.
3. Place trivet into the Instant Pot and pour in the broth. Set the peppers upright on the trivet. Lock lid.
4. Press the Manual button and adjust time to 15 minutes. When timer beeps, let pressure release naturally until float valve drops and then unlock lid.
5. Serve immediately and garnish with Parmesan cheese.

Per Serving calories: 265 | fat: 3.0g | protein: 8.1g | carbs: 53.1g | fiber: 8.0g | sodium: 834mg

Carrot and Turnip Purée

Prep time: 10 minutes | Cook time: 10 minutes | Serves 6

2 tablespoons olive oil, divided
3 large turnips, peeled and quartered
4 large carrots, peeled and cut into 2-inch pieces
2 cups vegetable broth
1 teaspoon salt
½ teaspoon ground nutmeg
2 tablespoons sour cream

1. Press the Sauté button on Instant Pot. Heat 1 tablespoon olive oil. Toss turnips and carrots in oil for 1 minute. Add broth. Lock lid. Press the Manual button and adjust time to 8 minutes. When timer beeps, quick release pressure until float valve drops and then unlock lid.
2. Drain vegetables and reserve liquid; set liquid aside. Add 2 tablespoons of reserved liquid plus remaining ingredients to vegetables in the Instant Pot.
3. Use an immersion blender to blend until desired smoothness. If too thick, add more liquid 1 tablespoon at a time. Serve warm.

Per Serving calories: 95 | fat: 5.2g | protein: 1.4g | carbs: 11.8g | fiber: 3.0g | sodium: 669mg

Brussels Sprouts Linguine

Prep time: 5 minutes | Cook time: 25 minutes | Serves 4

8 ounces (227 g) whole-wheat linguine
⅓ cup plus 2 tablespoons extra-virgin olive oil, divided
1 medium sweet onion, diced
2 to 3 garlic cloves, smashed
8 ounces (227 g) Brussels sprouts, chopped
½ cup chicken stock
⅓ cup dry white wine
½ cup shredded Parmesan cheese
1 lemon, quartered

1. Bring a large pot of water to a boil and cook the pasta for about 5 minutes, or until al dente. Drain the pasta and reserve 1 cup of the pasta water. Mix the cooked pasta with 2 tablespoons of the olive oil. Set aside.
2. In a large skillet, heat the remaining ⅓ cup of the olive oil over medium heat. Add the onion to the skillet and sauté for about 4 minutes, or until tender. Add the smashed garlic cloves and sauté for 1 minute, or until fragrant.
3. Stir in the Brussels sprouts and cook covered for 10 minutes. Pour in the chicken stock to prevent burning. Once the Brussels sprouts have wilted and are fork-tender, add white wine and cook for about 5 minutes, or until reduced.
4. Add the pasta to the skillet and add the pasta water as needed.
5. Top with the Parmesan cheese and squeeze the lemon over the dish right before eating.

Per Serving

calories: 502 | fat: 31.0g | protein: 15.0g | carbs: 50.0g | fiber: 9.0g | sodium: 246mg

Beet and Watercress Salad

Prep time: 15 minutes | Cook time: 8 minutes | Serves 4

2 pounds (907 g) beets, scrubbed, trimmed and cut into ¾-inch pieces
½ cup water
1 teaspoon caraway seeds
½ teaspoon table salt, plus more for seasoning
1 cup plain Greek yogurt
1 small garlic clove, minced
5 ounces (142 g) watercress, torn into bite-size pieces
1 tablespoon extra-virgin olive oil, divided, plus more for drizzling
1 tablespoon white wine vinegar, divided
Black pepper, to taste
1 teaspoon grated orange zest
2 tablespoons orange juice
¼ cup coarsely chopped fresh dill
¼ cup hazelnuts, toasted, skinned and chopped
Coarse sea salt, to taste

1. Combine the beets, water, caraway seeds and table salt in the Instant Pot. Set the lid in place. Select the Manual mode and set the cooking time for 8 minutes on High Pressure. When the timer goes off, do a quick pressure release.
2. Carefully open the lid. Using a slotted spoon, transfer the beets to a plate. Set aside to cool slightly.
3. In a small bowl, combine the yogurt, garlic and 3 tablespoons of the beet cooking liquid. In a large bowl, toss the watercress with 2 teaspoons of the oil and 1 teaspoon of the vinegar. Season with table salt and pepper.
4. Spread the yogurt mixture over a serving dish. Arrange the watercress on top of the yogurt mixture, leaving 1-inch border of the yogurt mixture. Add the beets to now-empty large bowl and toss with the orange zest and juice, the remaining 2 teaspoons of the vinegar and the remaining 1 teaspoon of the oil. Season with table salt and pepper.
5. Arrange the beets on top of the watercress mixture. Drizzle with the olive oil and sprinkle with the dill, hazelnuts and sea salt. Serve immediately.

Per Serving calories: 240 | fat: 15.0g | protein: 9.0g | carbs: 19.0g | fiber: 5.0g | sodium: 440mg

Garlicky Broccoli Rabe

Prep time: 10 minutes | Cook time: 5 to 6 minutes | Serves 4

14 ounces (397 g) broccoli rabe, trimmed and cut into 1-inch pieces
2 teaspoons salt, plus more for seasoning
Black pepper, to taste
2 tablespoons extra-virgin olive oil
3 garlic cloves, minced
¼ teaspoon red pepper flakes

1. Bring 3 quarts water to a boil in a large saucepan. Add the broccoli rabe and 2 teaspoons of the salt to the boiling water and cook for 2 to 3 minutes, or until wilted and tender. Drain the broccoli rabe. Transfer to ice water and let sit until chilled. Drain again and pat dry.
2. In a skillet over medium heat, heat the oil and add the garlic and red pepper flakes. Sauté for about 2 minutes, or until the garlic begins to sizzle. Increase the heat to medium-high. Stir in the broccoli rabe and cook for about 1 minute, or until heated through, stirring constantly. Season with salt and pepper. Serve immediately.

Per Serving calories: 87 | fat: 7.3g | protein: 3.4g | carbs: 4.0g | fiber: 2.9g | sodium: 1196mg

Sautéed Cabbage with Parsley

Prep time: 10 minutes | Cook time: 12 to 14 minutes | Serves 4 to 6

1 small head green cabbage (about 1¼ pounds / 567 g), cored and sliced thin	1 onion, halved and sliced thin
2 tablespoons extra-virgin olive oil, divided	¾ teaspoon salt, divided
	¼ teaspoon black pepper
	¼ cup chopped fresh parsley
	1½ teaspoons lemon juice

1. Place the cabbage in a large bowl with cold water. Let sit for 3 minutes. Drain well. Heat 1 tablespoon of the oil in a skillet over medium-high heat until shimmering. Add the onion and ¼ teaspoon of the salt and cook for 5 to 7 minutes, or until softened and lightly browned. Transfer to a bowl. Heat the remaining 1 tablespoon of the oil in now-empty skillet over medium-high heat until shimmering. Add the cabbage and sprinkle with the remaining ½ teaspoon of the salt and black pepper. Cover and cook for about 3 minutes, without stirring, or until cabbage is wilted and lightly browned on bottom.
2. Stir and continue to cook for about 4 minutes, uncovered, or until the cabbage is crisp-tender and lightly browned in places, stirring once halfway through cooking. Off heat, stir in the cooked onion, parsley and lemon juice.
3. Transfer to a plate and serve.

Per Serving calories: 117 | fat: 7.0g | protein: 2.7g | carbs: 13.4g | fiber: 5.1g | sodium: 472mg

Braised Cauliflower with White Wine

Prep time: 10 minutes | Cook time: 12 to 16 minutes | Serves 4 to 6

3 tablespoons plus 1 teaspoon extra-virgin olive oil, divided	¼ teaspoon salt, plus more for seasoning
3 garlic cloves, minced	Black pepper, to taste
⅛ teaspoon red pepper flakes	⅓ cup vegetable broth
1 head cauliflower (2 pounds / 907 g), cored and cut into 1½-inch florets	⅓ cup dry white wine
	2 tablespoons minced fresh parsley

1. Combine 1 teaspoon of the oil, garlic and pepper flakes in small bowl.
2. Heat the remaining 3 tablespoons of the oil in a skillet over medium-high heat until shimmering. Add the cauliflower and ¼ teaspoon of the salt and cook for 7 to 9 minutes, stirring occasionally, or until florets are golden brown.
3. Push the cauliflower to sides of the skillet. Add the garlic mixture to the center of the skillet. Cook for about 30 seconds, or until fragrant. Stir the garlic mixture into the cauliflower.
4. Pour in the broth and wine and bring to simmer. Reduce the heat to medium-low. Cover and cook for 4 to 6 minutes, or until the cauliflower is crisp-tender. Off heat, stir in the parsley and season with salt and pepper.
5. Serve immediately.

Per Serving
calories: 143 | fat: 11.7g | protein: 3.1g | carbs: 8.7g | fiber: 3.1g | sodium: 263mg

Cauliflower Steaks with Arugula

Prep time: 5 minutes | Cook time: 20 minutes | Serves 4

Cauliflower:	**Dressing:**
1 head cauliflower	1½ tablespoons extra-virgin olive oil
Cooking spray	
½ teaspoon garlic powder	1½ tablespoons honey mustard
4 cups arugula	
	1 teaspoon freshly squeezed lemon juice

1. Preheat the oven to 425ºF (220ºC).
2. Remove the leaves from the cauliflower head, and cut it in half lengthwise. Cut 1½-inch-thick steaks from each half.
3. Spritz both sides of each steak with cooking spray and season both sides with the garlic powder.
4. Place the cauliflower steaks on a baking sheet, cover with foil, and roast in the oven for 10 minutes.
5. Remove the baking sheet from the oven and gently pull back the foil to avoid the steam. Flip the steaks, then roast uncovered for 10 minutes more.
6. Meanwhile, make the dressing: Whisk together the olive oil, honey mustard and lemon juice in a small bowl.
7. When the cauliflower steaks are done, divide into four equal portions. Top each portion with one-quarter of the arugula and dressing.
8. Serve immediately.

Per Serving
calories: 115 | fat: 6.0g | protein: 5.0g | carbs: 14.0g | fiber: 4.0g | sodium: 97mg

Parmesan Stuffed Zucchini Boats

Prep time: 5 minutes | Cook time: 15 minutes | Serves 4

1 cup canned low-sodium chickpeas, drained and rinsed	2 zucchinis
	¼ cup shredded Parmesan cheese
1 cup no-sugar-added spaghetti sauce	

1. Preheat the oven to 425ºF (220ºC).
2. In a medium bowl, stir together the chickpeas and spaghetti sauce.
3. Cut the zucchini in half lengthwise and scrape a spoon gently down the length of each half to remove the seeds.
4. Fill each zucchini half with the chickpea sauce and top with one-quarter of the Parmesan cheese.
5. Place the zucchini halves on a baking sheet and roast in the oven for 15 minutes.
6. Transfer to a plate. Let rest for 5 minutes before serving.

Per Serving
calories: 139 | fat: 4.0g | protein: 8.0g | carbs: 20.0g | fiber: 5.0g | sodium: 344mg

Baby Kale and Cabbage Salad

Prep time: 10 minutes | Cook time: 0 minutes | Serves 6

2 bunches baby kale, thinly sliced

½ head green savoy cabbage, cored and thinly sliced

1 medium red bell pepper, thinly sliced

1 garlic clove, thinly sliced

1 cup toasted peanuts

Dressing:

Juice of 1 lemon

¼ cup apple cider vinegar

1 teaspoon ground cumin

¼ teaspoon smoked paprika

1. In a large mixing bowl, toss together the kale and cabbage.
2. Make the dressing: Whisk together the lemon juice, vinegar, cumin and paprika in a small bowl.
3. Pour the dressing over the greens and gently massage with your hands. Add the pepper, garlic and peanuts to the mixing bowl. Toss to combine. Serve immediately.

Per Serving calories: 199 | fat: 12.0g | protein: 10.0g | carbs: 17.0g | fiber: 5.0g | sodium: 46mg

Grilled Romaine Lettuce

Prep time: 5 minutes | Cook time: 3 to 5 minutes | Serves 4

Romaine:

2 heads romaine lettuce, halved lengthwise

2 tablespoons extra-virgin olive oil

Dressing:

½ cup unsweetened almond milk

1 tablespoon extra-virgin olive oil

¼ bunch fresh chives, thinly chopped

1 garlic clove, pressed

1 pinch red pepper flakes

1. Heat a grill pan over medium heat.
2. Brush each lettuce half with the olive oil. Place the lettuce halves, flat-side down, on the grill. Grill for 3 to 5 minutes, or until the lettuce slightly wilts and develops light grill marks. Meanwhile, whisk together all the ingredients for the dressing in a small bowl. Drizzle 2 tablespoons of the dressing over each romaine half and serve.

Per Serving calories: 126 | fat: 11.0g | protein: 2.0g | carbs: 7.0g | fiber: 1.0g | sodium: 41mg

Mini Crustless Spinach Quiches

Prep time: 10 minutes | Cook time: 20 minutes | Serves 6

2 tablespoons extra-virgin olive oil

1 onion, finely chopped

2 cups baby spinach

2 garlic cloves, minced

8 large eggs, beaten

¼ cup unsweetened almond milk

½ teaspoon sea salt

¼ teaspoon freshly ground black pepper

1 cup shredded Swiss cheese

Cooking spray

1. Preheat the oven to 375ºF (190ºC). Spritz a 6-cup muffin tin with cooking spray. Set aside.
2. In a large skillet over medium-high heat, heat the olive oil until shimmering. Add the onion and cook for about 4 minutes, or until soft. Add the spinach and cook for about 1 minute, stirring constantly, or until the spinach softens. Add the garlic and sauté for 30 seconds. Remove from the heat and let cool.
3. In a medium bowl, whisk together the eggs, milk, salt and pepper. Stir the cooled vegetables and the cheese into the egg mixture. Spoon the mixture into the prepared muffin tins. Bake for about 15 minutes, or until the eggs are set.
4. Let rest for 5 minutes before serving.

Per Serving calories: 218 | fat: 17.0g | protein: 14.0g | carbs: 4.0g | fiber: 1.0g | sodium: 237mg

Butternut Noodles with Mushrooms

Prep time: 10 minutes | Cook time: 12 minutes | Serves 4

¼ cup extra-virgin olive oil

1 pound (454 g) cremini mushrooms, sliced

½ red onion, finely chopped

1 teaspoon dried thyme

½ teaspoon sea salt

3 garlic cloves, minced

½ cup dry white wine

Pinch of red pepper flakes

4 cups butternut noodles

4 ounces (113 g) grated Parmesan cheese

1. In a large skillet over medium-high heat, heat the olive oil until shimmering. Add the mushrooms, onion, thyme, and salt to the skillet. Cook for about 6 minutes, stirring occasionally, or until the mushrooms start to brown. Add the garlic and sauté for 30 seconds. Stir in the white wine and red pepper flakes. Fold in the noodles. Cook for about 5 minutes, stirring occasionally, or until the noodles are tender. Serve topped with the grated Parmesan.

Per Serving calories: 244 | fat: 14.0g | protein: 4.0g | carbs: 22.0g | fiber: 4.0g | sodium: 159mg

Potato Tortilla with Leeks and Mushrooms

Prep time: 30 minutes | Cook time: 50 minutes | Serves 2

1 tablespoon olive oil

1 cup thinly sliced leeks

4 ounces (113 g) baby bella (cremini) mushrooms, stemmed and sliced

1 small potato, peeled and sliced ¼-inch thick

½ cup unsweetened almond milk

5 large eggs, beaten

1 teaspoon Dijon mustard

½ teaspoon salt

½ teaspoon dried thyme

Pinch freshly ground black pepper

3 ounces (85 g) Gruyère cheese, shredded

1. Preheat the oven to 350ºF (180ºC).
2. In a large sauté pan over medium-high heat, heat the olive oil. Add the leeks, mushrooms, and potato and sauté for about 10 minutes, or until the potato starts to brown.
3. Reduce the heat to medium-low, cover, and cook for an additional 10 minutes, or until the potato begins to soften. Add 1 to 2 tablespoons of water to prevent sticking to the bottom of the pan, if needed.
4. Meanwhile, whisk together the milk, beaten eggs, mustard, salt, thyme, black pepper, and cheese in a medium bowl until combined. When the potatoes are fork-tender, turn off the heat. Transfer the cooked vegetables to an oiled nonstick ovenproof pan and arrange them in a nice layer along the bottom and slightly up the sides of the pan. Pour the milk mixture evenly over the vegetables.
5. Bake in the preheated oven for 25 to 30 minutes, or until the eggs are completely set and the top is golden and puffed. Remove from the oven and cool for 5 minutes before cutting and serving.

Per Serving calories: 541 | fat: 33.1g | protein: 32.8g | carbs: 31.0g | fiber: 4.0g | sodium: 912mg

Mushrooms Ragu with Cheesy Polenta

Prep time: 20 minutes | Cook time: 30 minutes | Serves 2

½ ounce (14 g) dried porcini mushrooms

1 pound (454 g) baby bella (cremini) mushrooms, quartered

2 tablespoons olive oil

1 garlic clove, minced

1 large shallot, minced

1 tablespoon flour

2 teaspoons tomato paste

½ cup red wine

1 cup mushroom stock (or reserved liquid from soaking the porcini mushrooms, if using)

1 fresh rosemary sprig

½ teaspoon dried thyme

1½ cups water

½ teaspoon salt, plus more as needed

⅓ cup instant polenta

2 tablespoons grated Parmesan cheese

1. Soak the dried porcini mushrooms in 1 cup of hot water for about 15 minutes to soften them. When ready, scoop them out of the water, reserving the soaking liquid. Mince the porcini mushrooms. Heat the olive oil in a large sauté pan over medium-high heat. Add the mushrooms, garlic, and shallot and sauté for 10 minutes, or until the vegetables are beginning to caramelize.
2. Stir in the flour and tomato paste and cook for an additional 30 seconds. Add the red wine, mushroom stock, rosemary, and thyme. Bring the mixture to a boil, stirring constantly, or until it has thickened.
3. Reduce the heat and allow to simmer for 10 minutes.
4. Meanwhile, bring the water to a boil in a saucepan and sprinkle with the salt.
5. Add the instant polenta and stir quickly while it thickens. Scatter with the grated Parmesan cheese. Taste and season with more salt as needed. Serve warm.

Per Serving calories: 450 | fat: 16.0g | protein: 14.1g | carbs: 57.8g | fiber: 5.0g | sodium: 165mg

Veggie Rice Bowls with Pesto Sauce

Prep time: 15 minutes | Cook time: 1 minute | Serves 2

2 cups water

1 cup arborio rice, rinsed

Salt and ground black pepper, to taste

2 eggs

1 cup broccoli florets

½ pound (227 g) Brussels sprouts

1 carrot, peeled and chopped

1 small beet, peeled and cubed

¼ cup pesto sauce

Lemon wedges, for serving

1. Combine the water, rice, salt, and pepper in the Instant Pot. Insert a trivet over rice and place a steamer basket on top. Add the eggs, broccoli, Brussels sprouts, carrots, beet cubes, salt, and pepper to the steamer basket.
2. Lock the lid. Select the Manual mode and set the cooking time for 1 minute at High Pressure.
3. When the timer beeps, perform a natural pressure release for 10 minutes, then release any remaining pressure. Carefully open the lid. Remove the steamer basket and trivet from the pot and transfer the eggs to a bowl of ice water. Peel and halve the eggs. Use a fork to fluff the rice.
4. Divide the rice, broccoli, Brussels sprouts, carrot, beet cubes, and eggs into two bowls. Top with a dollop of pesto sauce and serve with the lemon wedges.

Per Serving calories: 590 | fat: 34.1g | protein: 21.9g | carbs: 50.0g | fiber: 19.6g | sodium: 670mg

Roasted Cauliflower and Carrots

Prep time: 10 minutes | Cook time: 30 minutes | Serves 2

4 cups cauliflower florets (about ½ small head)

2 medium carrots, peeled, halved, and then sliced into quarters lengthwise

2 tablespoons olive oil, divided

½ teaspoon salt, divided

½ teaspoon garlic powder, divided

2 teaspoons za'atar spice mix, divided

1 (15-ounce / 425-g) can chickpeas, drained, rinsed, and patted dry

¾ cup plain Greek yogurt

1 teaspoon harissa spice paste, plus additional as needed

1. Preheat the oven to 400°F (205°C). Line a sheet pan with foil or parchment paper.
2. Put the cauliflower and carrots in a large bowl. Drizzle with 1 tablespoon of olive oil and sprinkle with ¼ teaspoon of salt, ¼ teaspoon of garlic powder, and 1 teaspoon of za'atar. Toss to combine well.
3. Spread the vegetables onto one half of the prepared sheet pan in a single layer.
4. Put the chickpeas in the same bowl and season with the remaining 1 tablespoon of olive oil, ¼ teaspoon of salt, ¼ teaspoon of garlic powder, and the remaining 1 teaspoon of za'atar. Toss to combine well.
5. Spread the chickpeas onto the other half of the sheet pan.
6. Roast in the preheated oven for 30 minutes, or until the vegetables are crisp-tender. Flip the vegetables halfway through and give the chickpeas a stir so they cook evenly.
7. Meanwhile, whisk the yogurt and harissa together in a small bowl. Taste and add additional harissa as needed.
8. Serve the vegetables and chickpeas with the yogurt mixture on the side.

Per Serving calories: 468 | fat: 23.0g | protein: 18.1g | carbs: 54.1g | fiber: 13.8g | sodium: 631mg

Sauté ed Spinach and Leeks

Prep time: 5 minutes | Cook time: 8 minutes | Serves 2

3 tablespoons olive oil

2 garlic cloves, crushed

2 leeks, chopped

2 red onions, chopped

9 ounces (255 g) fresh spinach

1 teaspoon kosher salt

½ cup crumbled goat cheese

1. Coat the bottom of the Instant Pot with the olive oil.
2. Add the garlic, leek, and onions and stir-fry for about 5 minutes, on Sauté mode.
3. Stir in the spinach. Sprinkle with the salt and sauté for an additional 3 minutes, stirring constantly.
4. Transfer to a plate and scatter with the goat cheese before serving.

Per Serving

calories: 447 | fat: 31.2g | protein: 14.6g | carbs: 28.7g | fiber: 6.3g | sodium: 937mg

Zoodles with Beet Pesto

Prep time: 10 minutes | Cook time: 50 minutes | Serves 2

1 medium red beet, peeled, chopped
½ cup walnut pieces
½ cup crumbled goat cheese
3 garlic cloves
2 tablespoons freshly squeezed lemon juice
2 tablespoons plus 2 teaspoons extra-virgin olive oil, divided
¼ teaspoon salt
4 small zucchinis, spiralized

1. Preheat the oven to 375°F (190°C).
2. Wrap the chopped beet in a piece of aluminum foil and seal well.
3. Roast in the preheated oven for 30 to 40 minutes until tender.
4. Meanwhile, heat a skillet over medium-high heat until hot. Add the walnuts and toast for 5 to 7 minutes, or until fragrant and lightly browned.
5. Remove the cooked beets from the oven and place in a food processor. Add the toasted walnuts, goat cheese, garlic, lemon juice, 2 tablespoons of olive oil, and salt. Pulse until smoothly blended. Set aside.
6. Heat the remaining 2 teaspoons of olive oil in a large skillet over medium heat. Add the zucchini and toss to coat in the oil. Cook for 2 to 3 minutes, stirring gently, or until the zucchini is softened. Transfer the zucchini to a serving plate and toss with the beet pesto, then serve.

Per Serving

calories: 423 | fat: 38.8g | protein: 8.0g | carbs: 17.1g | fiber: 6.0g | sodium: 338mg

Fried Eggplant Rolls

Prep time: 20 minutes | Cook time: 10 minutes | Serves 4 to 6

1 large eggplants, trimmed and cut lengthwise into ¼-inch-thick slices
1 teaspoon salt
1 cup ricotta cheese
4 ounces (113 g) goat cheese, shredded
¼ cup finely chopped fresh basil
½ teaspoon freshly ground black pepper
Olive oil spray

1. Add the eggplant slices to a colander and season with salt. Set aside for 15 to 20 minutes.
2. Mix together the ricotta and goat cheese, basil, and black pepper in a large bowl and stir to combine. Set aside.
3. Dry the eggplant slices with paper towels and lightly mist them with olive oil spray.
4. Heat a large skillet over medium heat and lightly spray it with olive oil spray.
5. Arrange the eggplant slices in the skillet and fry each side for 3 minutes until golden brown.
6. Remove from the heat to a paper towel-lined plate and rest for 5 minutes.
7. Make the eggplant rolls: Lay the eggplant slices on a flat work surface and top each slice with a tablespoon of the prepared cheese mixture. Roll them up and serve immediately.

Per Serving

calories: 254 | fat: 14.9g | protein: 15.3g | carbs: 18.6g | fiber: 7.1g | sodium: 745mg

Roasted Veggies and Brown Rice Bowl

Prep time: 15 minutes | Cook time: 20 minutes | Serves 4

2 cups cauliflower florets
2 cups broccoli florets
1 (15-ounce / 425-g) can chickpeas, drained and rinsed
1 cup carrot slices (about 1 inch thick)
2 to 3 tablespoons extra-virgin olive oil, divided
Salt and freshly ground black pepper, to taste
Nonstick cooking spray
2 cups cooked brown rice
2 to 3 tablespoons sesame seeds, for garnish
Dressing:
3 to 4 tablespoons tahini
2 tablespoons honey
1 lemon, juiced
1 garlic clove, minced
Salt and freshly ground black pepper, to taste

1. Preheat the oven to 400°F (205°C). Spritz two baking sheets with nonstick cooking spray.
2. Spread the cauliflower and broccoli on the first baking sheet and the second with the chickpeas and carrot slices.
3. Drizzle each sheet with half of the olive oil and sprinkle with salt and pepper. Toss to coat well.
4. Roast the chickpeas and carrot slices in the preheated oven for 10 minutes, leaving the carrots tender but crisp, and the cauliflower and broccoli for 20 minutes until fork-tender. Stir them once halfway through the cooking time.
5. Meanwhile, make the dressing: Whisk together the tahini, honey, lemon juice, garlic, salt, and pepper in a small bowl.
6. Divide the cooked brown rice among four bowls. Top each bowl evenly with roasted vegetables and dressing. Sprinkle the sesame seeds on top for garnish before serving.

Per Serving

calories: 453 | fat: 17.8g | protein: 12.1g | carbs: 61.8g | fiber: 11.2g | sodium: 60mg

Cauliflower Hash with Carrots

Prep time: 10 minutes | Cook time: 10 minutes | Serves 4

3 tablespoons extra-virgin olive oil
1 large onion, chopped
1 tablespoon minced garlic
2 cups diced carrots
4 cups cauliflower florets
½ teaspoon ground cumin
1 teaspoon salt

1. In a large skillet, heat the olive oil over medium heat.
2. Add the onion and garlic and sauté for 1 minute. Stir in the carrots and stir-fry for 3 minutes.
3. Add the cauliflower florets, cumin, and salt and toss to combine.
4. Cover and cook for 3 minutes until lightly browned. Stir well and cook, uncovered, for 3 to 4 minutes, until softened.
5. Remove from the heat and serve warm.

Per Serving

calories: 158 | fat: 10.8g | protein: 3.1g | carbs: 14.9g | fiber: 5.1g | sodium: 656mg

Garlicky Zucchini Cubes with Mint

Prep time: 5 minutes | Cook time: 10 minutes | Serves 4

3 large green zucchini, cut into ½-inch cubes	1 large onion, chopped
3 tablespoons extra-virgin olive oil	3 cloves garlic, minced
	1 teaspoon salt
	1 teaspoon dried mint

1. Heat the olive oil in a large skillet over medium heat.
2. Add the onion and garlic and sauté for 3 minutes, stirring constantly, or until softened.
3. Stir in the zucchini cubes and salt and cook for 5 minutes, or until the zucchini is browned and tender.
4. Add the mint to the skillet and toss to combine, then continue cooking for 2 minutes. Serve warm.

Per Serving calories: 146 | fat: 10.6g | protein: 4.2g | carbs: 11.8g | fiber: 3.0g | sodium: 606mg

Zucchini and Artichokes Bowl with Farro

Prep time: 15 minutes | Cook time: 10 minutes | Serves 4 to 6

⅓ cup extra-virgin olive oil	Salt and freshly ground black pepper, to taste
⅓ cup chopped red onions	½ cup crumbled feta cheese, for serving (optional)
½ cup chopped red bell pepper	¼ cup sliced olives, for serving (optional)
2 garlic cloves, minced	
1 cup zucchini, cut into ½-inch-thick slices	2 tablespoons fresh basil, chiffonade, for serving (optional)
½ cup coarsely chopped artichokes	
½ cup canned chickpeas, drained and rinsed	3 tablespoons balsamic vinegar, for serving (optional)
3 cups cooked farro	

1. Heat the olive oil in a large skillet over medium heat until it shimmers. Add the onions, bell pepper, and garlic and sauté for 5 minutes, stirring occasionally, until softened.
2. Stir in the zucchini slices, artichokes, and chickpeas and sauté for about 5 minutes until slightly tender.
3. Add the cooked farro and toss to combine until heated through. Sprinkle the salt and pepper to season.
4. Divide the mixture into bowls. Top each bowl evenly with feta cheese, olive slices, and basil and sprinkle with the balsamic vinegar, if desired.

Per Serving calories: 366 | fat: 19.9g | protein: 9.3g | carbs: 50.7g | fiber: 9.0g | sodium: 86mg

Zucchini Fritters

Prep time: 15 minutes | Cook time: 5 minutes | Makes 14 fritters

4 cups grated zucchini	⅔ all-purpose flour
Salt, to taste	⅛ teaspoon black pepper
2 large eggs, lightly beaten	2 tablespoons olive oil
⅓ cup sliced scallions (green and white parts)	

1. Put the grated zucchini in a colander and lightly season with salt. Set aside to rest for 10 minutes. Squeeze out as much liquid from the grated zucchini as possible.
2. Pour the grated zucchini into a bowl. Fold in the beaten eggs, scallions, flour, salt, and pepper and stir until everything is well combined.
3. Heat the olive oil in a large skillet over medium heat until hot.
4. Drop 3 tablespoons mounds of the zucchini mixture onto the hot skillet to make each fritter, pressing them lightly into rounds and spacing them about 2 inches apart.
5. Cook for 2 to 3 minutes. Flip the zucchini fritters and cook for 2 minutes more, or until they are golden brown and cooked through.
6. Remove from the heat to a plate lined with paper towels. Repeat with the remaining zucchini mixture.
7. Serve hot.

Per Serving (2 fritters)
calories: 113 | fat: 6.1g | protein: 4.0g | carbs: 12.2g | fiber: 1.0g | sodium: 25mg

Moroccan Tagine with Vegetables

Prep time: 20 minutes | Cook time: 40 minutes | Serves 2

2 tablespoons olive oil	2 small red potatoes, cut into 1-inch pieces
½ onion, diced	
1 garlic clove, minced	1 cup water
2 cups cauliflower florets	1 teaspoon pure maple syrup
1 medium carrot, cut into 1-inch pieces	½ teaspoon cinnamon
	½ teaspoon turmeric
1 cup diced eggplant	1 teaspoon cumin
1 (28-ounce / 794-g) can whole tomatoes with their juices	½ teaspoon salt
	1 to 2 teaspoons harissa paste
1 (15-ounce / 425-g) can chickpeas, drained and rinsed	

1. In a Dutch oven, heat the olive oil over medium-high heat. Sauté the onion for 5 minutes, stirring occasionally, or until the onion is translucent.
2. Stir in the garlic, cauliflower florets, carrot, eggplant, tomatoes, and potatoes. Using a wooden spoon or spatula to break up the tomatoes into smaller pieces.
3. Add the chickpeas, water, maple syrup, cinnamon, turmeric, cumin, and salt and stir to incorporate. Bring the mixture to a boil.
4. Once it starts to boil, reduce the heat to medium-low. Stir in the harissa paste, cover, allow to simmer for about 40 minutes, or until the vegetables are softened. Taste and adjust seasoning as needed.
5. Let the mixture cool for 5 minutes before serving.

Per Serving
calories: 293 | fat: 9.9g | protein: 11.2g | carbs: 45.5g | fiber: 12.1g | sodium: 337mg

Vegan Lentil Bolognese

Prep time: 15 minutes | Cook time: 50 minutes | Serves 2

1 medium celery stalk	1 cup red wine
1 large carrot	½ teaspoon salt, plus more as needed
½ large onion	
1 garlic clove	½ teaspoon pure maple syrup
2 tablespoons olive oil	
1 (28-ounce / 794-g) can crushed tomatoes	1 cup cooked lentils (prepared from ½ cup dry)

1. Add the celery, carrot, onion, and garlic to a food processor and process until everything is finely chopped.
2. In a Dutch oven, heat the olive oil over medium-high heat. Add the chopped mixture and saut é for about 10 minutes, stirring occasionally, or until the vegetables are lightly browned.
3. Stir in the tomatoes, wine, salt, and maple syrup and bring to a boil.
4. Once the sauce starts to boil, cover, and reduce the heat to medium-low. Simmer for 30 minutes, stirring occasionally, or until the vegetables are softened.
5. Stir in the cooked lentils and cook for an additional 5 minutes until warmed through.
6. Taste and add additional salt, if needed. Serve warm.

Per Serving

calories: 367 | fat: 15.0g | protein: 13.7g | carbs: 44.5g | fiber: 17.6g | sodium: 1108mg

Grilled Vegetable Skewers

Prep time: 15 minutes | Cook time: 10 minutes | Serves 4

4 medium red onions, peeled and sliced into 6 wedges	2 orange bell peppers, cut into 2-inch squares
4 medium zucchinis, cut into 1-inch-thick slices	2 yellow bell peppers, cut into 2-inch squares
2 beefsteak tomatoes, cut into quarters	2 tablespoons plus 1 teaspoon olive oil, divided
4 red bell peppers, cut into 2-inch squares	Special Equipment:
	4 wooden skewers, soaked in water for at least 30 minutes

1. Preheat the grill to medium-high heat.
2. Skewer the vegetables by alternating between red onion, zucchini, tomatoes, and the different colored bell peppers. Brush them with 2 tablespoons of olive oil.
3. Oil the grill grates with 1 teaspoon of olive oil and grill the vegetable skewers for 5 minutes. Flip the skewers and grill for 5 minutes more, or until they are cooked to your liking.
4. Let the skewers cool for 5 minutes before serving.

Per Serving

calories: 115 | fat: 3.0g | protein: 3.5g | carbs: 18.7g | fiber: 4.7g | sodium: 12mg

Stuffed Portobello Mushroom with Tomatoes

Prep time: 10 minutes | Cook time: 15 minutes | Serves 4

4 large portobello mushroom caps	4 sun-dried tomatoes
3 tablespoons extra-virgin olive oil	1 cup shredded mozzarella cheese, divided
Salt and freshly ground black pepper, to taste	½ to ¾ cup low-sodium tomato sauce

1. Preheat the broiler to High.
2. Arrange the mushroom caps on a baking sheet and drizzle with olive oil.
1. Sprinkle with salt and pepper.
2. Broil for 1o minutes, flipping the mushroom caps halfway through, until browned on the top.
3. Remove from the broil. Spoon 1 tomato, 2 tablespoons of cheese, and 2 to 3 tablespoons of sauce onto each mushroom cap.
4. Return the mushroom caps to the broiler and continue broiling for 2 to 3 minutes.
5. Cool for 5 minutes before serving.

Per Serving

calories: 217 | fat: 15.8g | protein: 11.2g | carbs: 11.7g | fiber: 2.0g | sodium: 243mg

Wilted Dandelion Greens with Sweet Onion

Prep time: 15 minutes | Cook time: 15 minutes | Serves 4

1 tablespoon extra-virgin olive oil	2 bunches dandelion greens, roughly chopped
2 garlic cloves, minced	Freshly ground black pepper, to taste
1 Vidalia onion, thinly sliced	
½ cup low-sodium vegetable broth	

1. Heat the olive oil in a large skillet over low heat.
2. Add the garlic and onion and cook for 2 to 3 minutes, stirring occasionally, or until the onion is translucent.
3. Fold in the vegetable broth and dandelion greens and cook for 5 to 7 minutes until wilted, stirring frequently.
4. Sprinkle with the black pepper and serve on a plate while warm.

Per Serving

calories: 81 | fat: 3.9g | protein: 3.2g | carbs: 10.8g | fiber: 4.0g | sodium: 72mg

Celery and Mustard Greens

Prep time: 10 minutes | Cook time: 15 minutes | Serves 4

½ cup low-sodium vegetable broth	½ large red bell pepper, thinly sliced
1 celery stalk, roughly chopped	2 garlic cloves, minced
½ sweet onion, chopped	1 bunch mustard greens, roughly chopped

1. Pour the vegetable broth into a large cast iron pan and bring it to a simmer over medium heat.
2. Stir in the celery, onion, bell pepper, and garlic. Cook uncovered for about 3 to 5 minutes, or until the onion is softened.
3. Add the mustard greens to the pan and stir well. Cover, reduce the heat to low, and cook for an additional 10 minutes, or until the liquid is evaporated and the greens are wilted. Remove from the heat and serve warm.

Per Serving (1 cup) calories: 39 | fat: 0g | protein: 3.1g | carbs: 6.8g | fiber: 3.0g | sodium: 120mg

Vegetable and Tofu Scramble

Prep time: 5 minutes | Cook time: 10 minutes | Serves 2

2 tablespoons extra-virgin olive oil
½ red onion, finely chopped
1 cup chopped kale
8 ounces (227 g) mushrooms, sliced
8 ounces (227 g) tofu, cut into pieces
2 garlic cloves, minced
Pinch red pepper flakes
½ teaspoon sea salt
⅛ teaspoon freshly ground black pepper

1. Heat the olive oil in a medium nonstick skillet over medium-high heat until shimmering.
2. Add the onion, kale, and mushrooms to the skillet and cook for about 5 minutes, stirring occasionally, or until the vegetables start to brown.
3. Add the tofu and stir-fry for 3 to 4 minutes until softened.
4. Stir in the garlic, red pepper flakes, salt, and black pepper and cook for 30 seconds.
5. Let the mixture cool for 5 minutes before serving.

Per Serving

calories: 233 | fat: 15.9g | protein: 13.4g | carbs: 11.9g | fiber: 2.0g | sodium: 672mg

Zoodles

Prep time: 10 minutes | Cook time: 5 minutes | Serves 2

2 tablespoons avocado oil
2 medium zucchini, spiralized
¼ teaspoon salt
Freshly ground black pepper, to taste

1. Heat the avocado oil in a large skillet over medium heat until it shimmers.
2. Add the zucchini noodles, salt, and black pepper to the skillet and toss to coat. Cook for 1 to 2 minutes, stirring constantly, until tender.
3. Serve warm.

Per Serving

calories: 128 | fat: 14.0g | protein: 0.3g | carbs: 0.3g | fiber: 0.1g | sodium: 291mg

Lentil and Tomato Collard Wraps

Prep time: 15 minutes | Cook time: 0 minutes | Serves 4

2 cups cooked lentils
5 Roma tomatoes, diced
½ cup crumbled feta cheese
10 large fresh basil leaves, thinly sliced
¼ cup extra-virgin olive oil
1 tablespoon balsamic vinegar
2 garlic cloves, minced
½ teaspoon raw honey
½ teaspoon salt
¼ teaspoon freshly ground black pepper
4 large collard leaves, stems removed

1. Combine the lentils, tomatoes, cheese, basil leaves, olive oil, vinegar, garlic, honey, salt, and black pepper in a large bowl and stir until well blended.
2. Lay the collard leaves on a flat work surface. Spoon the equal-sized amounts of the lentil mixture onto the edges of the leaves. Roll them up and slice in half to serve.

Per Serving

calories: 318 | fat: 17.6g | protein: 13.2g | carbs: 27.5g | fiber: 9.9g | sodium: 475mg

Stir-Fry Baby Bok Choy

Prep time: 12 minutes | Cook time: 10 to 13 minutes | Serves 6

2 tablespoons coconut oil
1 large onion, finely diced
2 teaspoons ground cumin
1-inch piece fresh ginger, grated
1 teaspoon ground turmeric
½ teaspoon salt
12 baby bok choy heads, ends trimmed and sliced lengthwise
Water, as needed
3 cups cooked brown rice

1. Heat the coconut oil in a large pan over medium heat.
2. Sauté the onion for 5 minutes, stirring occasionally, or until the onion is translucent. Fold in the cumin, ginger, turmeric, and salt and stir to coat well.
3. Add the bok choy and cook for 5 to 8 minutes, stirring occasionally, or until the bok choy is tender but crisp. You can add 1 tablespoon of water at a time, if the skillet gets dry until you finish sautéing. Transfer the bok choy to a plate and serve over the cooked brown rice.

Per Serving calories: 443 | fat: 8.8g | protein: 30.3g | carbs: 75.7g | fiber: 19.0g | sodium: 1289mg

Sweet Pepper Stew

Prep time: 20 minutes | Cook time: 50 minutes | Serves 2

2 tablespoons olive oil
2 sweet peppers, diced (about 2 cups)
½ large onion, minced
1 garlic clove, minced
1 tablespoon gluten-free Worcestershire sauce
1 teaspoon oregano
1 cup low-sodium tomato juice
1 cup low-sodium vegetable stock
¼ cup brown rice
¼ cup brown lentils
Salt, to taste

1. In a Dutch oven, heat the olive oil over medium-high heat.
2. Sauté the sweet peppers and onion for 10 minutes, stirring occasionally, or until the onion begins to turn golden and the peppers are wilted.
3. Stir in the garlic, Worcestershire sauce, and oregano and cook for 30 seconds more. Add the tomato juice, vegetable stock, rice, and lentils to the Dutch oven and stir to mix well. Bring the mixture to a boil and then reduce the heat to medium-low. Let it simmer covered for about 45 minutes, or until the rice is cooked through and the lentils are tender. Sprinkle with salt and serve warm.

Per Serving

calories: 378 | fat: 15.6g | protein: 11.4g | carbs: 52.8g | fiber: 7.0g | sodium: 391mg

Vegetable and Red Lentil Stew

Prep time: 10 minutes | Cook time: 35 minutes | Serves 6

1 tablespoon extra-virgin olive oil	4 celery stalks, finely diced
2 onions, peeled and finely diced	3 cups red lentils
6½ cups water	1 teaspoon dried oregano
2 zucchini, finely diced	1 teaspoon salt, plus more as needed

1. Heat the olive oil in a large pot over medium heat.
2. Add the onions and sauté for about 5 minutes, stirring constantly, or until the onions are softened.
3. Stir in the water, zucchini, celery, lentils, oregano, and salt and bring the mixture to a boil.
4. Reduce the heat to low and let simmer covered for 30 minutes, stirring occasionally, or until the lentils are tender.
5. Taste and adjust the seasoning as needed.

Per Serving calories: 387 | fat: 4.4g | protein: 24.0g | carbs: 63.7g | fiber: 11.7g | sodium: 418mg

Roasted Vegetables

Prep time: 20 minutes | Cook time: 35 minutes | Serves 2

6 teaspoons extra-virgin olive oil, divided	2 cups fresh cauliflower florets
12 to 15 Brussels sprouts, halved	1 medium zucchini, cut into 1-inch rounds
1 medium sweet potato, peeled and cut into 2-inch cubes	1 red bell pepper, cut into 1-inch slices
	Salt, to taste

1. Preheat the oven to 425ºF (220ºC).
2. Add 2 teaspoons of olive oil, Brussels sprouts, sweet potato, and salt to a large bowl and toss until they are completely coated.
3. Transfer them to a large roasting pan and roast for 10 minutes, or until the Brussels sprouts are lightly browned.
4. Meantime, combine the cauliflower florets with 2 teaspoons of olive oil and salt in a separate bowl.
5. Remove from the oven. Add the cauliflower florets to the roasting pan and roast for 10 minutes more.
6. Meanwhile, toss the zucchini and bell pepper with the remaining olive oil in a medium bowl until well coated. Season with salt.
7. Remove the roasting pan from the oven and stir in the zucchini and bell pepper. Continue roasting for 15 minutes, or until the vegetables are fork-tender.
8. Divide the roasted vegetables between two plates and serve warm. **Per Serving** calories: 333 | fat: 16.8g | protein: 12.2g | carbs: 37.6g | fiber: 11.0g | sodium: 329mg

Ratatouille

Prep time: 10 minutes | Cook time: 30 minutes | Serves 4

4 tablespoons extra-virgin olive oil, divided	1 (15-ounce / 425-g) can no-salt-added diced tomatoes
1 cup diced zucchini	½ teaspoon garlic powder
2 cups diced eggplant	1 teaspoon ground thyme
1 cup diced onion	Salt and freshly ground black pepper, to taste
1 cup chopped green bell pepper	

1. Heat 2 tablespoons of olive oil in a large saucepan over medium heat until it shimmers.
2. Add the zucchini and eggplant and sauté for 10 minutes, stirring occasionally. If necessary, add the remaining olive oil. Stir in the onion and bell pepper and sauté for 5 minutes until softened.
3. Add the diced tomatoes with their juice, garlic powder, and thyme and stir to combine. Continue cooking for 15 minutes until the vegetables are cooked through, stirring occasionally. Sprinkle with salt and black pepper.
4. Remove from the heat and serve on a plate.

Per Serving calories: 189 | fat: 13.7g | protein: 3.1g | carbs: 14.8g | fiber: 4.0g | sodium: 27mg

Sautéed Green Beans with Tomatoes

Prep time: 10 minutes | Cook time: 20 minutes | Serves 4

¼ cup extra-virgin olive oil	1½ teaspoons salt, divided
1 large onion, chopped	1 (15-ounce / 425-g) can diced tomatoes
4 cloves garlic, finely chopped	½ teaspoon freshly ground black pepper
1 pound (454 g) green beans, fresh or frozen, cut into 2-inch pieces	

1. Heat the olive oil in a large skillet over medium heat.
2. Add the onion and garlic and sauté for 1 minute until fragrant.
3. Stir in the green beans and sauté for 3 minutes. Sprinkle with ½ teaspoon of salt.
4. Add the tomatoes, remaining salt, and pepper and stir to mix well. Cook for an additional 12 minutes, stirring occasionally, or until the green beans are crisp and tender.
5. Remove from the heat and serve warm.

Per Serving calories: 219 | fat: 13.9g | protein: 4.0g | carbs: 17.7g | fiber: 6.2g | sodium: 843mg

Baked Tomatoes and Chickpeas

Prep time: 15 minutes | Cook time: 40 to 45 minutes | Serves 4

1 tablespoon extra-virgin olive oil	2 (15-ounce / 425-g) cans chickpeas, drained and rinsed
½ medium onion, chopped	4 cups halved cherry tomatoes
3 garlic cloves, chopped	
¼ teaspoon ground cumin	½ cup plain Greek yogurt, for serving
2 teaspoons smoked paprika	1 cup crumbled feta cheese, for serving

1. Preheat the oven to 425ºF (220ºC).
2. Heat the olive oil in an ovenproof skillet over medium heat.
3. Add the onion and garlic and sauté for about 5 minutes, stirring occasionally, or until tender and fragrant.
4. Add the paprika and cumin and cook for 2 minutes. Stir in the chickpeas and tomatoes and allow to simmer for 5 to 10 minutes.
5. Transfer the skillet to the preheated oven and roast for 25 to 30 minutes, or until the mixture bubbles and thickens.
6. Remove from the oven and serve topped with yogurt and crumbled feta cheese.

Per Serving calories: 411 | fat: 14.9g | protein: 20.2g | carbs: 50.7g | fiber: 13.3g | sodium: 443mg

Creamy Cauliflower Chickpea Curry

Prep time: 5 minutes | Cook time: 15 minutes | Serves 4

3 cups fresh or frozen cauliflower florets

2 cups unsweetened almond milk

1 (15-ounce / 425-g) can low-sodium chickpeas, drained and rinsed

1 tablespoon curry powder

¼ teaspoon garlic powder

¼ teaspoon ground ginger

⅛ teaspoon onion powder

¼ teaspoon salt

1 (15-ounce / 425-g) can coconut milk

1. Add the cauliflower florets, almond milk, chickpeas, coconut milk, curry powder, garlic powder, ginger, and onion powder to a large stockpot and stir to combine.
2. Cover and cook over medium-high heat for 10 minutes, stirring occasionally.
3. Reduce the heat to low and continue cooking uncovered for 5 minutes, or until the cauliflower is tender.
4. Sprinkle with the salt and stir well. Serve warm.

Per Serving

calories: 409 | fat: 29.6g | protein: 10.0g | carbs: 29.8g | fiber: 9.1g | sodium: 117mg

Cauliflower Rice Risotto with Mushrooms

Prep time: 5 minutes | Cook time: 10 minutes | Serves 4

1 teaspoon extra-virgin olive oil

½ cup chopped portobello mushrooms

4 cups cauliflower rice

½ cup plain Greek yogurt

¼ cup low-sodium vegetable broth

1 cup shredded Parmesan cheese

1. In a medium skillet, heat the olive oil over medium-low heat until shimmering.
2. Add the mushrooms and stir-fry for 3 minutes.
3. Stir in the cauliflower rice, yogurt, and vegetable broth. Cover and bring to a boil over high heat for 5 minutes, stirring occasionally.
4. Add the Parmesan cheese and stir to combine. Continue cooking for an additional 3 minutes until the cheese is melted.
5. Divide the mixture into four bowls and serve warm.

Per Serving calories: 167 | fat: 10.7g | protein: 12.1g | carbs: 8.1g | fiber: 3.0g | sodium: 326mg

Sweet Potato Chickpea Buddha Bowl

Prep time: 10 minutes | Cook time: 10 to 15 minutes | Serves 2

Sauce:

1 tablespoon tahini

2 tablespoons plain Greek yogurt

2 tablespoons hemp seeds

1 garlic clove, minced Pinch salt

Freshly ground black pepper, to taste

Bowl:

1 small sweet potato, peeled and finely diced

1 teaspoon extra-virgin olive oil

1 cup from 1 (15-ounce / 425-g) can low-sodium chickpeas, drained and rinsed

2 cups baby kale

Make the Sauce

1. Whisk together the tahini and yogurt in a small bowl.
2. Stir in the hemp seeds and minced garlic. Season with salt pepper. Add 2 to 3 tablespoons water to create a creamy yet pourable consistency and set aside.

Make the Bowl

3. Preheat the oven to 425ºF (220ºC). Line a baking sheet with parchment paper.
4. Place the sweet potato on the prepared baking sheet and drizzle with the olive oil. Toss well
5. Roast in the preheated oven for 10 to 15 minutes, stirring once during cooking, or until fork-tender and browned.
6. In each of 2 bowls, place ½ cup of chickpeas, 1 cup of baby kale, and half of the cooked sweet potato. Serve drizzled with half of the prepared sauce.

Per Serving

calories: 323 | fat: 14.1g | protein: 17.0g | carbs: 36.0 g | fiber: 7.9g | sodium: 304mg

Zucchini Patties

Prep time: 15 minutes | Cook time: 5 minutes | Serves 2

2 medium zucchinis, shredded

1 teaspoon salt, divided

2 eggs

2 tablespoons chickpea flour

1 tablespoon chopped fresh mint

1 scallion, chopped

2 tablespoons extra-virgin olive oil

1. Put the shredded zucchini in a fine-mesh strainer and season with ½ teaspoon of salt. Set aside.
2. Beat together the eggs, chickpea flour, mint, scallion, and remaining ½ teaspoon of salt in a medium bowl.
3. Squeeze the zucchini to drain as much liquid as possible. Add the zucchini to the egg mixture and stir until well incorporated.
4. Heat the olive oil in a large skillet over medium-high heat.
5. Drop the zucchini mixture by spoonfuls into the skillet. Gently flatten the zucchini with the back of a spatula.
6. Cook for 2 to 3 minutes or until golden brown. Flip and cook for an additional 2 minutes.
7. Remove from the heat and serve on a plate.

Per Serving

calories: 264 | fat: 20.0g | protein: 9.8g | carbs: 16.1g | fiber: 4.0g | sodium: 1780mg

Zucchini Crisp

Prep time: 10 minutes | Cook time: 20 minutes | Serves 2

4 zucchinis, sliced into ½-inch rounds
½ cup unsweetened almond milk
1 teaspoon fresh lemon juice
1 teaspoon arrowroot powder
½ teaspoon salt, divided
½ cup whole wheat bread crumbs
¼ cup nutritional yeast
¼ cup hemp seeds
½ teaspoon garlic powder
¼ teaspoon crushed red pepper
¼ teaspoon black pepper

1. Preheat the oven to 375ºF (190ºC). Line two baking sheets with parchment paper and set aside.
2. Put the zucchini in a medium bowl with the almond milk, lemon juice, arrowroot powder, and ¼ teaspoon of salt. Stir to mix well.
3. In a large bowl with a lid, thoroughly combine the bread crumbs, nutritional yeast, hemp seeds, garlic powder, crushed red pepper and black pepper. Add the zucchini in batches and shake until the slices are evenly coated.
4. Arrange the zucchini on the prepared baking sheets in a single layer.
5. Bake in the preheated oven for about 20 minutes, or until the zucchini slices are golden brown.
6. Season with the remaining ¼ teaspoon of salt before serving.

Per Serving

calories: 255 | fat: 11.3g | protein: 8.6g | carbs: 31.9g | fiber: 3.8g | sodium: 826mg

Creamy Sweet Potatoes and Collards

Prep time: 20 minutes | Cook time: 35 minutes | Serves 2

1 tablespoon avocado oil
3 garlic cloves, chopped
1 yellow onion, diced
½ teaspoon crushed red pepper flakes
1 large sweet potato, peeled and diced
2 bunches collard greens (about 2 pounds/907 g), stemmed, leaves chopped int
1-inch squares
1 (14.5-ounce / 411-g) can diced tomatoes with juice
1 (15-ounce / 425-g) can red kidney beans or chickpeas, drained and rinsed
1½ cups water
½ cup unsweetened coconut milk
Salt and black pepper, to taste

1. In a large, deep skillet over medium heat, melt the avocado oil.
2. Add the garlic, onion, and red pepper flakes and cook for 3 minutes. Stir in the sweet potato and collards.
3. Add the tomatoes with their juice, beans, water, and coconut milk and mix well. Bring the mixture just to a boil.
4. Reduce the heat to medium-low, cover, and simmer for about 30 minutes, or until softened.
5. Season to taste with salt and pepper and serve.

Per Serving calories: 445 | fat: 9.6g | protein: 18.1g | carbs: 73.1g | fiber: 22.1g | sodium: 703mg

Paprika Cauliflower Steaks with Walnut Sauce

Prep time: 5 minutes | Cook time: 30 minutes | Serves 2

Walnut Sauce:
½ cup raw walnut halves
2 tablespoons virgin olive oil, divided
1 clove garlic, chopped
1 small yellow onion, chopped
½ cup unsweetened almond milk
Salt and pepper, to taste
2 tablespoons fresh lemon juice
Paprika Cauliflower:
1 medium head cauliflower
1 teaspoon sweet paprika
1 teaspoon minced fresh thyme leaves (about 2 sprigs)

1. Preheat the oven to 350ºF (180ºC).
2. Make the walnut sauce: Toast the walnuts in a large, ovenproof skillet over medium heat until fragrant and slightly darkened, about 5 minutes. Transfer the walnuts to a blender. Heat 1 tablespoon of olive oil in the skillet. Add the garlic and onion and sauté for about 2 minutes, or until slightly softened. Transfer the garlic and onion into the blender, along with the almond milk, lemon juice, salt, and pepper. Blend the ingredients until smooth and creamy. Keep the sauce warm while you prepare the cauliflower.
3. Make the paprika cauliflower: Cut two 1-inch-thick "steaks" from the center of the cauliflower. Lightly moisten the steaks with water and season both sides with paprika, thyme, salt, and pepper. Heat the remaining 1 tablespoon of olive oil in the skillet over medium-high heat. Add the cauliflower steaks and sear for about 3 minutes until evenly browned. Flip the cauliflower steaks and transfer the skillet to the oven. Roast in the preheated oven for about 20 minutes until crisp-tender. Serve the cauliflower steaks warm with the walnut sauce on the side.

Per Serving calories: 367 | fat: 27.9g | protein: 7.0g | carbs: 22.7g | fiber: 5.8g | sodium: 173mg

Potato and Kale Bowls

Prep time: 10 minutes | Cook time: 10 minutes | Serves 4

1 tablespoon olive oil
1 small onion, peeled and diced
1 stalk celery, diced
2 cloves garlic, minced
4 medium potatoes, peeled and diced
2 bunches kale, washed, deveined, and chopped
1½ cups vegetable broth
2 teaspoons salt
½ teaspoon ground black pepper
¼ teaspoon caraway seeds
1 tablespoon apple cider vinegar
4 tablespoons sour cream

1. Press the Sauté button on Instant Pot. Heat oil. Add onion and celery and stir-fry for 3 to 5 minutes until onions are translucent. Add garlic and cook for an additional minute. Add potatoes in an even layer. Add chopped kale in an even layer. Add broth. Lock lid.
2. Press the Manual button and adjust time to 5 minutes. Let the pressure release naturally for 10 minutes. Quick release any additional pressure until float valve drops and then unlock lid; then drain broth. Stir in salt, pepper, caraway seeds, and vinegar; slightly mash the potatoes in the Instant Pot. Garnish each serving with 1 tablespoon sour cream.

Per Serving calories: 259 | fat: 5.5g | protein: 7.9g | carbs: 47.6g | fiber: 7.6g | sodium: 1422mg

Eggplant and Millet Pilaf

Prep time: 5 minutes | Cook time: 17 minutes | Serves 4

1 tablespoon olive oil	2 cups vegetable broth
¼ cup peeled and diced onion	1 teaspoon sea salt
1 cup peeled and diced eggplant	¼ teaspoon ground black pepper
1 small Roma tomato, seeded and diced	⅛ teaspoon saffron
1 cup millet	⅛ teaspoon cayenne pepper
	1 tablespoon chopped fresh chives

1. Press Sauté button on Instant Pot. Add the olive oil. Add onion and cook for 3 to 5 minutes until translucent. Toss in eggplant and stir-fry for 2 more minutes. Add diced tomato.
2. Add millet to Instant Pot in an even layer. Gently pour in broth. Lock lid.
3. Press the Rice button (the Instant Pot will determine the time, about 10 minutes pressurized cooking time). When timer beeps, let pressure release naturally for 5 minutes. Quick release any additional pressure until float valve drops and then unlock lid.
4. Transfer pot ingredients to a serving bowl. Season with salt, pepper, saffron, and cayenne pepper. Garnish with chives.

Per Serving

calories: 238 | fat: 5.6g | protein: 6.0g | carbs: 40.8g | fiber: 5.3g | sodium: 861mg

Chapter 7

<u>Poultry and Meats</u>

<u>Herbed-Mustard-Coated Pork Tenderloin</u>
Prep time: 10 minutes | Cook time: 15 minutes | Serves 4

3 tablespoons fresh rosemary leaves
¼ cup Dijon mustard
½ cup fresh parsley leaves
6 garlic cloves
½ teaspoon sea salt
¼ teaspoon freshly ground black pepper
1 tablespoon extra-virgin olive oil
1 (1½-pound / 680-g) pork tenderloin

1. Preheat the oven to 400°F (205°C).
2. Put all the ingredients, except for the pork tenderloin, in a food processor. Pulse until it has a thick consistency.
3. Put the pork tenderloin on a baking sheet, then rub with the mixture to coat well.
4. Put the sheet in the preheated oven and bake for 15 minutes or until the internal temperature of the pork reaches at least 165°F (74°C). Flip the tenderloin halfway through the cooking time.
5. Transfer the cooked pork tenderloin to a large plate and allow to cool for 5 minutes before serving.

Per Serving calories: 363 | fat: 18.1g | protein: 2.2g | carbs: 4.9g | fiber: 2.0g | sodium: 514mg

<u>Macadamia Pork</u>
Prep time: 10 minutes | Cook time: 10 minutes | Serves 4

1 (1-pound / 454-g) pork tenderloin, cut into ½-inch slices and pounded thin
1 teaspoon sea salt, divided
¼ teaspoon freshly ground black pepper, divided
½ cup macadamia nuts
1 cup unsweetened coconut milk
1 tablespoon extra-virgin olive oil

1. Preheat the oven to 400°F (205°C).
2. On a clean work surface, rub the pork with ½ teaspoon of the salt and ⅛ teaspoon of the ground black pepper. Set aside. Ground the macadamia nuts in a food processor, then combine with remaining salt and black pepper in a bowl. Stir to mix well and set aside.
3. Combine the coconut milk and olive oil in a separate bowl. Stir to mix well.
4. Dredge the pork chops into the bowl of coconut milk mixture, then dunk into the bowl of macadamia nut mixture to coat well. Shake the excess off.
5. Put the well-coated pork chops on a baking sheet, then bake for 10 minutes or until the internal temperature of the pork reaches at least 165°F (74°C).
6. Transfer the pork chops to a serving plate and serve immediately.

Per Serving calories: 436 | fat: 32.8g | protein: 33.1g | carbs: 5.9g | fiber: 3.0g | sodium: 310mg

<u>Grilled Chicken and Zucchini Kebabs</u>
Prep time: 10 minutes | Cook time: 20 minutes | Serves 4

¼ cup extra-virgin olive oil
2 tablespoons balsamic vinegar
1 teaspoon dried oregano, crushed between your fingers
1 pound (454 g) boneless, skinless chicken breasts, cut into 1½-inch pieces
2 medium zucchinis, cut into 1-inch pieces
½ cup Kalamata olives, pitted and halved
2 tablespoons olive brine
¼ cup torn fresh basil leaves
Nonstick cooking spray

Special Equipment:
14 to 15 (12-inch) wooden skewers, soaked for at least 30 minutes

1. Spray the grill grates with nonstick cooking spray. Preheat the grill to medium-high heat.
2. In a small bowl, whisk together the olive oil, vinegar, and oregano. Divide the marinade between two large plastic zip-top bags.
3. Add the chicken to one bag and the zucchini to another. Seal and massage the marinade into both the chicken and zucchini.
4. Thread the chicken onto 6 wooden skewers. Thread the zucchini onto 8 or 9 wooden skewers.
5. Cook the kebabs in batches on the grill for 5 minutes, flip, and grill for 5 minutes more, or until any chicken juices run clear.
6. Remove the chicken and zucchini from the skewers to a large serving bowl. Toss with the olives, olive brine, and basil and serve.

Per Serving
calories: 283 | fat: 15.0g | protein: 11.0g | carbs: 26.0g | fiber: 3.0g | sodium: 575mg

Almond-Crusted Chicken Tenders with Honey

Prep time: 10 minutes | Cook time: 20 minutes | Serves 4

1 tablespoon honey

1 tablespoon whole-grain or Dijon mustard

¼ teaspoon freshly ground black pepper

¼ teaspoon kosher or sea salt

1 pound (454 g) boneless, skinless chicken breast tenders or tenderloins

1 cup almonds, roughly chopped

Nonstick cooking spray

1. Preheat the oven to 425°F (220°C). Line a large, rimmed baking sheet with parchment paper. Place a wire cooling rack on the parchment-lined baking sheet, and spray the rack well with nonstick cooking spray.
2. In a large bowl, combine the honey, mustard, pepper, and salt. Add the chicken and toss gently to coat. Set aside.
3. Dump the almonds onto a large sheet of parchment paper and spread them out. Press the coated chicken tenders into the nuts until evenly coated on all sides. Place the chicken on the prepared wire rack.
4. Bake in the preheated oven for 15 to 20 minutes, or until the internal temperature of the chicken measures 165°F (74°C) on a meat thermometer and any juices run clear.
5. Cool for 5 minutes before serving.

Per Serving calories: 222 | fat: 7.0g | protein: 11.0g | carbs: 29.0g | fiber: 2.0g | sodium: 448mg

Parsley-Dijon Chicken and Potatoes

Prep time: 5 minutes | Cook time: 22 minutes | Serves 6

1 tablespoon extra-virgin olive oil

1½ pounds (680 g) boneless, skinless chicken thighs, cut into 1-inch cubes, patted dry

1½ pounds (680 g) Yukon Gold potatoes, unpeeled, cut into ½-inch cubes

2 garlic cloves, minced

¼ cup dry white wine

1 cup low-sodium or no-salt-added chicken broth

1 tablespoon Dijon mustard

¼ teaspoon freshly ground black pepper

¼ teaspoon kosher or sea salt

1 cup chopped fresh flat-leaf (Italian) parsley, including stems

1 tablespoon freshly squeezed lemon juice

1. In a large skillet over medium-high heat, heat the oil. Add the chicken and cook for 5 minutes, stirring only after the chicken has browned on one side. Remove the chicken and reserve on a plate.
2. Add the potatoes to the skillet and cook for 5 minutes, stirring only after the potatoes have become golden and crispy on one side. Push the potatoes to the side of the skillet, add the garlic, and cook, stirring constantly, for 1 minute. Add the wine and cook for 1 minute, until nearly evaporated. Add the chicken broth, mustard, salt, pepper, and reserved chicken. Turn the heat to high and bring to a boil. Once boiling, cover, reduce the heat to medium-low, and cook for 10 to 12 minutes, until the potatoes are tender and the internal temperature of the chicken measures 165°F (74°C) on a meat thermometer and any juices run clear. During the last minute of cooking, stir in the parsley. Remove from the heat, stir in the lemon juice, and serve.

Per Serving calories: 324 | fat: 9.0g | protein: 16.0g | carbs: 45.0g | fiber: 5.0g | sodium: 560mg

Potato Lamb and Olive Stew

Prep time: 20 minutes | Cook time: 3 hours 42 minutes | Serves 10

4 tablespoons almond flour

¾ cup low-sodium chicken stock

1¼ pounds (567 g) small potatoes, halved

3 cloves garlic, minced

4 large shallots, cut into ½-inch wedges

3 sprigs fresh rosemary

1 tablespoon lemon zest

Coarse sea salt and black pepper, to taste

3½ pounds (1.6 kg) lamb shanks, fat trimmed and cut crosswise into 1½-inch pieces

2 tablespoons extra-virgin olive oil

½ cup dry white wine

1 cup pitted green olives, halved

2 tablespoons lemon juice

1. Combine 1 tablespoon of almond flour with chicken stock in a bowl. Stir to mix well. Put the flour mixture, potatoes, garlic, shallots, rosemary, and lemon zest in the slow cooker. Sprinkle with salt and black pepper. Stir to mix well. Set aside.
2. Combine the remaining almond flour with salt and black pepper in a large bowl, then dunk the lamb shanks in the flour and toss to coat.
3. Heat the olive oil in a nonstick skillet over medium-high heat until shimmering.
4. Add the well-coated lamb and cook for 10 minutes or until golden brown. Flip the lamb pieces halfway through the cooking time. Transfer the cooked lamb to the slow cooker.
5. Pour the wine in the same skillet, then cook for 2 minutes or until it reduces in half. Pour the wine in the slow cooker.
6. Put the slow cooker lid on and cook on high for 3 hours and 30 minutes or until the lamb is very tender.
7. In the last 20 minutes of the cooking, open the lid and fold in the olive halves to cook.
8. Pour the stew on a large plate, let them sit for 5 minutes, then skim any fat remains over the face of the liquid.
9. Drizzle with lemon juice and sprinkle with salt and pepper. Serve warm.

Per Serving

calories: 309 | fat: 10.3g | protein: 36.9g | carbs: 16.1g | fiber: 2.2g | sodium: 239mg

Slow Cook Lamb Shanks with Cannellini Beans Stew

Prep time: 20 minutes | Cook time: 10 hours 15 minutes | Serves 12

1 (19-ounce / 539-g) can cannellini beans, rinsed and drained
1 large yellow onion, chopped
2 medium-sized carrots, diced
1 large stalk celery, chopped
2 cloves garlic, thinly sliced
4 (1½-pound / 680-g) lamb shanks, fat trimmed
2 teaspoons tarragon
½ teaspoon sea salt
¼ teaspoon ground black pepper
1 (28-ounce / 794-g) can diced tomatoes, with the juice

1. Combine the beans, onion, carrots, celery, and garlic in the slow cooker. Stir to mix well.
2. Add the lamb shanks and sprinkle with tarragon, salt, and ground black pepper.
3. Pour in the tomatoes with juice, then cover the lid and cook on high for an hour.
4. Reduce the heat to low and cook for 9 hours or until the lamb is super tender.
5. Transfer the lamb on a plate, then pour the bean mixture in a colander over a separate bowl to reserve the liquid.
6. Let the liquid sit for 5 minutes until set, then skim the fat from the surface of the liquid. Pour the bean mixture back to the liquid.
7. Remove the bones from the lamb heat and discard the bones. Put the lamb meat and bean mixture back to the slow cooker. Cover and cook to reheat for 15 minutes or until heated through.
8. Pour them on a large serving plate and serve immediately.

Per Serving
calories: 317 | fat: 9.7g | protein: 52.1g | carbs: 7.0g | fiber: 2.1g | sodium: 375mg

Beef Kebabs with Onion and Pepper

Prep time: 15 minutes | Cook time: 10 minutes | Serves 6

2 pounds (907 g) beef fillet
1½ teaspoons salt
1 teaspoon freshly ground black pepper
½ teaspoon ground nutmeg
½ teaspoon ground allspice
⅓ cup extra-virgin olive oil
1 large onion, cut into 8 quarters
1 large red bell pepper, cut into 1-inch cubes

1. Preheat the grill to high heat.
2. Cut the beef into 1-inch cubes and put them in a large bowl.
3. In a small bowl, mix together the salt, black pepper, allspice, and nutmeg.
4. Pour the olive oil over the beef and toss to coat. Evenly sprinkle the seasoning over the beef and toss to coat all pieces.
5. Skewer the beef, alternating every 1 or 2 pieces with a piece of onion or bell pepper.
6. To cook, place the skewers on the preheated grill, and flip every 2 to 3 minutes until all sides have cooked to desired doneness, 6 minutes for medium-rare, 8 minutes for well done. Serve hot.

Per Serving calories: 485 | fat: 36.0g | protein: 35.0g | carbs: 4.0g | fiber: 1.0g | sodium: 1453mg

Grilled Pork Chops

Prep time: 20 minutes | Cook time: 10 minutes | Serves 4

¼ cup extra-virgin olive oil
2 tablespoons fresh thyme leaves
1 teaspoon smoked paprika
1 teaspoon salt
4 pork loin chops, ½-inch-thick

1. In a small bowl, mix together the olive oil, thyme, paprika, and salt. Put the pork chops in a plastic zip-top bag or a bowl and coat them with the spice mix. Let them marinate for 15 minutes.
2. Preheat the grill to high heat. Cook the pork chops for 4 minutes on each side until cooked through. Serve warm.

Per Serving calories: 282 | fat: 23.0g | protein: 21.0g | carbs: 1.0g | fiber: 0g | sodium: 832mg

Greek-Style Lamb Burgers

Prep time: 10 minutes | Cook time: 10 minutes | Serves 4

1 pound (454 g) ground lamb
½ teaspoon salt
½ teaspoon freshly ground black pepper
4 tablespoons crumbled feta cheese
Buns, toppings, and tzatziki, for serving (optional)

1. Preheat the grill to high heat. In a large bowl, using your hands, combine the lamb with the salt and pepper.
2. Divide the meat into 4 portions. Divide each portion in half to make a top and a bottom. Flatten each half into a 3-inch circle. Make a dent in the center of one of the halves and place 1 tablespoon of the feta cheese in the center. Place the second half of the patty on top of the feta cheese and press down to close the 2 halves together, making it resemble a round burger. Grill each side for 3 minutes, for medium-well. Serve on a bun with your favorite toppings and tzatziki sauce, if desired.

Per Serving calories: 345 | fat: 29.0g | protein: 20.0g | carbs: 1.0g | fiber: 0g | sodium: 462mg

Chicken Bruschetta Burgers

Prep time: 10 minutes | Cook time: 16 minutes | Serves 2

1 tablespoon olive oil
2 garlic cloves, minced
3 tablespoons finely minced onion
1 teaspoon dried basil
3 tablespoons minced sun-dried tomatoes packed in olive oil
8 ounces (227 g) ground chicken breast
¼ teaspoon salt
3 pieces small Mozzarella balls, minced

1. Heat the olive oil in a nonstick skillet over medium-high heat. Add the garlic and onion and sauté for 5 minutes until tender. Stir in the basil. Remove from the skillet to a medium bowl. Add the tomatoes, ground chicken, and salt and stir until incorporated. Mix in the Mozzarella balls.
2. Divide the chicken mixture in half and form into two burgers, each about ¾-inch thick.
3. Heat the same skillet over medium-high heat and add the burgers. Cook each side for 5 to 6 minutes, or until they reach an internal temperature of 165°F (74°C).
4. Serve warm.

Per Serving calories: 300 | fat: 17.0g | protein: 32.2g | carbs: 6.0g | fiber: 1.1g | sodium: 724mg

Chicken Cacciatore

Prep time: 15 minutes | Cook time: 1 hour and 30 minutes | Serves 2

1½ pounds (680 g) bone-in chicken thighs, skin removed and patted dry	1 (15-ounce / 425-g) can crushed fire-roasted tomatoes
Salt, to taste	1 fresh rosemary sprig
2 tablespoons olive oil	½ cup dry red wine
½ large onion, thinly sliced	1 teaspoon Italian herb seasoning
4 ounces (113 g) baby bella mushrooms, sliced	½ teaspoon garlic powder
1 red sweet pepper, cut into 1-inch pieces	3 tablespoons flour

1. Season the chicken thighs with a generous pinch of salt.
2. Heat the olive oil in a Dutch oven over medium-high heat. Add the chicken and brown for 5 minutes per side.
3. Add the onion, mushrooms, and sweet pepper to the Dutch oven and sauté for another 5 minutes.
4. Add the tomatoes, rosemary, wine, Italian seasoning, garlic powder, and salt, stirring well.
5. Bring the mixture to a boil, then reduce the heat to low. Allow to simmer slowly for at least 1 hour, stirring occasionally, or until the chicken is tender and easily pulls away from the bone.
6. Measure out 1 cup of the sauce from the pot and put it into a bowl. Add the flour and whisk well to make a slurry.
7. Increase the heat to medium-high and slowly whisk the slurry into the pot. Stir until it comes to a boil and cook until the sauce is thickened.
8. Remove the chicken from the bones and shred it, and add it back to the sauce before serving, if desired.

Per Serving calories: 520 | fat: 23.1g | protein: 31.8g | carbs: 37.0g | fiber: 6.0g | sodium: 484mg

Chicken Gyros with Tzatziki Sauce

Prep time: 15 minutes | Cook time: 10 minutes | Serves 2

2 tablespoons freshly squeezed lemon juice	1 small zucchini, cut into ½-inch strips lengthwise
2 tablespoons olive oil, divided, plus more for oiling the grill	½ red pepper, seeded and cut in half lengthwise
1 teaspoon minced fresh oregano	½ English cucumber, peeled and minced
½ teaspoon garlic powder	¾ cup plain Greek yogurt
Salt, to taste	1 tablespoon minced fresh dill
8 ounces (227 g) chicken tenders	2 (8-inch) pita breads
1 small eggplant, cut into 1-inch strips lengthwise	

1. Combine the lemon juice, 1 tablespoon of olive oil, oregano, garlic powder, and salt in a medium bowl. Add the chicken and let marinate for 30 minutes.
2. Place the eggplant, zucchini, and red pepper in a large mixing bowl and sprinkle with salt and the remaining 1 tablespoon of olive oil. Toss well to coat. Let the vegetables rest while the chicken is marinating.
3. Make the tzatziki sauce: Combine the cucumber, yogurt, salt, and dill in a medium bowl. Stir well to incorporate and set aside in the refrigerator.
4. When ready, preheat the grill to medium-high heat and oil the grill grates.
5. Drain any liquid from the vegetables and put them on the grill.
6. Remove the chicken tenders from the marinade and put them on the grill.
7. Grill the chicken and vegetables for 3 minutes per side, or until the chicken is no longer pink inside.
8. Remove the chicken and vegetables from the grill and set aside. On the grill, heat the pitas for about 30 seconds, flipping them frequently.
9. Divide the chicken tenders and vegetables between the pitas and top each with ¼ cup of the prepared sauce. Roll the pitas up like a cone and serve.

Per Serving

calories: 586 | fat: 21.9g | protein: 39.0g | carbs: 62.0g | fiber: 11.8g | sodium: 955mg

Crispy Pesto Chicken

Prep time: 15 minutes | Cook time: 50 minutes | Serves 2

12 ounces (340 g) small red potatoes (3 or 4 potatoes), scrubbed and diced into 1-inch pieces	½ teaspoon garlic powder
	¼ teaspoon salt
1 tablespoon olive oil	1 (8-ounce / 227-g) boneless, skinless chicken breast
	3 tablespoons prepared pesto

1. Preheat the oven to 425ºF (220ºC). Line a baking sheet with parchment paper.
2. Combine the potatoes, olive oil, garlic powder, and salt in a medium bowl. Toss well to coat.
3. Arrange the potatoes on the parchment paper and roast for 10 minutes. Flip the potatoes and roast for an additional 10 minutes.
4. Meanwhile, put the chicken in the same bowl and toss with the pesto, coating the chicken evenly.
5. Check the potatoes to make sure they are golden brown on the top and bottom. Toss them again and add the chicken breast to the pan.
6. Turn the heat down to 350ºF (180ºC) and roast the chicken and potatoes for 30 minutes. Check to make sure the chicken reaches an internal temperature of 165ºF (74ºC) and the potatoes are fork-tender.
7. Let cool for 5 minutes before serving.

Per Serving

calories: 378 | fat: 16.0g | protein: 29.8g | carbs: 30.1g | fiber: 4.0g | sodium: 425mg

Beef Stew with Beans and Zucchini

Prep time: 20 minutes | Cook time: 6 to 8 hours | Serves 2

1 (15-ounce / 425-g) can diced or crushed tomatoes with basil
1 teaspoon beef base
2 tablespoons olive oil, divided
8 ounces (227 g) baby bella (cremini) mushrooms, quartered
2 garlic cloves, minced
½ large onion, diced
1 pound (454 g) cubed beef stew meat
3 tablespoons flour
¼ teaspoon salt
Pinch freshly ground black pepper
¾ cup dry red wine
¼ cup minced brined olives
1 fresh rosemary sprig
1 (15-ounce / 425-g) can white cannellini beans, drained and rinsed
1 medium zucchini, cut in half lengthwise and then cut into 1-inch pieces.

1. Place the tomatoes into a slow cooker and set it to low heat. Add the beef base and stir to incorporate.
2. Heat 1 tablespoon of olive oil in a large sauté pan over medium heat. Add the mushrooms and onion and sauté for 10 minutes, stirring occasionally, or until they're golden. Add the garlic and cook for 30 seconds more. Transfer the vegetables to the slow cooker.
3. In a plastic food storage bag, combine the stew meat with the flour, salt, and pepper. Seal the bag and shake well to combine. Heat the remaining 1 tablespoon of olive oil in the sauté pan over high heat.
4. Add the floured meat and sear to get a crust on the outside edges. Deglaze the pan by adding about half of the red wine and scraping up any browned bits on the bottom. Stir so the wine thickens a bit and transfer to the slow cooker along with any remaining wine.
5. Stir the stew to incorporate the ingredients. Stir in the olives and rosemary, cover, and cook for 6 to 8 hours on Low. About 30 minutes before the stew is finished, add the beans and zucchini to let them warm through. Serve warm.

Per Serving calories: 389 | fat: 15.1g | protein: 30.8g | carbs: 25.0g | fiber: 8.0g | sodium: 582mg

Greek Beef Kebabs

Prep time: 15 minutes | Cook time: 20 minutes | Serves 2

6 ounces (170 g) beef sirloin tip, trimmed of fat and cut into 2-inch pieces
3 cups of any mixture of vegetables: mushrooms, summer squash, zucchini, onions, red peppers, cherry tomatoes
½ cup olive oil
¼ cup freshly squeezed lemon juice
2 tablespoons balsamic vinegar
2 teaspoons dried oregano
1 teaspoon garlic powder
1 teaspoon salt
1 teaspoon minced fresh rosemary
Cooking spray

1. Put the beef in a plastic freezer bag.
2. Slice the vegetables into similar-size pieces and put them in a second freezer bag.
3. Make the marinade: Mix the olive oil, lemon juice, balsamic vinegar, oregano, garlic powder, salt, and rosemary in a measuring cup. Whisk well to combine. Pour half of the marinade over the beef, and the other half over the vegetables.
4. Put the beef and vegetables in the refrigerator to marinate for 4 hours.
5. When ready, preheat the grill to medium-high heat and spray the grill grates with cooking spray.
6. Thread the meat onto skewers and the vegetables onto separate skewers.
7. Grill the meat for 3 minutes per side. They should only take 10 to 12 minutes to cook, depending on the thickness of the meat.
8. Grill the vegetables for about 3 minutes per side, or until they have grill marks and are softened. Serve hot.

Per Serving calories: 284 | fat: 18.2g | protein: 21.0g | carbs: 9.0g | fiber: 3.9g | sodium: 122mg

Gyro Burgers with Tahini Sauce

Prep time: 15 minutes | Cook time: 10 minutes | Serves 4

2 tablespoons extra-virgin olive oil
1 tablespoon dried oregano
1¼ teaspoons garlic powder, divided
1 teaspoon ground cumin
½ teaspoon freshly ground black pepper
¼ teaspoon kosher or sea salt
1 pound (454 g) beef flank steak, top round steak, or lamb leg steak, center cut, about 1 inch thick
1 medium green bell pepper, halved and seeded
2 tablespoons tahini or peanut butter
1 tablespoon hot water (optional)
½ cup plain Greek yogurt
1 tablespoon freshly squeezed lemon juice
1 cup thinly sliced red onion
4 (6-inch) whole-wheat pita breads, warmed
Nonstick cooking spray

1. Set an oven rack about 4 inches below the broiler element. Preheat the oven broiler to high. Line a large, rimmed baking sheet with aluminum foil. Place a wire cooling rack on the foil, and spray the rack with nonstick cooking spray. Set aside.
2. In a small bowl, whisk together the olive oil, oregano, 1 teaspoon of garlic powder, cumin, pepper, and salt. Rub the oil mixture on all sides of the steak, reserving 1 teaspoon of the mixture. Place the steak on the prepared rack. Rub the remaining oil mixture on the bell pepper, and place on the rack, cut-side down. Press the pepper with the heel of your hand to flatten.
3. Broil for 5 minutes. Flip the steak and the pepper pieces, and broil for 2 to 5 minutes more, until the pepper is charred and the internal temperature of the meat measures 145ºF (63ºC) on a meat thermometer. Put the pepper and steak on a cutting board to rest for 5 minutes.
4. Meanwhile, in a small bowl, whisk the tahini until smooth (adding 1 tablespoon of hot water if your tahini is sticky). Add the remaining ¼ teaspoon of garlic powder and the yogurt and lemon juice, and whisk thoroughly.
5. Slice the steak crosswise into ¼-inch-thick strips. Slice the bell pepper into strips. Divide the steak, bell pepper, and onion among the warm pita breads. Drizzle with tahini sauce and serve.

Per Serving

calories: 348 | fat: 15.0g | protein: 33.0g | carbs: 20.0g | fiber: 3.0g | sodium: 530mg

Grilled Lemon Chicken

Prep time: 10 minutes | Cook time: 12 to 14 minutes | Serves 2

1 (4-ounce / 113-g) boneless, skinless chicken breasts	1 teaspoon dried basil
	1 teaspoon paprika
Marinade:	½ teaspoon dried thyme
4 tablespoons freshly squeezed lemon juice	¼ teaspoon salt
	¼ teaspoon garlic powder
2 tablespoons olive oil, plus more for greasing the grill grates	

1. Make the marinade: Whisk together the lemon juice, olive oil, basil, paprika, thyme, salt, and garlic powder in a large bowl until well combined.
2. Add the chicken breasts to the bowl and let marinate for at least 30 minutes.
3. When ready to cook, preheat the grill to medium-high heat. Lightly grease the grill grates with the olive oil.
4. Discard the marinade and arrange the chicken breasts on the grill grates.
5. Grill for 12 to 14 minutes, flipping the chicken halfway through, or until a meat thermometer inserted in the center of the chicken reaches 165ºF (74ºC).
6. Let the chicken cool for 5 minutes and serve warm.

Per Serving

calories: 251 | fat: 15.5g | protein: 27.3g | carbs: 1.9g | fiber: 1.0g | sodium: 371mg

Quick Chicken Salad Wraps

Prep time: 15 minutes | Cook time: 0 minutes | Serves 2

Tzatziki Sauce:	**Salad Wraps:**
½ cup plain Greek yogurt	2 (8-inch) whole-grain pita bread
1 tablespoon freshly squeezed lemon juice	1 cup shredded chicken meat
Pinch garlic powder	2 cups mixed greens
1 teaspoon dried dill	2 roasted red bell peppers, thinly sliced
Salt and freshly ground black pepper, to taste	½ English cucumber, peeled if desired and thinly sliced
	¼ cup pitted black olives
	1 scallion, chopped

1. Make the tzatziki sauce: In a bowl, whisk together the yogurt, lemon juice, garlic powder, dill, salt, and pepper until creamy and smooth.
2. Make the salad wraps: Place the pita bread on a clean work surface and spoon ¼ cup of the tzatziki sauce onto each piece of pita bread, spreading it all over. Top with the shredded chicken, mixed greens, red pepper slices, cucumber slices, black olives, finished by chopped scallion.
3. Roll the salad wraps and enjoy.

Per Serving

calories: 428 | fat: 10.6g | protein: 31.1g | carbs: 50.9g | fiber: 6.0g | sodium: 675mg

Roasted Chicken Thighs With Basmati Rice

Prep time: 15 minutes | Cook time: 50 to 55 minutes | Serves 2

Chicken:	10 ounces (284 g) boneless, skinless chicken thighs (about 4 pieces)
½ teaspoon cumin	
½ teaspoon cinnamon	
½ teaspoon paprika	**Rice:**
¼ teaspoon ginger powder	1 tablespoon olive oil
¼ teaspoon garlic powder	½ small onion, minced
¼ teaspoon coriander	½ cup basmati rice 2 pinches saffron
¼ teaspoon salt	1 cup low-sodium chicken stock
⅛ teaspoon cayenne pepper	¼ teaspoon salt

Make the Chicken

1. Preheat the oven to 350ºF (180ºC).
2. Combine the cumin, cinnamon, paprika, ginger powder, garlic powder, coriander, salt, and cayenne pepper in a small bowl. Using your hands to rub the spice mixture all over the chicken thighs.
3. Transfer the chicken thighs to a baking dish. Roast in the preheated oven for 35 to 40 minutes, or until the internal temperature reaches 165ºF (74ºC) on a meat thermometer.

Make the Rice

4. Meanwhile, heat the olive oil in a skillet over medium-high heat. Sauté the onion for 5 minutes until fragrant, stirring occasionally.
5. Stir in the basmati rice, saffron, chicken stock, and salt. Reduce the heat to low, cover, and bring to a simmer for 15 minutes, until light and fluffy.
6. Remove the chicken from the oven to a plate and serve with the rice.

Per Serving calories: 400 | fat: 9.6g | protein: 37.2g | carbs: 40.7g | fiber: 2.1g | sodium: 714mg

Panko Grilled Chicken Patties

Prep time: 10 minutes | Cook time: 8 to 10 minutes | Serves 4

1 pound (454 g) ground chicken	1 garlic clove, minced
3 tablespoons crumbled feta cheese	1 teaspoon chopped fresh oregano
3 tablespoons finely chopped red pepper	¼ teaspoon salt
¼ cup finely chopped red onion	⅛ teaspoon freshly ground black pepper
3 tablespoons panko bread crumbs	Cooking spray

1. Mix together the ground chicken, feta cheese, red pepper, red onion, bread crumbs, garlic, oregano, salt, and black pepper in a large bowl, and stir to incorporate.
2. Divide the chicken mixture into 8 equal portions and form each portion into a patty with your hands.
3. Preheat a grill to medium-high heat and oil the grill grates with cooking spray.
4. Arrange the patties on the grill grates and grill each side for 4 to 5 minutes, or until the patties are cooked through.
5. Rest for 5 minutes before serving.

Per Serving calories: 241 | fat: 13.5g | protein: 23.2g | carbs:6.7g | fiber: 1.1g | sodium: 321mg

Spiced Roast Chicken

Prep time: 10 minutes | Cook time: 35 minutes | Serves 6

1 teaspoon garlic powder	½ teaspoon salt
1 teaspoon ground paprika	¼ teaspoon ground cayenne pepper
½ teaspoon ground cumin	
½ teaspoon ground coriander	6 chicken legs
	1 teaspoon extra-virgin olive oil

1. Preheat the oven to 400°F (205°C).
2. Combine the garlic powder, paprika, cumin, coriander, salt, and cayenne pepper in a small bowl.
3. On a clean work surface, rub the spices all over the chicken legs until completely coated.
4. Heat the olive oil in an ovenproof skillet over medium heat.
5. Add the chicken thighs and sear each side for 8 to 10 minutes, or until the skin is crispy and browned.
6. Transfer the skillet to the preheated oven and continue cooking for 10 to 15 minutes, or until the juices run clear and it registers an internal temperature of 165°F (74°C).
7. Remove from the heat and serve on plates.

Per Serving

calories: 275 | fat: 15.6g | protein: 30.3g | carbs: 0.9g | fiber: 0g | sodium: 255mg

Yogurt Chicken Breasts

Prep time: 10 minutes | Cook time: 10 minutes | Serves 4

1 pound (454 g) boneless, skinless chicken breasts, cut into 2-inch strips	Pinch saffron (3 or 4 threads)
1 tablespoon extra-virgin olive oil	3 garlic cloves, minced
	½ onion, chopped
Yogurt Sauce:	2 tablespoons chopped fresh cilantro
½ cup plain Greek yogurt	Juice of ½ lemon
2 tablespoons water	½ teaspoon salt

1. Make the yogurt sauce: Place the yogurt, water, saffron, garlic, onion, cilantro, lemon juice, and salt in a blender, and pulse until completely mixed.
2. Transfer the yogurt sauce to a large bowl, along with the chicken strips. Toss to coat well.
3. Cover with plastic wrap and marinate in the refrigerator for at least 1 hour, or up to overnight.
4. When ready to cook, heat the olive oil in a large skillet over medium heat.
5. Add the chicken strips to the skillet, discarding any excess marinade. Cook each side for 5 minutes, or until cooked through.
6. Let the chicken cool for 5 minutes before serving.

Per Serving

calories: 154 | fat: 4.8g | protein: 26.3g | carbs: 2.9g | fiber: 0g | sodium: 500mg

Coconut Chicken Tenders

Prep time: 10 minutes | Cook time: 15 to 20 minutes | Serves 6

4 chicken breasts, each cut lengthwise into 3 strips	½ cup coconut flour
	2 eggs
½ teaspoon salt	2 tablespoons unsweetened plain almond milk
¼ teaspoon freshly ground black pepper	
	1 cup unsweetened coconut flakes

1. Preheat the oven to 400°F (205°C). Line a baking sheet with parchment paper.
2. On a clean work surface, season the chicken with salt and pepper.
3. In a small bowl, add the coconut flour. In a separate bowl, whisk the eggs with almond milk until smooth. Place the coconut flakes on a plate.
4. One at a time, roll the chicken strips in the coconut flour, then dredge them in the egg mixture, shaking off any excess, and finally in the coconut flakes to coat.
5. Arrange the coated chicken pieces on the baking sheet. Bake in the preheated oven for 15 to 20 minutes, flipping the chicken halfway through, or until the chicken is golden brown and cooked through.
6. Remove from the oven and serve on plates.

Per Serving

calories: 215 | fat: 12.6g | protein: 20.2g | carbs: 8.9g | fiber: 6.1g | sodium: 345mg

Sautéed Ground Turkey with Brown Rice

Prep time: 20 minutes | Cook time: 45 minutes | Serves 2

1 tablespoon olive oil	¼ cup sun-dried tomatoes, minced
½ medium onion, minced	
2 garlic cloves, minced	1¼ cups low-sodium chicken stock
8 ounces (227 g) ground turkey breast	
	½ cup brown rice
½ cup chopped roasted red peppers, (about 2 jarred peppers)	1 teaspoon dried oregano
	Salt, to taste
	2 cups lightly packed baby spinach

1. In a skillet, heat the olive oil over medium heat. Sauté the onion for 5 minutes, stirring occasionally.
2. Stir in the garlic and sauté for 30 seconds more until fragrant.
3. Add the turkey breast and cook for about 7 minutes, breaking apart with a wooden spoon, until the turkey is no longer pink.
4. Stir in the roasted red peppers, tomatoes, chicken stock, brown rice, and oregano and bring to a boil.
5. When the mixture starts to boil, cover, and reduce the heat to medium-low. Bring to a simmer until the rice is tender, stirring occasionally, about 30 minutes. Sprinkle with the salt.
6. Add the baby spinach and keep stirring until wilted.
7. Remove from the heat and serve warm.

Per Serving

calories: 445 | fat: 16.8g | protein: 30.2g | carbs: 48.9g | fiber: 5.1g | sodium: 662mg

Baked Teriyaki Turkey Meatballs

Prep time: 20 minutes | Cook time: 20 minutes | Serves 6

1 pound (454 g) lean ground turkey	2 tablespoons reduced-sodium tamari or gluten-free soy sauce
1 egg, whisked	
¼ cup finely chopped scallions, both white and green parts	1 teaspoon grated fresh ginger
2 garlic cloves, minced	1 tablespoon honey
	2 teaspoons mirin
	1 teaspoon olive oil

1. Preheat the oven to 400ºF (205ºC). Line a baking sheet with parchment paper and set aside.
2. Mix together the ground turkey, whisked egg, scallions, garlic, tamari, ginger, honey, mirin, and olive oil in a large bowl, and stir until well blended.
3. Using a tablespoon to scoop out rounded heaps of the turkey mixture, and then roll them into balls with your hands. Transfer the balls to the prepared baking sheet.
4. Bake in the preheated oven for 20 minutes, flipping the balls with a spatula halfway through, or until the meatballs are browned and cooked through.
5. Serve warm.

Per Serving

calories: 158 | fat: 8.6g | protein: 16.2g | carbs: 4.0g | fiber: 0.2g | sodium: 269mg

Beef, Tomato, and Lentils Stew

Prep time: 10 minutes | Cook time: 10 minutes | Serves 4

1 tablespoon extra-virgin olive oil	1 (14-ounce / 397-g) can lentils, drained
1 pound (454 g) extra-lean ground beef	½ teaspoon sea salt
1 onion, chopped	⅛ teaspoon freshly ground black pepper
1 (14-ounce / 397-g) can chopped tomatoes with garlic and basil, drained	

1. Heat the olive oil in a pot over medium-high heat until shimmering.
2. Add the beef and onion to the pot and sauté for 5 minutes or until the beef is lightly browned.
3. Add the remaining ingredients. Bring to a boil. Reduce the heat to medium and cook for 4 more minutes or until the lentils are tender. Keep stirring during the cooking.
4. Pour them in a large serving bowl and serve immediately.

Per Serving calories: 460 | fat: 14.8g | protein: 44.2g | carbs: 36.9g | fiber: 17.0g | sodium: 320mg

Ground Beef, Tomato, and Kidney Bean Chili

Prep time: 10 minutes | Cook time: 15 minutes | Serves 4

1 tablespoon extra-virgin olive oil	2 (28-ounce / 794-g) cans chopped tomatoes, juice reserved
1 pound (454 g) extra-lean ground beef	Chili Spice:
1 onion, chopped	1 teaspoon garlic powder
2 (14-ounce / 397-g) cans kidney beans	1 tablespoon chili powder
	½ teaspoon sea salt

1. Heat the olive oil in a pot over medium-high heat until shimmering.

2. Add the beef and onion to the pot and sauté for 5 minutes or until the beef is lightly browned and the onion is translucent.
3. Add the remaining ingredients. Bring to a boil. Reduce the heat to medium and cook for 10 more minutes. Keep stirring during the cooking.
4. Pour them in a large serving bowl and serve immediately.

Per Serving

calories: 891 | fat: 20.1g | protein: 116.3g | carbs: 62.9g | fiber: 17.0g | sodium: 561mg

Lamb Tagine with Couscous and Almonds

Prep time: 15 minutes | Cook time: 7 hours 7 minutes | Serves 6

2 tablespoons almond flour	¼ teaspoon crushed saffron threads
Juice and zest of 1 navel orange	1 teaspoon ground cumin
2 tablespoons extra-virgin olive oil	¼ teaspoon ground red pepper flakes
2 pounds (907 g) boneless lamb leg, fat trimmed and cut into 1½-inch cubes	½ teaspoon sea salt
	2 tablespoons raw honey
½ cup low-sodium chicken stock	1 cup pitted dates
	3 cups cooked couscous, for serving
2 large white onions, chopped	2 tablespoons toasted slivered almonds, for serving
1 teaspoon pumpkin pie spice	

1. Combine the almond flour with orange juice in a large bowl. Stir until smooth, then mix in the orange zest. Set aside.
2. Heat the olive oil in a nonstick skillet over medium-high heat until shimmering.
3. Add the lamb cubes and sauté for 7 minutes or until lightly browned.
4. Pour in the flour mixture and chicken stock, then add the onions, pumpkin pie spice, saffron, cumin, ground red pepper flakes, and salt. Stir to mix well.
5. Pour them in the slow cooker. Cover and cook on low for 6 hours or until the internal temperature of the lamb reaches at least 145ºF (63ºC).
6. When the cooking is complete, mix in the honey and dates, then cook for another an hour.
7. Put the couscous in a tagine bowl or a large bowl, then top with lamb mixture. Scatter with slivered almonds and serve immediately.

Per Serving

calories: 447 | fat: 10.2g | protein: 36.3g | carbs: 53.5g | fiber: 4.9g | sodium: 329mg

Chermoula Roasted Pork Tenderloin

Prep time: 15 minutes | Cook time: 20 minutes | Serves 2

½ cup fresh cilantro	2 teaspoons cumin
½ cup fresh parsley	1 teaspoon smoked paprika
6 small garlic cloves	½ teaspoon salt, divided
3 tablespoons olive oil, divided	Pinch freshly ground black pepper
3 tablespoons freshly squeezed lemon juice	1 (8-ounce / 227-g) pork tenderloin

1. Preheat the oven to 425°F (220°C).
2. In a food processor, combine the cilantro, parsley, garlic, 2 tablespoons of olive oil, lemon juice, cumin, paprika, and ¼ teaspoon of salt. Pulse 15 to 20 times, or until the mixture is fairly smooth. Scrape the sides down as needed to incorporate all the ingredients. Transfer the sauce to a small bowl and set aside.
3. Season the pork tenderloin on all sides with the remaining ¼ teaspoon of salt and a generous pinch of black pepper.
4. Heat the remaining 1 tablespoon of olive oil in a sauté pan.
5. Sear the pork for 3 minutes, turning often, until golden brown on all sides.
6. Transfer the pork to a baking dish and roast in the preheated oven for 15 minutes, or until the internal temperature registers 145°F (63°C).
7. Cool for 5 minutes before serving.

Per Serving

calories: 169 | fat: 13.1g | protein: 11.0g | carbs: 2.9g | fiber: 1.0g | sodium: 332mg

Lamb Kofta (Spiced Meatballs)

Prep time: 15 minutes | Cook time: 30 minutes | Serves 2

¼ cup walnuts	¼ teaspoon cumin
1 garlic clove	¼ teaspoon allspice
½ small onion	¼ teaspoon salt
1 roasted piquillo pepper	Pinch cayenne pepper
2 tablespoons fresh mint	8 ounces (227 g) lean ground lamb
2 tablespoons fresh parsley	

1. Preheat the oven to 350°F (180°C). Line a baking sheet with aluminum foil.
2. In a food processor, combine the walnuts, garlic, onion, roasted pepper, mint, parsley, cumin, allspice, salt, and cayenne pepper. Pulse about 10 times to combine everything.
3. Transfer the spice mixture to a large bowl and add the ground lamb. With your hands or a spatula, mix the spices into the lamb.
4. Roll the lamb into 1½-inch balls (about the size of golf balls).
5. Arrange the meatballs on the prepared baking sheet and bake for 30 minutes, or until cooked to an internal temperature of 165°F (74°C).
6. Serve warm.

Per Serving

calories: 409 | fat: 22.9g | protein: 22.0g | carbs: 7.1g | fiber: 3.0g | sodium: 428mg

Chapter 8

Fish and Seafood

Cioppino (Seafood Tomato Stew)

Prep time: 10 minutes | Cook time: 20 minutes | Serves 2

2 tablespoons olive oil
½ small onion, diced
½ green pepper, diced
2 teaspoons dried basil
2 teaspoons dried oregano
½ cup dry white wine
1 (14.5-ounce / 411-g) can diced tomatoes with basil
1 (8-ounce / 227-g) can no-salt-added tomato sauce
1 (6.5-ounce / 184-g) can minced clams with their juice
8 ounces (227 g) peeled, deveined raw shrimp
4 ounces (113 g) any white fish (a thick piece works best)
3 tablespoons fresh parsley
Salt and freshly ground black pepper, to taste

1. In a Dutch oven, heat the olive oil over medium heat.
2. Sauté the onion and green pepper for 5 minutes, or until tender. Stir in the basil, oregano, wine, diced tomatoes, and tomato sauce and bring to a boil.
3. Once boiling, reduce the heat to low and bring to a simmer for 5 minutes.
4. Add the clams, shrimp, and fish and cook for about 10 minutes, or until the shrimp are pink and cooked through.
5. Scatter with the parsley and add the salt and black pepper to taste. Remove from the heat and serve warm.

Per Serving calories: 221 | fat: 7.7g | protein: 23.1g | carbs: 10.9g | fiber: 4.2g | sodium: 720mg

Lemon Grilled Shrimp

Prep time: 20 minutes | Cook time: 4 to 6 minutes | Serves 4

2 tablespoons garlic, minced
3 tablespoons fresh Italian parsley, finely chopped
¼ cup extra-virgin olive oil
½ cup lemon juice
1 teaspoon salt
2 pounds (907 g) jumbo shrimp (21 to 25), peeled and deveined
Special Equipment:
4 wooden skewers, soaked in water for at least 30 minutes

1. Whisk together the garlic, parsley, olive oil, lemon juice, and salt in a large bowl.
2. Add the shrimp to the bowl and toss well, making sure the shrimp are coated in the marinade. Set aside to sit for 15 minutes.
3. When ready, skewer the shrimps by piercing through the center. You can place about 5 to 6 shrimps on each skewer.
4. Preheat the grill to high heat.
5. Grill the shrimp for 4 to 6 minutes, flipping the shrimp halfway through, or until the shrimp are pink on the outside and opaque in the center. Serve hot.

Per Serving calories: 401 | fat: 17.8g | protein: 56.9g | carbs: 3.9g | fiber: 0g | sodium: 1223mg

Garlic Shrimp with Mushrooms

Prep time: 10 minutes | Cook time: 15 minutes | Serves 4

1 pound (454 g) fresh shrimp, peeled, deveined, and patted dry
1 teaspoon salt
1 cup extra-virgin olive oil
8 large garlic cloves, thinly sliced
4 ounces (113 g) sliced mushrooms (shiitake, baby bella, or button)
½ teaspoon red pepper flakes
¼ cup chopped fresh flat-leaf Italian parsley

1. In a bowl, season the shrimp with salt. Set aside.
2. Heat the olive oil in a large skillet over medium-low heat.
3. Add the garlic and cook for 3 to 4 minutes until fragrant, stirring occasionally.
4. Sauté the mushrooms for 5 minutes, or until they start to exude their juices. Stir in the shrimp and sprinkle with red pepper flakes and sauté for 3 to 4 minutes more, or until the shrimp start to turn pink.
5. Remove the skillet from the heat and add the parsley. Stir to combine and serve warm.

Per Serving
calories: 619 | fat: 55.5g | protein: 24.1g | carbs: 3.7g | fiber: 0g | sodium: 735mg

Lemony Shrimp with Orzo Salad

Prep time: 10 minutes | Cook time: 22 minutes | Serves 4

1 cup orzo
1 hothouse cucumber, deseeded and chopped
½ cup finely diced red onion
2 tablespoons extra-virgin olive oil
2 pounds (907 g) shrimp, peeled and deveined
3 lemons, juiced
Salt and freshly ground black pepper, to taste
¾ cup crumbled feta cheese
2 tablespoons dried dill
1 cup chopped fresh flat-leaf parsley

1. Bring a large pot of water to a boil. Add the orzo and cook covered for 15 to 18 minutes, or until the orzo is tender. Transfer to a colander to drain and set aside to cool.
2. Mix the cucumber and red onion in a bowl. Set aside.
3. Heat the olive oil in a medium skillet over medium heat until it shimmers.
4. Reduce the heat, add the shrimp, and cook each side for 2 minutes until cooked through.
5. Add the cooked shrimp to the bowl of cucumber and red onion. Mix in the cooked orzo and lemon juice and toss to combine. Sprinkle with salt and pepper. Scatter the top with the feta cheese and dill. Garnish with the parsley and serve immediately.

Per Serving
calories: 565 | fat: 17.8g | protein: 63.3g | carbs: 43.9g | fiber: 4.1g | sodium: 2225mg

Avocado Shrimp Ceviche

Prep time: 15 minutes | Cook time: 0 minutes | Serves 4

1 pound (454 g) fresh shrimp, peeled, deveined, and cut in half lengthwise
1 small red or yellow bell pepper, cut into ½-inch chunks
½ small red onion, cut into thin slivers
½ English cucumber, peeled and cut into ½-inch chunks
¼ cup chopped fresh cilantro
½ cup extra-virgin olive oil
⅓ cup freshly squeezed lime juice
2 tablespoons freshly squeezed clementine juice
2 tablespoons freshly squeezed lemon juice
1 teaspoon salt
½ teaspoon freshly ground black pepper
2 ripe avocados, peeled, pitted, and cut into ½-inch chunks

1. Place the shrimp, bell pepper, red onion, cucumber, and cilantro in a large bowl and toss to combine.
2. In a separate bowl, stir together the olive oil, lime, clementine, and lemon juice, salt, and black pepper until smooth. Pour the mixture into the bowl of shrimp and vegetable mixture and toss until they are completely coated.
3. Cover the bowl with plastic wrap and transfer to the refrigerator to marinate for at least 2 hours, or up to 8 hours.
4. When ready, stir in the avocado chunks and toss to incorporate. Serve immediately.

Per Serving
calories: 496 | fat: 39.5g | protein: 25.3g | carbs: 13.8g | fiber: 6.0g | sodium: 755mg

Spicy Grilled Shrimp with Lemon Wedges

Prep time: 15 minutes | Cook time: 6 minutes | Serves 6

1 large clove garlic, crushed
1 teaspoon coarse salt
1 teaspoon paprika
½ teaspoon cayenne pepper
2 teaspoons lemon juice
2 tablespoons plus 1 teaspoon olive oil, divided
2 pounds (907 g) large shrimp, peeled and deveined
8 wedges lemon, for garnish

1. Preheat the grill to medium heat.
2. Stir together the garlic, salt, paprika, cayenne pepper, lemon juice, and 2 tablespoons of olive oil in a small bowl until a paste forms. Add the shrimp and toss until well coated.
3. Grease the grill grates lightly with remaining 1 teaspoon of olive oil.
4. Grill the shrimp for 4 to 6 minutes, flipping the shrimp halfway through, or until the shrimp is totally pink and opaque.
5. Garnish the shrimp with lemon wedges and serve hot.

Per Serving
calories: 163 | fat: 5.8g | protein: 25.2g | carbs: 2.8g | fiber: 0.4g | sodium: 585mg

Cod with Parsley Pistou

Prep time: 15 minutes | Cook time: 10 minutes | Serves 4

1 cup packed roughly chopped fresh flat-leaf Italian parsley
Zest and juice of 1 lemon
1 to 2 small garlic cloves, minced
1 teaspoon salt
½ teaspoon freshly ground black pepper
1 cup extra-virgin olive oil, divided
1 pound (454 g) cod fillets, cut into 4 equal-sized pieces

1. Make the pistou: Place the parsley, lemon zest and juice, garlic, salt, and pepper in a food processor until finely chopped. With the food processor running, slowly drizzle in ¾ cup of olive oil until a thick sauce forms. Set aside.
2. Heat the remaining ¼ cup of olive oil in a large skillet over medium-high heat.
3. Add the cod fillets, cover, and cook each side for 4 to 5 minutes, until browned and cooked through.
4. Remove the cod fillets from the heat to a plate and top each with generous spoonfuls of the prepared pistou. Serve immediately.

Per Serving calories: 580 | fat: 54.6g | protein: 21.1g | carbs: 2.8g | fiber: 1.0g | sodium: 651mg

Fried Cod Fillets

Prep time: 5 minutes | Cook time: 10 minutes | Serves 4

½ cup all-purpose flour
1 teaspoon garlic powder
1 teaspoon salt
4 (4- to 5-ounce / 113- to 142-g) cod fillets
1 tablespoon extra-virgin olive oil

1. Mix together the flour, garlic powder, and salt in a shallow dish. Dredge each piece of fish in the seasoned flour until they are evenly coated.
2. Heat the olive oil in a medium skillet over medium-high heat. Once hot, add the cod fillets and fry for 6 to 8 minutes, flipping the fish halfway through, or until the fish is opaque and flakes easily.
3. Remove from the heat and serve on plates.

Per Serving calories: 333 | fat: 18.8g | protein: 21.2g | carbs: 20.0g | fiber: 5.7g | sodium: 870mg

Mediterranean Braised Cod with Vegetables

Prep time: 10 minutes | Cook time: 18 minutes | Serves 2

1 tablespoon olive oil
½ medium onion, minced
2 garlic cloves, minced
1 teaspoon oregano
1 (15-ounce / 425-g) can artichoke hearts in water, drained and halved
1 (15-ounce / 425-g) can diced tomatoes with basil
¼ cup pitted Greek olives, drained
10 ounces (284 g) wild cod
Salt and freshly ground black pepper, to taste

1. In a skillet, heat the olive oil over medium-high heat.
2. Sauté the onion for about 5 minutes, stirring occasionally, or until tender. Stir in the garlic and oregano and cook for 30 seconds more until fragrant.
3. Add the artichoke hearts, tomatoes, and olives and stir to combine. Top with the cod. Cover and cook for 10 minutes, or until the fish flakes easily with a fork and juices run clean. Sprinkle with the salt and pepper. Serve warm.

Per Serving calories: 332 | fat: 10.5g | protein: 29.2g | carbs: 30.7g | fiber: 8.0g | sodium: 1906mg

Lemon-Parsley Swordfish

Prep time: 10 minutes | Cook time: 17 to 20 minutes | Serves 4

1 cup fresh Italian parsley	2 cloves garlic
¼ cup lemon juice	½ teaspoon salt
¼ cup extra-virgin olive oil	4 swordfish steaks
¼ cup fresh thyme	Olive oil spray

1. Preheat the oven to 450ºF (235ºC). Grease a large baking dish generously with olive oil spray.
2. Place the parsley, lemon juice, olive oil, thyme, garlic, and salt in a food processor and pulse until smoothly blended.
3. Arrange the swordfish steaks in the greased baking dish and spoon the parsley mixture over the top.
4. Bake in the preheated oven for 17 to 20 minutes until flaky.
5. Divide the fish among four plates and serve hot.

Per Serving

calories: 396 | fat: 21.7g | protein: 44.2g | carbs: 2.9g | fiber: 1.0g | sodium: 494mg

Baked Salmon with Tarragon Mustard Sauce

Prep time: 5 minutes | Cook time: 12 minutes | Serves 4

1¼ pounds (567 g) salmon fillet (skin on or removed), cut into 4 equal pieces	2 tablespoons chopped fresh tarragon
¼ cup Dijon mustard	½ teaspoon salt
¼ cup avocado oil mayonnaise	¼ teaspoon freshly ground black pepper
Zest and juice of ½ lemon	4 tablespoons extra-virgin olive oil, for serving

1. Preheat the oven to 425ºF (220ºC). Line a baking sheet with parchment paper. Arrange the salmon pieces on the prepared baking sheet, skin-side down.
2. Stir together the mustard, avocado oil mayonnaise, lemon zest and juice, tarragon, salt, and pepper in a small bowl. Spoon the mustard mixture over the salmon.
3. Bake for 10 to 12 minutes, or until the top is golden and salmon is opaque in the center.
4. Divide the salmon among four plates and drizzle each top with 1 tablespoon of olive oil before serving.

Per Serving

calories: 386 | fat: 27.7g | protein: 29.3g | carbs: 3.8g | fiber: 1.0g | sodium: 632mg

Baked Lemon Salmon

Prep time: 5 minutes | Cook time: 20 minutes | Serves 4

¼ teaspoon dried thyme	½ teaspoon freshly ground black pepper
Zest and juice of ½ lemon	1 pound (454 g) salmon fillet
¼ teaspoon salt	Nonstick cooking spray

1. Preheat the oven to 425ºF (220ºC). Coat a baking sheet with nonstick cooking spray.
2. Mix together the thyme, lemon zest and juice, salt, and pepper in a small bowl and stir to incorporate.
3. Arrange the salmon, skin-side down, on the coated baking sheet. Spoon the thyme mixture over the salmon and spread it all over.
4. Bake in the preheated oven for about 15 to 20 minutes, or until the fish flakes apart easily. Serve warm.

Per Serving calories: 162 | fat: 7.0g | protein: 23.1g | carbs: 1.0g | fiber: 0g | sodium: 166mg

Glazed Broiled Salmon

Prep time: 5 minutes | Cook time: 5 to 10 minutes | Serves 4

4 (4-ounce / 113-g) salmon fillets	1 teaspoon coconut aminos
3 tablespoons miso paste	1 teaspoon rice vinegar
2 tablespoons raw honey	

1. Preheat the broiler to High. Line a baking dish with aluminum foil and add the salmon fillets.
2. Whisk together the miso paste, honey, coconut aminos, and vinegar in a small bowl. Pour the glaze over the fillets and spread it evenly with a brush.
3. Broil for about 5 minutes, or until the salmon is browned on top and opaque. Brush any remaining glaze over the salmon and broil for an additional 5 minutes if needed. The cooking time depends on the thickness of the salmon.
4. Let the salmon cool for 5 minutes before serving.

Per Serving

calories: 263 | fat: 8.9g | protein: 30.2g | carbs: 12.8g | fiber: 0.7g | sodium: 716mg

Baked Salmon with Basil and Tomato

Prep time: 10 minutes | Cook time: 20 minutes | Serves 2

2 (6-ounce / 170-g) boneless salmon fillets	1 tablespoon olive oil
1 tablespoon dried basil	2 tablespoons grated Parmesan cheese
1 tomato, thinly sliced	Nonstick cooking spray

1. Preheat the oven to 375ºF (190ºC). Line a baking sheet with a piece of aluminum foil and mist with nonstick cooking spray.
2. Arrange the salmon fillets onto the aluminum foil and scatter with basil. Place the tomato slices on top and drizzle with olive oil. Top with the grated Parmesan cheese.
3. Bake for about 20 minutes, or until the flesh is opaque and it flakes apart easily.
4. Remove from the oven and serve on a plate.

Per Serving

calories: 403 | fat: 26.5g | protein: 36.3g | carbs: 3.8g | fiber: 0.1g | sodium: 179mg

Honey-Mustard Roasted Salmon

Prep time: 5 minutes | Cook time: 15 to 20 minutes | Serves 4

2 tablespoons whole-grain mustard	¼ teaspoon freshly ground black pepper
2 garlic cloves, minced	1 pound (454 g) salmon fillet
1 tablespoon honey	Nonstick cooking spray
¼ teaspoon salt	

1. Preheat the oven to 425ºF (220ºC). Coat a baking sheet with nonstick cooking spray.
2. Stir together the mustard, garlic, honey, salt, and pepper in a small bowl.
3. Arrange the salmon fillet, skin-side down, on the coated baking sheet. Spread the mustard mixture evenly over the salmon fillet.
4. Roast in the preheated oven for 15 to 20 minutes, or until it flakes apart easily and reaches an internal temperature of 145ºF (63ºC).Serve hot.

Per Serving

calories: 185 | fat: 7.0g | protein: 23.2g | carbs: 5.8g | fiber: 0g | sodium: 311mg

Baked Fish with Pistachio Crust

Prep time: 10 minutes | Cook time: 15 to 20 minutes | Serves 4

½ cup extra-virgin olive oil, divided	½ cup ground flaxseed
1 pound (454 g) flaky white fish (such as cod, haddock, or halibut), skin removed	Zest and juice of 1 lemon, divided
	1 teaspoon ground cumin
½ cup shelled finely chopped pistachios	1 teaspoon ground allspice
	½ teaspoon salt
	¼ teaspoon freshly ground black pepper

1. Preheat the oven to 400ºF (205ºC).
2. Line a baking sheet with parchment paper or aluminum foil and drizzle 2 tablespoons of olive oil over the sheet, spreading to evenly coat the bottom.
3. Cut the fish into 4 equal pieces and place on the prepared baking sheet. In a small bowl, combine the pistachios, flaxseed, lemon zest, cumin, allspice, salt, and pepper. Drizzle in ¼ cup of olive oil and stir well.
4. Divide the nut mixture evenly on top of the fish pieces. Drizzle the lemon juice and remaining 2 tablespoons of olive oil over the fish and bake until cooked through, 15 to 20 minutes, depending on the thickness of the fish.
5. Cool for 5 minutes before serving.

Per Serving

calories: 509 | fat: 41.0g | protein: 26.0g | carbs: 9.0g | fiber: 6.0g | sodium: 331mg

Dill Baked Sea Bass

Prep time: 10 minutes | Cook time: 10 to 15 minutes | Serves 6

¼ cup olive oil	1 garlic clove, minced
2 pounds (907 g) sea bass	¼ cup dry white wine
Sea salt and freshly ground pepper, to taste	3 teaspoons fresh dill
	2 teaspoons fresh thyme

1. Preheat the oven to 425ºF (220ºC).
2. Brush the bottom of a roasting pan with the olive oil. Place the fish in the pan and brush the fish with oil.
3. Season the fish with sea salt and freshly ground pepper. Combine the remaining ingredients and pour over the fish.
4. Bake in the preheated oven for 10 to 15 minutes, depending on the size of the fish. Serve hot.

Per Serving calories: 224 | fat: 12.1g | protein: 28.1g | carbs: 0.9g | fiber: 0.3g | sodium: 104mg

Sole Piccata with Capers

Prep time: 10 minutes | Cook time: 17 minutes | Serves 4

1 teaspoon extra-virgin olive oil	2 tablespoons all-purpose flour
4 (5-ounce / 142-g) sole fillets, patted dry	2 cups low-sodium chicken broth
3 tablespoons almond butter	Juice and zest of ½ lemon
2 teaspoons minced garlic	2 tablespoons capers

1. Place a large skillet over medium-high heat and add the olive oil.
2. Sear the sole fillets until the fish flakes easily when tested with a fork, about 4 minutes on each side. Transfer the fish to a plate and set aside.

3. Return the skillet to the stove and add the butter.
4. Sauté the garlic until translucent, about 3 minutes.
5. Whisk in the flour to make a thick paste and cook, stirring constantly, until the mixture is golden brown, about 2 minutes.
6. Whisk in the chicken broth, lemon juice and zest.
7. Cook for about 4 minutes until the sauce is thickened.
8. Stir in the capers and serve the sauce over the fish.

Per Serving

calories: 271 | fat:13.0g | protein: 30.0g | carbs: 7.0g | fiber: 0g | sodium: 413mg

Haddock with Cucumber Sauce

Prep time: 10 minutes | Cook time: 10 minutes | Serves 4

¼ cup plain Greek yogurt	1 teaspoon honey
½ scallion, white and green parts, finely chopped	Sea salt and freshly ground black pepper, to taste
½ English cucumber, grated, liquid squeezed out	4 (5-ounce / 142-g) haddock fillets, patted dry
2 teaspoons chopped fresh mint	Nonstick cooking spray

1. In a small bowl, stir together the yogurt, cucumber, scallion, mint, honey, and a pinch of salt. Set aside.
2. Season the fillets lightly with salt and pepper.
3. Place a large skillet over medium-high heat and spray lightly with cooking spray.
4. Cook the haddock, turning once, until it is just cooked through, about 5 minutes per side.
5. Remove the fish from the heat and transfer to plates.
6. Serve topped with the cucumber sauce.

Per Serving

calories: 164 | fat: 2.0g | protein: 27.0g | carbs: 4.0g | fiber: 0g | sodium: 104mg

Crispy Herb Crusted Halibut

Prep time: 10 minutes | Cook time: 20 minutes | Serves 4

4 (5-ounce / 142-g) halibut fillets, patted dry	1 tablespoon chopped fresh parsley
Extra-virgin olive oil, for brushing	1 teaspoon chopped fresh basil
½ cup coarsely ground unsalted pistachios	1 teaspoon chopped fresh thyme
	Pinch sea salt
	Pinch freshly ground black pepper

1. Preheat the oven to 350ºF (180ºC). Line a baking sheet with parchment paper.
2. Place the fillets on the baking sheet and brush them generously with olive oil.
3. In a small bowl, stir together the pistachios, parsley, basil, thyme, salt, and pepper.
4. Spoon the nut mixture evenly on the fish, spreading it out so the tops of the fillets are covered.
5. Bake in the preheated oven until it flakes when pressed with a fork, about 20 minutes.
6. Serve immediately.

Per Serving

calories: 262 | fat: 11.0g | protein: 32.0g | carbs: 4.0g | fiber: 2.0g | sodium: 77mg

Breaded Shrimp

Prep time: 10 minutes | Cook time: 4 to 6 minutes | Serves 4

2 large eggs
1 tablespoon water
2 cups seasoned Italian bread crumbs
1 teaspoon salt
1 cup flour
1 pound (454 g) large shrimp (21 to 25), peeled and deveined
Extra-virgin olive oil, as needed

1. In a small bowl, beat the eggs with the water, then transfer to a shallow dish. Add the bread crumbs and salt to a separate shallow dish, then mix well.
2. Place the flour into a third shallow dish.
3. Coat the shrimp in the flour, then the beaten egg, and finally the bread crumbs. Place on a plate and repeat with all of the shrimp. Heat a skillet over high heat. Pour in enough olive oil to coat the bottom of the skillet. Cook the shrimp in the hot skillet for 2 to 3 minutes on each side. Remove and drain on a paper towel. Serve warm.

Per Serving

calories: 714 | fat: 34.0g | protein: 37.0g | carbs: 63.0g | fiber: 3.0g | sodium: 1727mg

Pesto Shrimp over Zoodles

Prep time: 15 minutes | Cook time: 10 minutes | Serves 4

1 pound (454 g) fresh shrimp, peeled and deveined
Salt and freshly ground black pepper, to taste
2 tablespoons extra-virgin olive oil
½ small onion, slivered
8 ounces (227 g) store-bought jarred pesto
¾ cup crumbled goat or feta cheese, plus additional for serving
2 large zucchini, spiralized, for serving
¼ cup chopped flat-leaf Italian parsley, for garnish

1. In a bowl, season the shrimp with salt and pepper. Set aside.
2. In a large skillet, heat the olive oil over medium-high heat. Sauté the onion until just golden, 5 to 6 minutes.
3. Reduce the heat to low and add the pesto and cheese, whisking to combine and melt the cheese. Bring to a low simmer and add the shrimp. Reduce the heat back to low and cover. Cook until the shrimp is cooked through and pink, about 3 to 4 minutes.
4. Serve the shrimp warm over zoodles, garnishing with chopped parsley and additional crumbled cheese.

Per Serving

calories: 491 | fat: 35.0g | protein: 29.0g | carbs: 15.0g | fiber: 4.0g | sodium: 870mg

Salt and Pepper Calamari and Scallops

Prep time: 5 minutes | Cook time: 10 minutes | Serves 4

8 ounces (227 g) calamari steaks, cut into ½-inch-thick rings
8 ounces (227 g) sea scallops
1½ teaspoons salt, divided
1 teaspoon garlic powder
1 teaspoon freshly ground black pepper
⅓ cup extra-virgin olive oil
2 tablespoons almond butter

1. Place the calamari and scallops on several layers of paper towels and pat dry. Sprinkle with 1 teaspoon of salt and allow to sit for 15 minutes at room temperature.
2. Pat dry with additional paper towels. Sprinkle with pepper and garlic powder.
3. In a deep medium skillet, heat the olive oil and butter over medium-high heat. When the oil is hot but not smoking, add the scallops and calamari in a single layer to the skillet and sprinkle with the remaining ½ teaspoon of salt. Cook for 2 to 4 minutes on each side, depending on the size of the scallops, until just golden but still slightly opaque in center.
4. Using a slotted spoon, remove from the skillet and transfer to a serving platter. Allow the cooking oil to cool slightly and drizzle over the seafood before serving.

Per Serving

calories: 309 | fat: 25.0g | protein: 18.0g | carbs: 3.0g | fiber: 0g | sodium: 928mg

Baked Cod with Vegetables

Prep time: 15 minutes | Cook time: 25 minutes | Serves 2

1 pound (454 g) thick cod fillet, cut into 4 even portions
¼ teaspoon onion powder (optional)
¼ teaspoon paprika
3 tablespoons extra-virgin olive oil
4 medium scallions
½ cup fresh chopped basil, divided
3 tablespoons minced garlic (optional)
2 teaspoons salt
2 teaspoons freshly ground black pepper
¼ teaspoon dry marjoram (optional)
6 sun-dried tomato slices
½ cup dry white wine
½ cup crumbled feta cheese
1 (15-ounce / 425-g) can oil-packed artichoke hearts, drained
1 lemon, sliced
1 cup pitted kalamata olives
1 teaspoon capers (optional)
4 small red potatoes, quartered

1. Preheat the oven to 375°F (190°C).
2. Season the fish with paprika and onion powder (if desired).
3. Heat an ovenproof skillet over medium heat and sear the top side of the cod for about 1 minute until golden. Set aside.
4. Heat the olive oil in the same skillet over medium heat. Add the scallions, ¼ cup of basil, garlic (if desired), salt, pepper, marjoram (if desired), tomato slices, and white wine and stir to combine. Bring to a boil and remove from heat.
5. Evenly spread the sauce on the bottom of skillet. Place the cod on top of the tomato basil sauce and scatter with feta cheese. Place the artichokes in the skillet and top with the lemon slices.
6. Scatter with the olives, capers (if desired), and the remaining ¼ cup of basil. Remove from the heat and transfer to the preheated oven. Bake for 15 to 20 minutes, or until it flakes easily with a fork.
7. Meanwhile, place the quartered potatoes on a baking sheet or wrapped in aluminum foil. Bake in the oven for 15 minutes until fork-tender.
8. Cool for 5 minutes before serving.

Per Serving

calories: 1168 | fat: 60.0g | protein: 63.8g | carbs: 94.0g | fiber: 13.0g | sodium: 4620mg

Slow Cooker Salmon in Foil

Prep time: 5 minutes | Cook time: 2 hours | Serves 2

2 (6-ounce / 170-g) salmon fillets
1 tablespoon olive oil
2 cloves garlic, minced
½ tablespoon lime juice
1 teaspoon finely chopped fresh parsley
¼ teaspoon black pepper

1. Spread a length of foil onto a work surface and place the salmon fillets in the middle. Mix together the olive oil, garlic, lime juice, parsley, and black pepper in a small bowl. Brush the mixture over the fillets. Fold the foil over and crimp the sides to make a packet.
2. Place the packet into the slow cooker, cover, and cook on High for 2 hours, or until the fish flakes easily with a fork.
3. Serve hot.

Per Serving calories: 446 | fat: 20.7g | protein: 65.4g | carbs: 1.5g | fiber: 0.2g | sodium: 240mg

Dill Chutney Salmon

Prep time: 5 minutes | Cook time: 3 minutes | Serves 2

Chutney:
¼ cup fresh dill
¼ cup extra virgin olive oil
Juice from ½ lemon
Sea salt, to taste

Fish:
2 cups water
2 salmon fillets
Juice from ½ lemon
¼ teaspoon paprika
Salt and freshly ground pepper to taste

1. Pulse all the chutney ingredients in a food processor until creamy. Set aside. Add the water and steamer basket to the Instant Pot. Place salmon fillets, skin-side down, on the steamer basket. Drizzle the lemon juice over salmon and sprinkle with the paprika. Secure the lid. Select the Manual mode and set the cooking time for 3 minutes at High Pressure.
2. Once cooking is complete, do a quick pressure release. Carefully open the lid. Season the fillets with pepper and salt to taste. Serve topped with the dill chutney.

Per Serving calories: 636 | fat: 41.1g | protein: 65.3g | carbs: 1.9g | fiber: 0.2g | sodium: 477mg

Garlic-Butter Parmesan Salmon and Asparagus

Prep time: 10 minutes | Cook time: 15 minutes | Serves 2

2 (6-ounce / 170-g) salmon fillets, skin on and patted dry
Pink Himalayan salt
Freshly ground black pepper, to taste
1 pound (454 g) fresh asparagus, ends snapped off
3 tablespoons almond butter
2 garlic cloves, minced
¼ cup grated Parmesan cheese

1. Preheat the oven to 400°F (205°C). Line a baking sheet with aluminum foil. Season both sides of the salmon fillets with salt and pepper. Put the salmon in the middle of the baking sheet and arrange the asparagus around the salmon.
2. Heat the almond butter in a small saucepan over medium heat. Add the minced garlic and cook for about 3 minutes, or until the garlic just begins to brown. Drizzle the garlic-butter sauce over the salmon and asparagus and scatter the Parmesan cheese on top. Bake in the preheated oven for about 12 minutes, or until the salmon is cooked through and the asparagus is crisp-tender.

3. You can switch the oven to broil at the end of cooking time for about 3 minutes to get a nice char on the asparagus.
4. Let cool for 5 minutes before serving.

Per Serving calories: 435 | fat: 26.1g | protein: 42.3g | carbs: 10.0g | fiber: 5.0g | sodium: 503mg

Lemon Rosemary Roasted Branzino

Prep time: 15 minutes | Cook time: 30 minutes | Serves 2

4 tablespoons extra-virgin olive oil, divided
2 (8-ounce / 227-g) branzino fillets, preferably at least 1 inch thick
1 garlic clove, minced
1 bunch scallions (white part only), thinly sliced
10 to 12 small cherry tomatoes, halved
1 large carrot, cut into ¼-inch rounds
½ cup dry white wine
2 tablespoons paprika
2 teaspoons kosher salt
½ tablespoon ground chili pepper
2 rosemary sprigs or 1 tablespoon dried rosemary
1 small lemon, thinly sliced
½ cup sliced pitted kalamata olives

1. Heat a large ovenproof skillet over high heat until hot, about 2 minutes. Add 1 tablespoon of olive oil and heat for 10 to 15 seconds until it shimmers.
2. Add the branzino fillets, skin-side up, and sear for 2 minutes. Flip the fillets and cook for an additional 2 minutes. Set aside. Swirl 2 tablespoons of olive oil around the skillet to coat evenly.
3. Add the garlic, scallions, tomatoes, and carrot, and sauté for 5 minutes, or until softened.
4. Add the wine, stirring until all ingredients are well combined. Carefully place the fish over the sauce.
5. Preheat the oven to 450°F (235°C).
6. Brush the fillets with the remaining 1 tablespoon of olive oil and season with paprika, salt, and chili pepper. Top each fillet with a rosemary sprig and lemon slices. Scatter the olives over fish and around the skillet.
7. Roast for about 10 minutes until the lemon slices are browned. Serve hot.

Per Serving calories: 724 | fat: 43.0g | protein: 57.7g | carbs: 25.0g | fiber: 10.0g | sodium: 2950mg

Grilled Lemon Pesto Salmon

Prep time: 5 minutes | Cook time: 6 to 10 minutes | Serves 2

10 ounces (283 g) salmon fillet (1 large piece or 2 smaller ones)
Salt and freshly ground black pepper, to taste
2 tablespoons prepared pesto sauce
1 large fresh lemon, sliced
Cooking spray

1. reheat the grill to medium-high heat. Spray the grill grates with cooking spray. Season the salmon with salt and black pepper. Spread the pesto sauce on top.
2. Make a bed of fresh lemon slices about the same size as the salmon fillet on the hot grill, and place the salmon on top of the lemon slices. Put any additional lemon slices on top of the salmon. Grill the salmon for 6 to 10 minutes, or until the fish is opaque and flakes apart easily. Serve hot.

Per Serving calories: 316 | fat: 21.1g | protein: 29.0g | carbs: 1.0g | fiber: 0g | sodium: 175mg

Steamed Trout with Lemon Herb Crust

Prep time: 10 minutes | Cook time: 15 minutes | Serves 2

3 tablespoons olive oil
3 garlic cloves, chopped
2 tablespoons fresh lemon juice
1 tablespoon chopped fresh mint
1 tablespoon chopped fresh parsley
¼ teaspoon dried ground thyme
1 teaspoon sea salt
1 pound (454 g) fresh trout (2 pieces)
2 cups fish stock

1. Stir together the olive oil, garlic, lemon juice, mint, parsley, thyme, and salt in a small bowl. Brush the marinade onto the fish. Insert a trivet in the Instant Pot. Pour in the fish stock and place the fish on the trivet.
2. Secure the lid. Select the Steam mode and set the cooking time for 15 minutes at High Pressure. Once cooking is complete, do a quick pressure release. Carefully open the lid. Serve warm.

Per Serving

calories: 477 | fat: 29.6g | protein: 51.7g | carbs: 3.6g | fiber: 0.2g | sodium: 2011mg

Roasted Trout Stuffed with Veggies

Prep time: 10 minutes | Cook time: 25 minutes | Serves 2

2 (8-ounce / 227-g) whole trout fillets, dressed (cleaned but with bones and skin intact)
1 tablespoon extra-virgin olive oil
¼ teaspoon salt
⅛ teaspoon freshly ground black pepper
1 small onion, thinly sliced
½ red bell pepper, seeded and thinly sliced
1 poblano pepper, seeded and thinly sliced
2 or 3 shiitake mushrooms, sliced
1 lemon, sliced
Nonstick cooking spray

1. Preheat the oven to 425°F (220°C). Spray a baking sheet with nonstick cooking spray. Rub both trout fillets, inside and out, with the olive oil. Season with salt and pepper.
2. Mix together the onion, bell pepper, poblano pepper, and mushrooms in a large bowl. Stuff half of this mixture into the cavity of each fillet. Top the mixture with 2 or 3 lemon slices inside each fillet.
3. Place the fish on the prepared baking sheet side by side. Roast in the preheated oven for 25 minutes, or until the fish is cooked through and the vegetables are tender.
4. Remove from the oven and serve on a plate.

Per Serving

calories: 453 | fat: 22.1g | protein: 49.0g | carbs: 13.8g | fiber: 3.0g | sodium: 356mg

Lemony Trout with Caramelized Shallots

Prep time: 10 minutes | Cook time: 20 minutes | Serves 2

Shallots:
1 teaspoon almond butter
2 shallots, thinly sliced Dash salt
Trout:
1 tablespoon plus 1 teaspoon almond butter, divided
2 (4-ounce / 113-g) trout fillets
3 tablespoons capers
¼ cup freshly squeezed lemon juice
¼ teaspoon salt
Dash freshly ground black pepper
1 lemon, thinly sliced

Make the Shallots

1. In a large skillet over medium heat, cook the butter, shallots, and salt for 20 minutes, stirring every 5 minutes, or until the shallots are wilted and caramelized. Make the Trout Meanwhile, in another large skillet over medium heat, heat 1 teaspoon of almond butter.
2. Add the trout fillets and cook each side for 3 minutes, or until flaky. Transfer to a plate and set aside.
3. In the skillet used for the trout, stir in the capers, lemon juice, salt, and pepper, then bring to a simmer. Whisk in the remaining 1 tablespoon of almond butter. Spoon the sauce over the fish.
4. Garnish the fish with the lemon slices and caramelized shallots before serving.

Per Serving

calories: 344 | fat: 18.4g | protein: 21.1g | carbs: 14.7g | fiber: 5.0g | sodium: 1090mg

Tomato Tuna Melts

Prep time: 5 minutes | Cook time: 3 to 4 minutes | Serves 2

1 (5-ounce / 142-g) can chunk light tuna packed in water, drained
2 tablespoons plain Greek yogurt
2 tablespoons finely chopped celery
1 tablespoon finely chopped red onion
2 teaspoons freshly squeezed lemon juice
Pinch cayenne pepper
1 large tomato, cut into ¾-inch-thick rounds
½ cup shredded Cheddar cheese

1. Preheat the broiler to High. Stir together the tuna, yogurt, celery, red onion, lemon juice, and cayenne pepper in a medium bowl. Place the tomato rounds on a baking sheet. Top each with some tuna salad and Cheddar cheese.
2. Broil for 3 to 4 minutes until the cheese is melted and bubbly. Cool for 5 minutes before serving.

Per Serving

calories: 244 | fat: 10.0g | protein: 30.1g | carbs: 6.9g | fiber: 1.0g | sodium: 445mg

Mackerel and Green Bean Salad

Prep time: 10 minutes | Cook time: 10 minutes | Serves 2

2 cups green beans
1 tablespoon avocado oil
2 mackerel fillets
4 cups mixed salad greens
2 hard-boiled eggs, sliced
1 avocado, sliced
2 tablespoons lemon juice
2 tablespoons olive oil
1 teaspoon Dijon mustard
Salt and black pepper, to taste

1. Cook the green beans in a medium saucepan of boiling water for about 3 minutes until crisp-tender. Drain and set aside.
2. Melt the avocado oil in a pan over medium heat. Add the mackerel fillets and cook each side for 4 minutes.
3. Divide the greens between two salad bowls. Top with the mackerel, sliced egg, and avocado slices.
4. In another bowl, whisk together the lemon juice, olive oil, mustard, salt, and pepper, and drizzle over the salad. Add the cooked green beans and toss to combine, then serve.

Per Serving calories: 737 | fat: 57.3g | protein: 34.2g | carbs: 22.1g | fiber: 13.4g | sodium: 398mg

Hazelnut Crusted Sea Bass

Prep time: 10 minutes | Cook time: 15 minutes | Serves 2

2 tablespoons almond butter   ⅓ cup roasted hazelnuts

2 sea bass fillets   A pinch of cayenne pepper

1. Preheat the oven to 425°F (220°C). Line a baking dish with waxed paper. Brush the almond butter over the fillets.
2. Pulse the hazelnuts and cayenne in a food processor.
3. Coat the sea bass with the hazelnut mixture, then transfer to the baking dish. Bake in the preheated oven for about 15 minutes. Cool for 5 minutes before serving.

Per Serving calories: 468 | fat: 30.8g | protein: 40.0g | carbs: 8.8g | fiber: 4.1g | sodium: 90mg

Shrimp and Pea Paella

Prep time: 20 minutes | Cook time: 60 minutes | Serves 2

2 tablespoons olive oil

1 garlic clove, minced

½ large onion, minced

1 cup diced tomato

½ cup short-grain rice

½ teaspoon sweet paprika

½ cup dry white wine

1¼ cups low-sodium chicken stock

8 ounces (227 g) large raw shrimp

1 cup frozen peas

¼ cup jarred roasted red peppers, cut into strips

Salt, to taste

1. Heat the olive oil in a large skillet over medium-high heat.
2. Add the garlic and onion and sauté for 3 minutes, or until the onion is softened. Add the tomato, rice, and paprika and stir for 3 minutes to toast the rice.
3. Add the wine and chicken stock and stir to combine. Bring the mixture to a boil.
4. Cover and reduce the heat to medium-low, and simmer for 45 minutes, or until the rice is just about tender and most of the liquid has been absorbed.
5. Add the shrimp, peas, and roasted red peppers. Cover and cook for an additional 5 minutes. Season with salt to taste and serve.

Per Serving calories: 646 | fat: 27.1g | protein: 42.0g | carbs: 59.7g | fiber: 7.0g | sodium: 687mg

Garlic Shrimp with Arugula Pesto

Prep time: 20 minutes | Cook time: 5 minutes | Serves 2

3 cups lightly packed arugula

½ cup lightly packed basil leaves

¼ cup walnuts

3 tablespoons olive oil

3 medium garlic cloves

2 tablespoons grated Parmesan cheese

1 tablespoon freshly squeezed lemon juice

Salt and freshly ground black pepper, to taste

1 (10-ounce / 283-g) package zucchini noodles

8 ounces (227 g) cooked, shelled shrimp

2 Roma tomatoes, diced

1. Process the arugula, basil, walnuts, olive oil, garlic, Parmesan cheese, and lemon juice in a food processor until smooth, scraping down the sides as needed. Season with salt and pepper to taste.
2. Heat a skillet over medium heat. Add the pesto, zucchini noodles, and cooked shrimp. Toss to combine the sauce over the noodles and shrimp, and cook until heated through. Taste and season with more salt and pepper as needed. Serve topped with the diced tomatoes.

Per Serving calories: 435 | fat: 30.2g | protein: 33.0g | carbs: 15.1g | fiber: 5.0g | sodium: 413mg

Baked Oysters with Vegetables

Prep time: 30 minutes | Cook time: 15 to 17 minutes | Serves 2

2 cups coarse salt, for holding the oysters

1 dozen fresh oysters, scrubbed

1 tablespoon almond butter

¼ cup finely chopped scallions, both white and green parts

½ cup finely chopped artichoke hearts

¼ cup finely chopped red bell pepper

1 garlic clove, minced

1 tablespoon finely chopped fresh parsley

Zest and juice of ½ lemon

Pinch salt

Freshly ground black pepper, to taste

1. Pour the salt into a baking dish and spread to evenly fill the bottom of the dish.
2. Prepare a clean work surface to shuck the oysters. Using a shucking knife, insert the blade at the joint of the shell, where it hinges open and shut. Firmly apply pressure to pop the blade in, and work the knife around the shell to open. Discard the empty half of the shell. Using the knife, gently loosen the oyster, and remove any shell particles. Set the oysters in their shells on the salt, being careful not to spill the juices. Preheat the oven to 425°F (220°C).
3. Heat the almond butter in a large skillet over medium heat. Add the scallions, artichoke hearts, and bell pepper, and cook for 5 to 7 minutes. Add the garlic and cook for 1 minute more. Remove from the heat and stir in the parsley, lemon zest and juice, and season to taste with salt and pepper. Divide the vegetable mixture evenly among the oysters. Bake in the preheated oven for 10 to 12 minutes, or until the vegetables are lightly browned. Serve warm.

Per Serving calories: 135 | fat: 7.2g | protein: 6.0g | carbs: 10.7g | fiber: 2.0g | sodium: 280mg

Steamed Cod

Prep time: 15 minutes | Cook time: 7 minutes | Serves 4

1 pound (454 g) cherry tomatoes, halved	2 cups water
1 bunch fresh thyme sprigs	1 cup white rice
4 fillets cod	1 cup Kalamata olives
1 teaspoon olive oil	2 tablespoons pickled capers
1 clove garlic, pressed	1 tablespoon olive oil
3 pinches salt	1 pinch ground black pepper

1. Line a parchment paper on the basket of your instant pot. Place about half the tomatoes in a single layer on the paper. Sprinkle with thyme, reserving some for garnish.
2. Arrange cod fillets on top. Sprinkle with a little bit of olive oil. Spread the garlic, pepper, salt, and remaining tomatoes over the fish. In the pot, mix rice and water.
3. Lay a trivet over the rice and water. Lower steamer basket onto the trivet. Seal the lid, and cook for 7 minutes on Low Pressure. Release the pressure quickly.
4. Remove the steamer basket and trivet from the pot. Use a fork to fluff rice. Plate the fish fillets and apply a garnish of olives, reserved thyme, pepper, remaining olive oil, and capers. Serve with rice.

Per Serving calories: 352 | fat: 9.1g | protein: 22.2g | carbs: 44.7g | fiber: 3.9g | sodium: 827mg

Steamed Bass

Prep time: 10 minutes | Cook time: 8 minutes | Serves 4

1½ cups water	2 turnips, chopped
1 lemon, sliced	2 pinches salt
4 sea bass fillets	1 pinch ground black pepper
4 sprigs thyme	2 teaspoons olive oil
1 white onion, cut into thin rings	

1. Add water and set a rack into the pot.
2. Line a parchment paper to the bottom of the steamer basket. Place lemon slices in a single layer on the rack.
3. Arrange fillets on the top of the lemons, cover with onion and thyme sprigs. Top with turnip slices.
4. Drizzle pepper, salt, and olive oil over the mixture. Put steamer basket onto the rack. Seal lid and cook on Low pressure for 8 minutes. Release the pressure quickly.
5. Serve over the delicate onion rings and thinly turnips.

Per Serving

calories: 177 | fat: 4.9g | protein: 24.7g | carbs: 7.8g | fiber: 2.0g | sodium: 209mg

Catfish and Shrimp Jambalaya

Prep time: 20 minutes | Cook time: 4 hours 45 minutes | Serves

4 ounces (113 g) catfish (cut into 1-inch cubes)	1 cup canned diced tomatoes
4 ounces (113 g) shrimp (peeled and deveined)	1 cup uncooked long-grain white rice
1 tablespoon olive oil	½ tablespoon Cajun seasoning
2 bacon slices, chopped	¼ teaspoon dried thyme
1¼ cups vegetable broth	¼ teaspoon cayenne pepper
¾ cup sliced celery stalk	½ teaspoon dried oregano
¼ teaspoon minced garlic	Salt and freshly ground black pepper, to taste
½ cup chopped onion	

1. Select the Sauté function on your Instant Pot and add the oil into it.
2. Put the onion, garlic, celery, and bacon to the pot and cook for 10 minutes.
3. Add all the remaining ingredients to the pot except seafood.
4. Stir well, then secure the cooker lid.
5. Select the Slow Cook function on a medium mode.
6. Keep the pressure release handle on venting position. Cook for 4 hours.
7. Once done, remove the lid and add the seafood to the gravy.
8. Secure the lid again, keep the pressure handle in the venting position.
9. Cook for another 45 minutes then serve.

Per Serving calories: 437 | fat: 13.1g | protein: 21.3g | carbs: 56.7g | fiber: 2.6g | sodium: 502mg

Salmon and Potato Casserole

Prep time: 20 minutes | Cook time: 8 hours | Serves 4

½ tablespoon olive oil	3 tablespoons flour
8 ounces (227 g) cream of mushroom soup	1 (1-pound / 454-g) can salmon (drained and flaked)
¼ cup water	½ cup chopped scallion
3 medium potatoes (peeled and sliced)	¼ teaspoon ground nutmeg
	Salt and freshly ground black pepper, to taste

1. Pour mushroom soup and water in a separate bowl and mix them well.
2. Add the olive oil to the Instant Pot and grease it lightly.
3. Place half of the potatoes in the pot and sprinkle salt, pepper, and half of the flour over it.
4. Now add a layer of half of the salmon over potatoes, then a layer of half of the scallions.
5. Repeat these layers and pour mushroom soup mix on top.
6. Top it with nutmeg evenly.
7. Secure the lid and set its pressure release handle to the venting position.
8. Select the Slow Cook function with Medium heat on your Instant Pot.
9. Let it cook for 8 hours then serve.

Per Serving

calories: 388 | fat: 11.6g | protein: 34.6g | carbs: 37.2g | fiber: 4.4g | sodium: 842mg

Salmon and Tomato Curry

Prep time: 10 minutes | Cook time: 12 minutes | Serves 8

3 pounds (1.4 kg) salmon fillets (cut into pieces)
2 tablespoons olive oil
2 Serrano peppers, chopped
1 teaspoon ground turmeric
4 tablespoons curry powder
4 teaspoons ground cumin
4 curry leaves

4 teaspoons ground coriander
2 small yellow onions, chopped
2 teaspoons red chili powder
4 garlic cloves, minced
4 cups unsweetened coconut milk
2½ cups tomatoes, chopped
2 tablespoons fresh lemon juice
Fresh cilantro leaves to garnish

1. Put the oil and curry leaves to the insert of the Instant Pot. Select the Sauté function to cook for 30 secs.
2. Add the garlic and onions to the pot, cook for 5 minutes.
3. Stir in all the spices and cook for another 1 minute.
4. Put the fish, Serrano pepper, coconut milk, and tomatoes while cooking.
5. Cover and lock the lid. Seal the pressure release valve.
6. Select the Manual function at Low Pressure for 5 minutes.
7. After the beep, do a Natural release to release all the steam.
8. Remove the lid and squeeze in lemon juice.
9. Garnish with fresh cilantro leaves and serve.

Per Serving

calories: 551 | fat: 40.6g | protein: 38.9g | carbs: 10.6g | fiber: 3.2g | sodium: 778mg

Lemony Salmon

Prep time: 10 minutes | Cook time: 3 minutes | Serves 3

1 cup water
3 lemon slices
1 (5-ounce / 142-g) salmon fillet

1 teaspoon fresh lemon juice
Salt and ground black pepper, to taste
Fresh cilantro to garnish

1. Add the water to the Instant pot and place a trivet inside.
2. In a shallow bowl, place the salmon fillet. Sprinkle salt and pepper over it.
3. Squeeze some lemon juice on top then place a lemon slice over the salmon fillet.
4. Cover the lid and lock it. Set its pressure release handle to Sealing position.
5. Use Steam function on your cooker for 3 minutes to cook.
6. After the beep, do a Quick release and release the pressure.
7. Remove the lid, then serve with the lemon slice and fresh cilantro on top.

Per Serving

calories: 161 | fat: 5.0g | protein: 26.6g | carbs: 0.7g | fiber: 0.2g | sodium: 119mg

Spicy Cumin Salmon

Prep time: 10 minutes | Cook time: 2 minutes | Serves 8

2 cups water
2 garlic cloves, minced
2 teaspoons powdered stevia
8 lemon slices
2 tablespoons red chili powder

2 teaspoons ground cumin
Salt and freshly grated black pepper, to taste
2 pounds (907 g) salmon fillet, cut into 8 pieces

1. Pour two cups of water in the insert of the Instant Pot. Set the trivet in it.
2. In a separate bowl, add all the ingredients except the lemon slices and mix them well.
3. Pour this mixture over the salmon fillets and rub it all over it.
4. Place the salmon slices over the trivet in a single layer.
5. Top each fillet with a lemon slice.
6. Secure the lid and select Steam function for 2 minutes.
7. After the beep, do a Quick release and then remove the lid.
8. Serve immediately.

Per Serving

calories: 151 | fat: 4.7g | protein: 23.3g | carbs: 3.1g | fiber: 1.0g | sodium: 117mg

Rosemary Salmon with Feta Cheese

Prep time: 5 minutes | Cook time: 3 minutes | Serves 6

1½ pounds (680 g) salmon fillets
1½ cups water
¼ cup olive oil
1½ garlic cloves, minced
1½ tablespoons feta cheese, crumbled

½ teaspoon dried oregano
3 tablespoons fresh lemon juice
Salt and freshly ground black pepper, to taste
3 fresh rosemary sprigs
3 lemon slices

1. Take a large bowl and add the garlic, feta cheese, salt, pepper, lemon juice, and oregano. Whisk well all the ingredients.
2. Add the water to the Instant pot then place the steamer trivet in it.
3. Arrange the salmon fillets over the trivet in a single layer.
4. Pour the cheese mixture over these fillets.
5. Place a lemon slice and a rosemary sprig over each fillet.
6. Secure the lid.
7. Select the Steam function on your cooker and set 3 minutes cooking time.
8. After it is done, carefully do a Quick release. Remove the lid.
9. Serve hot.

Per Serving

calories: 229 | fat: 14.0g | protein: 23.4g | carbs: 1.3g | fiber: 0.2g | sodium: 88mg

Mahi-Mahi Meal

Prep time: 15 minutes | Cook time: 7 minutes | Serves 4

1½ cups water	4 garlic cloves, minced
4 (4-ounce / 113-g) mahi-mahi fillets	4 tablespoons fresh lime juice
Salt and freshly ground black pepper, to taste	4 tablespoons erythritol
	2 teaspoons red pepper flakes, crushed

1. Sprinkle some salt and pepper over Mahi-Mahi fillets for seasoning. In a separate bowl add all the remaining ingredients and mix well.
2. Add the water to the Instant pot and place the trivet in it.
3. Arrange the seasoned fillets over the trivet in a single layer.
4. Pour the prepared sauce on top of each fillet.
5. Cover and secure the lid.
6. Set the Steam function on your cooker for 5 minutes.
7. Once it beeps, do a quick release then remove the lid.
8. Serve the steaming hot Mahi-Mahi and enjoy.

Per Serving calories: 228 | fat: 1.4g | protein: 38.0g | carbs: 14.2g | fiber: 0.1g | sodium: 182mg

Rosemary Cod with Cherry Tomato

Prep time: 20 minutes | Cook time: 5 minutes | Serves 6

1½ pounds (680 g) cherry tomatoes, halved	3 garlic cloves, minced
2½ tablespoons fresh rosemary, chopped	2 tablespoons olive oil
6 (4-ounce / 113-g) cod fillets	Salt and freshly ground black pepper, to taste

1. Add the olive oil, half of the tomatoes and rosemary to the insert of the Instant Pot. Place the cod fillets over these tomatoes. Then add more tomatoes to the pot.
2. Add the garlic to the pot. Then secure the lid.
3. Select the Manual function with High Pressure for 5 minutes. After the beep, use the quick release to discharge all the steam. Serve cod fillets with tomatoes and sprinkle a pinch of salt and pepper on top.

Per Serving calories: 143 | fat: 5.2g | protein: 18.8g | carbs: 5.0g | fiber: 1.5g | sodium: 358mg

Mussels with Onions

Prep time: 10 minutes | Cook time: 7 minutes | Serves 8

2 tablespoons olive oil	4 pounds (1.8 kg) mussels, cleaned and debearded
2 medium yellow onions, chopped	¼ cup fresh lemon juice
1 teaspoon dried rosemary, crushed	Salt and ground black pepper as needed
2 garlic cloves, minced	
2 cups chicken broth	

1. Put the oil to the Instant Pot and select the Sauté function for cooking. Add the onions and cook for 5 minutes with occasional stirring.
2. Add the rosemary and garlic to the pot. Stir and cook for 1 minute. Pour the chicken broth and lemon juice into the cooker, sprinkle some salt and black pepper over it.
3. Place the trivet inside the cooker and arrange the mussels over it.
4. Select the Manual function at Low Pressure for 1 minute.
5. Secure the lid and let the mussels cook.

6. After the beep, do a Quick release then remove the lid.
7. Serve the mussels with its steaming hot soup in a bowl.

Per Serving calories: 249 | fat: 8.8g | protein: 28.5g | carbs: 11.9g | fiber: 0.5g | sodium: 844mg

Cod Curry

Prep time: 5 minutes | Cook time: 12 minutes | Serves 8

3 pounds (1.4 kg) cod fillets, cut into bite-sized pieces	4 teaspoons ground cumin
2 tablespoons olive oil	4 teaspoons ground coriander
4 curry leaves	2 teaspoons red chili powder
4 medium onions, chopped	1 teaspoon ground turmeric
2 tablespoons fresh ginger, grated finely	4 cups unsweetened coconut milk
4 garlic cloves, minced	2½ cups tomatoes, chopped
4 tablespoons curry powder	2 Serrano peppers, seeded and chopped
	2 tablespoons fresh lemon juice

1. Add the oil to the Instant Pot and select Sauté function for cooking. Add the curry leaves and cook for 30 seconds. Stir the onion, garlic, and ginger into the pot and cook 5 minutes. Add all the spices to the mixture and cook for another 1½ minutes. Hit Cancel then add the coconut milk, Serrano pepper, tomatoes, and fish to the pot.
2. Secure the lid and select the Manual settings with Low Pressure and 5 minutes cooking time. After the beep, do a Quick release and remove the lid. Drizzle lemon juice over the curry then stir. Serve immediately.

Per Serving
calories: 424 | fat: 29.1g | protein: 30.2g | carbs: 14.4g | fiber: 3.8g | sodium: 559mg

Shrimps with Northern Beans

Prep time: 10 minutes | Cook time: 25 minutes | Serves 3

1½ tablespoons olive oil	½ teaspoon cayenne pepper
1 medium onion, chopped	½ pound (227 g) great northern beans, rinsed, soaked, and drained
½ small green bell pepper, seeded and chopped	1 cup chicken broth
½ celery stalk, chopped	1 bay leaf
1 garlic clove, minced	½ pound (227 g) medium shrimp, peeled and deveined
1 tablespoon fresh parsley, chopped	
½ teaspoon red pepper flakes, crushed	

1. Select the Sauté function on your Instant pot, then add the oil, onion, celery, bell pepper and cook for 5 minutes.
2. Now add the parsley, garlic, spices, and bay leaf to the pot and cook for another 2 minutes. Pour in the chicken broth then add the beans to it. Secure the cooker lid.
3. Select the Manual function for 15 minutes with medium pressure. After the beep, do a Natural release for 10 minutes and remove the lid. Add the shrimp to the beans and cook them together on the Manual function for 2 minutes at High Pressure. Do a Quick release, keep it aside for 10 minutes, then remove the lid. Serve hot.

Per Serving calories: 405 | fat: 9.1g | protein: 29.1g | carbs: 53.1g | fiber: 16.4g | sodium: 702mg

Shrimp and Potato Curry

Prep time: 5 minutes | Cook time: 9 minutes | Serves 8

2 tablespoons olive oil	6 medium tomatoes, chopped
1½ medium onions, chopped	2 pounds (907 g) medium shrimp, peeled and deveined
1½ teaspoons ground cumin	1½ tablespoons fresh lemon juice
2 teaspoons red chili powder	Salt, to taste
2 teaspoons ground turmeric	½ cup fresh cilantro, chopped
3 medium white rose potatoes, diced	

1. Select the Sauté function on your Instant Pot. Add the oil and onions then cook for 2 minutes.
2. Add the tomatoes, potatoes, cilantro, lemon juice and all the spices into the pot and secure the lid.
3. Select the Manual function at medium pressure for 5 minutes. Do a natural release then remove the lid. Stir shrimp into the pot. Secure the lid again then set the Manual function with High Pressure for 2 minutes.
4. After the beep, use Natural release and let it stand for 10 minutes. Remove the lid and serve hot.

Per Serving

calories: 197 | fat: 5.0g | protein: 18.1g | carbs: 20.3g | fiber: 3.9g | sodium: 700mg

Sardines and Plum Tomato Curry

Prep time: 10 minutes | Cook time: 8 hours 2 minutes | Serves 4

1 tablespoon olive oil	1 garlic clove, minced
1 pound (454 g) fresh sardines, cubed	½ cup tomato purée
2 plum tomatoes, chopped finely	Salt and ground black pepper, to taste
½ large onion, sliced	

1. Select the Sauté function on your Instant pot then add the oil and sardines to it. Let it sauté for 2 minutes then add all the remaining ingredients.
2. Cover the lid and select Slow Cook function for 8 hours.
3. Remove the lid and stir the cooked curry. Serve warm.

Per Serving

calories: 292 | fat: 16.5g | protein: 28.9g | carbs: 6.0g | fiber: 1.3g | sodium: 398mg

Salmon and Mushroom Hash with Pesto

Prep time: 15 minutes | Cook time: 20 minutes | Serves 6

Pesto:	Hash:
¼ cup extra-virgin olive oil	2 tablespoons extra-virgin olive oil
1 bunch fresh basil	6 cups mixed mushrooms (brown, white, shiitake, cremini, portobello, etc.), sliced
Juice and zest of 1 lemon	
⅓ cup water	
¼ teaspoon salt, plus additional as needed	1 pound (454 g) wild salmon, cubed

1. Make the pesto: Pulse the olive oil, basil, juice and zest, water, and salt in a blender or food processor until smoothly blended. Set aside.
2. Heat the olive oil in a large skillet over medium heat.
3. Stir-fry the mushrooms for 6 to 8 minutes, or until they begin to exude their juices.
4. Add the salmon and cook each side for 5 to 6 minutes until cooked through.
5. Fold in the prepared pesto and stir well. Taste and add additional salt as needed. Serve warm.

Per Serving

calories: 264 | fat: 14.7g | protein: 7.0g | carbs: 30.9g | fiber: 4.0g | sodium: 480mg

Spiced Citrus Sole

Prep time: 10 minutes | Cook time: 10 minutes | Serves 4

1 teaspoon garlic powder	¼ teaspoon freshly ground black pepper Pinch sea salt
1 teaspoon chili powder	
½ teaspoon lemon zest	4 (6-ounce / 170-g) sole fillets, patted dry
½ teaspoon lime zest	1 tablespoon extra-virgin olive oil
¼ teaspoon smoked paprika	2 teaspoons freshly squeezed lime juice

1. Preheat the oven to 450°F (235°C). Line a baking sheet with aluminum foil and set aside.
2. Mix together the garlic powder, chili powder, lemon zest, lime zest, paprika, pepper, and salt in a small bowl until well combined.
3. Arrange the sole fillets on the prepared baking sheet and rub the spice mixture all over the fillets until well coated. Drizzle the olive oil and lime juice over the fillets.
4. Bake in the preheated oven for about 8 minutes until flaky.
5. Remove from the heat to a plate and serve.

Per Serving

calories: 183 | fat: 5.0g | protein: 32.1g | carbs: 0g | fiber: 0g | sodium: 136mg

Asian-Inspired Tuna Lettuce Wraps

Prep time: 10 minutes | Cook time: 0 minutes | Serves 2

⅓ cup almond butter	½ cup canned water chestnuts, drained and chopped
1 tablespoon freshly squeezed lemon juice	
1 teaspoon low-sodium soy sauce	2 (2.6-ounce / 74-g) package tuna packed in water, drained
1 teaspoon curry powder	
½ teaspoon sriracha, or to taste	2 large butter lettuce leaves

1. Stir together the almond butter, lemon juice, soy sauce, curry powder, sriracha in a medium bowl until well mixed. Add the water chestnuts and tuna and stir until well incorporated.
2. Place 2 butter lettuce leaves on a flat work surface, spoon half of the tuna mixture onto each leaf and roll up into a wrap. Serve immediately.

Per Serving

calories: 270 | fat: 13.9g | protein: 19.1g | carbs: 18.5g | fiber: 3.0g | sodium: 626mg

Crispy Tilapia with Mango Salsa

Prep time: 5 minutes | Cook time: 10 minutes | Serves 2

Salsa:
1 cup chopped mango
2 tablespoons chopped fresh cilantro
2 tablespoons chopped red onion
2 tablespoons freshly squeezed lime juice
½ jalapeño pepper, seeded and minced
Pinch salt

Tilapia:
1 tablespoon paprika
1 teaspoon onion powder
½ teaspoon dried thyme
½ teaspoon freshly ground black pepper
¼ teaspoon cayenne pepper
½ teaspoon garlic powder
¼ teaspoon salt
½ pound (227 g) boneless tilapia fillets
2 teaspoons extra-virgin olive oil
1 lime, cut into wedges, for serving

1. Make the salsa: Place the mango, cilantro, onion, lime juice, jalapeño, and salt in a medium bowl and toss to combine. Set aside.
2. Make the tilapia: Stir together the paprika, onion powder, thyme, black pepper, cayenne pepper, garlic powder, and salt in a small bowl until well mixed. Rub both sides of fillets generously with the mixture.
3. Heat the olive oil in a large skillet over medium heat.
4. Add the fish fillets and cook each side for 3 to 5 minutes until golden brown and cooked through.
5. Divide the fillets among two plates and spoon half of the prepared salsa onto each fillet. Serve the fish alongside the lime wedges.

Per Serving
calories: 239 | fat: 7.8g | protein: 25.0g | carbs: 21.9g | fiber: 4.0g | sodium: 416mg

Mediterranean Grilled Sea Bass

Prep time: 20 minutes | Cook time: 20 minutes | Serves 6

¼ teaspoon onion powder
¼ teaspoon garlic powder
¼ teaspoon paprika
Lemon pepper and sea salt to taste
2 pounds (907 g) sea bass
3 tablespoons extra-virgin olive oil, divided
2 large cloves garlic, chopped
1 tablespoon chopped Italian flat leaf parsley

1. Preheat the grill to high heat.
2. Place the onion powder, garlic powder, paprika, lemon pepper, and sea salt in a large bowl and stir to combine.
3. Dredge the fish in the spice mixture, turning until well coated.
4. Heat 2 tablespoon of olive oil in a small skillet. Add the garlic and parsley and cook for 1 to 2 minutes, stirring occasionally. Remove the skillet from the heat and set aside. Brush the grill grates lightly with remaining 1 tablespoon olive oil.
5. Grill the fish for about 7 minutes. Flip the fish and drizzle with the garlic mixture and cook for an additional 7 minutes, or until the fish flakes when pressed lightly with a fork. Serve hot.

Per Serving calories: 200 | fat: 10.3g | protein: 26.9g | carbs: 0.6g | fiber: 0.1g | sodium: 105mg

Braised Branzino with Wine Sauce

Prep time: 15 minutes | Cook time: 15 minutes | Serves 2 to 3

Sauce:
¾ cup dry white wine
2 tablespoons white wine vinegar
2 tablespoons cornstarch
1 tablespoon honey

Fish:
1 large branzino, butterflied and patted dry
2 tablespoons onion powder
2 tablespoons paprika
½ tablespoon salt
6 tablespoons extra-virgin olive oil, divided
4 garlic cloves, thinly sliced
4 scallions, both green and white parts, thinly sliced
1 large tomato, cut into ¼-inch cubes
4 kalamata olives, pitted and chopped

1. Make the sauce: Mix together the white wine, vinegar, cornstarch, and honey in a bowl and keep stirring until the honey has dissolved. Set aside.
2. Make the fish: Place the fish on a clean work surface, skin-side down. Sprinkle the onion powder, paprika, and salt to season. Drizzle 2 tablespoons of olive oil all over the fish.
3. Heat 2 tablespoons of olive oil in a large skillet over high heat until it shimmers.
4. Add the fish, skin-side up, to the skillet and brown for about 2 minutes. Carefully flip the fish and cook for another 3 minutes. Remove from the heat to a plate and set aside.
5. Add the remaining 2 tablespoons olive oil to the skillet and swirl to coat. Stir in the garlic cloves, scallions, tomato, and kalamata olives and sauté for 5 minutes. Pour in the prepared sauce and stir to combine.
6. Return the fish (skin-side down) to the skillet, flipping to coat in the sauce. Reduce the heat to medium-low, and cook for an additional 5 minutes until cooked through.
7. Using a slotted spoon, transfer the fish to a plate and serve warm.

Per Serving calories: 1059 | fat: 71.9g | protein: 46.2g | carbs: 55.8g | fiber: 5.1g | sodium: 2807mg

Peppercorn-Seared Tuna Steaks

Prep time: 5 minutes | Cook time: 10 minutes | Serves 2

2 (5-ounce / 142-g) ahi tuna steaks
1 teaspoon kosher salt
¼ teaspoon cayenne pepper
2 tablespoons olive oil
1 teaspoon whole peppercorns

1. On a plate, Season the tuna steaks on both sides with salt and cayenne pepper.
2. In a skillet, heat the olive oil over medium-high heat until it shimmers.
3. Add the peppercorns and cook for about 5 minutes, or until they soften and pop.
4. Carefully put the tuna steaks in the skillet and sear for 1 to 2 minutes per side, depending on the thickness of the tuna steaks, or until the fish is cooked to the desired level of doneness.
5. Cool for 5 minutes before serving.

Per Serving
calories: 260 | fat: 14.3g | protein: 33.4g | carbs: 0.2g | fiber: 0.1g | sodium: 1033mg

Canned Sardine Donburi (Rice Bowl)

Prep time: 10 minutes | Cook time: 40 to 50 minutes | Serves 4 to 6

4 cups water	3 scallions, sliced thin
2 cups brown rice, rinsed well	1-inch piece fresh ginger, grated
½ teaspoon salt	4 tablespoons sesame oil
3 (4-ounce / 113-g) cans sardines packed in water, drained	

1. Place the water, brown rice, and salt to a large saucepan and stir to combine. Allow the mixture to boil over high heat.
2. Once boiling, reduce the heat to low, and cook covered for 45 to 50 minutes, or until the rice is tender.
3. Meanwhile, roughly mash the sardines with a fork in a medium bowl.
4. When the rice is done, stir in the mashed sardines, scallions, and ginger.
5. Divide the mixture into four bowls. Top each bowl with a drizzle of sesame oil. Serve warm.

Per Serving

calories: 603 | fat: 23.6g | protein: 25.2g | carbs: 73.8g | fiber: 4.0g | sodium: 498mg

Baked Halibut Steaks with Vegetables

Prep time: 15 minutes | Cook time: 20 minutes | Serves 4

2 teaspoon olive oil, divided	2 tablespoons chopped fresh basil
1 clove garlic, peeled and minced	¼ teaspoon salt
½ cup minced onion	¼ teaspoon ground black pepper
1 cup diced zucchini	4 (6-ounce / 170-g) halibut steaks
2 cups diced fresh tomatoes	⅓ cup crumbled feta cheese

1. Preheat oven to 450°F (235°C). Coat a shallow baking dish lightly with 1 teaspoon of olive oil.
2. In a medium saucepan, heat the remaining 1 teaspoon of olive oil.
3. Add the garlic, onion, and zucchini and mix well. Cook for 5 minutes, stirring occasionally, or until the zucchini is softened.
4. Remove the saucepan from the heat and stir in the tomatoes, basil, salt, and pepper.
5. Place the halibut steaks in the coated baking dish in a single layer. Spread the zucchini mixture evenly over the steaks. Scatter the top with feta cheese.
6. Bake in the preheated oven for about 15 minutes, or until the fish flakes when pressed lightly with a fork. Serve hot.

Per Serving

calories: 258 | fat: 7.6g | protein: 38.6g | carbs: 6.5g | fiber: 1.2g | sodium: 384mg

Spicy Haddock Stew

Prep time: 15 minutes | Cook time: 35 minutes | Serves 6

¼ cup coconut oil	1 cup coconut milk
1 tablespoon minced garlic	1 cup low-sodium chicken broth
1 onion, chopped	¼ teaspoon red pepper flakes
2 celery stalks, chopped	12 ounces (340 g) haddock, cut into 1-inch chunks
½ fennel bulb, thinly sliced	
1 carrot, diced	2 tablespoons chopped fresh cilantro, for garnish
1 sweet potato, diced	
1 (15-ounce / 425-g) can low-sodium diced tomatoes	

1. In a large saucepan, heat the coconut oil over medium-high heat.
2. Add the garlic, onion, and celery and sauté for about 4 minutes, stirring occasionally, or until they are tender.
3. Stir in the fennel bulb, carrot, and sweet potato and sauté for 4 minutes more.
4. Add the diced tomatoes, coconut milk, chicken broth, and red pepper flakes and stir to incorporate, then bring the mixture to a boil.
5. Once it starts to boil, reduce the heat to low, and bring to a simmer for about 15 minutes, or until the vegetables are fork-tender.
6. Add the haddock chunks and continue simmering for about 10 minutes, or until the fish is cooked through.
7. Sprinkle the cilantro on top for garnish before serving.

Per Serving

calories: 276 | fat: 20.9g | protein: 14.2g | carbs: 6.8g | fiber: 3.0g | sodium: 226mg

Orange Flavored Scallops

Prep time: 10 minutes | Cook time: 10 minutes | Serves 4

2 pounds (907 g) sea scallops, patted dry	1 tablespoon minced garlic
	¼ cup freshly squeezed orange juice
Sea salt and freshly ground black pepper, to taste	1 teaspoon orange zest
2 tablespoons extra-virgin olive oil	2 teaspoons chopped fresh thyme, for garnish

1. In a bowl, lightly season the scallops with salt and pepper. Set aside.
2. Heat the olive oil in a large skillet over medium-high heat until it shimmers.
3. Add the garlic and sauté for about 3 minutes, or until fragrant.
4. Stir in the seasoned scallops and sear each side for about 4 minutes, or until the scallops are browned.
5. Remove the scallops from the heat to a plate and set aside.
6. Add the orange juice and zest to the skillet, scraping up brown bits from bottom of skillet.
7. Drizzle the sauce over the scallops and garnish with the thyme before serving.

Per Serving

calories: 266 | fat: 7.6g | protein: 38.1g | carbs: 7.9g | fiber: 0g | sodium: 360mg

Garlic Skillet Salmon

Prep time: 5 minutes | Cook time: 14 to 16 minutes | Serves 4

1 tablespoon extra-virgin olive oil
2 garlic cloves, minced
1 teaspoon smoked paprika
1½ cups grape or cherry tomatoes, quartered
1 (12-ounce / 340-g) jar roasted red peppers, drained and chopped
1 tablespoon water
¼ teaspoon freshly ground black pepper
¼ teaspoon kosher or sea salt
1 pound (454 g) salmon fillets, skin removed and cut into 8 pieces
1 tablespoon freshly squeezed lemon juice

1. In a large skillet over medium heat, heat the oil. Add the garlic and smoked paprika and cook for 1 minute, stirring often. Add the tomatoes, roasted peppers, water, black pepper, and salt. Turn up the heat to medium-high, bring to a simmer, and cook for 3 minutes, stirring occasionally and smashing the tomatoes with a wooden spoon toward the end of the cooking time.
2. Add the salmon to the skillet, and spoon some of the sauce over the top. Cover and cook for 10 to 12 minutes, or until the salmon is cooked through and just starts to flake.
3. Remove the skillet from the heat, and drizzle lemon juice over the top of the fish. Stir the sauce, then break up the salmon into chunks with a fork. Serve hot.

Per Serving

calories: 255 | fat: 11.7g | protein: 24.2g | carbs: 5.9g | fiber: 1.2g | sodium: 809mg

Salmon Baked in Foil

Prep time: 5 minutes | Cook time: 25 minutes | Serves 4

2 cups cherry tomatoes
3 tablespoons extra-virgin olive oil
3 tablespoons lemon juice
3 tablespoons almond butter
1 teaspoon oregano
½ teaspoon salt
4 (5-ounce / 142-g) salmon fillets

1. Preheat the oven to 400°F (205°C).
2. Cut the tomatoes in half and put them in a bowl.
3. Add the olive oil, lemon juice, butter, oregano, and salt to the tomatoes and gently toss to combine.
4. Cut 4 pieces of foil, about 12-by-12 inches each.
5. Place the salmon fillets in the middle of each piece of foil.
6. Divide the tomato mixture evenly over the 4 pieces of salmon. Bring the ends of the foil together and seal to form a closed pocket.
7. Place the 4 pockets on a baking sheet. Bake in the preheated oven for 25 minutes.
8. Remove from the oven and serve on a plate.

Per Serving

calories: 410 | fat: 32.0g | protein: 30.0g | carbs: 4.0g | fiber: 1.0g | sodium: 370mg

Instant Pot Poached Salmon

Prep time: 10 minutes | Cook time: 3 minutes | Serves 4

1 lemon, sliced ¼ inch thick
4 (6-ounce / 170-g) skinless salmon fillets, 1½ inches thick
½ teaspoon salt
¼ teaspoon pepper
½ cup water

1. Layer the lemon slices in the bottom of the Instant Pot.
2. Season the salmon with salt and pepper, then arrange the salmon (skin- side down) on top of the lemon slices. Pour in the water. Secure the lid. Select the Manual mode and set the cooking time for 3 minutes at High Pressure.
3. Once cooking is complete, do a quick pressure release. Carefully open the lid. Serve warm.

Per Serving calories: 350 | fat: 23.0g | protein: 35.0g | carbs: 0g | fiber: 0g | sodium: 390mg

Balsamic-Honey Glazed Salmon

Prep time: 2 minutes | Cook time: 8 minutes | Serves 4

½ cup balsamic vinegar
1 tablespoon honey
4 (8-ounce / 227-g) salmon fillets
Sea salt and freshly ground pepper, to taste
1 tablespoon olive oil

1. Heat a skillet over medium-high heat. Combine the vinegar and honey in a small bowl.
2. Season the salmon fillets with the sea salt and freshly ground pepper; brush with the honey-balsamic glaze.
3. Add olive oil to the skillet, and sear the salmon fillets, cooking for 3 to 4 minutes on each side until lightly browned and medium rare in the center.
4. Let sit for 5 minutes before serving.

Per Serving calories: 454 | fat: 17.3g | protein: 65.3g | carbs: 9.7g | fiber: 0g | sodium: 246mg

Seared Salmon with Lemon Cream Sauce

Prep time: 10 minutes | Cook time: 20 minutes | Serves 4

4 (5-ounce / 142-g) salmon fillets
Sea salt and freshly ground black pepper, to taste
1 tablespoon extra-virgin olive oil
½ cup low-sodium vegetable broth
Juice and zest of 1 lemon
1 teaspoon chopped fresh thyme
½ cup fat-free sour cream
1 teaspoon honey
1 tablespoon chopped fresh chives

1. Preheat the oven to 400°F (205°C).
2. Season the salmon lightly on both sides with salt and pepper. Place a large ovenproof skillet over medium-high heat and add the olive oil.
3. Sear the salmon fillets on both sides until golden, about 3 minutes per side. Transfer the salmon to a baking dish and bake in the preheated oven until just cooked through, about 10 minutes.
4. Meanwhile, whisk together the vegetable broth, lemon juice and zest, and thyme in a small saucepan over medium-high heat until the liquid reduces by about one-quarter, about 5 minutes.
5. Whisk in the sour cream and honey.
6. Stir in the chives and serve the sauce over the salmon.

Per Serving calories: 310 | fat: 18.0g | protein: 29.0g | carbs: 6.0g | fiber: 0g | sodium: 129mg

Tuna and Zucchini Patties

Prep time: 10 minutes | Cook time: 12 minutes | Serves 4

3 slices whole-wheat sandwich bread, toasted
2 (5-ounce / 142-g) cans tuna in olive oil, drained
1 cup shredded zucchini
1 large egg, lightly beaten
¼ cup diced red bell pepper
1 tablespoon dried oregano
1 teaspoon lemon zest
¼ teaspoon freshly ground black pepper
¼ teaspoon kosher or sea salt
1 tablespoon extra-virgin olive oil
Salad greens or 4 whole-wheat rolls, for serving (optional)

1. Crumble the toast into bread crumbs with your fingers (or use a knife to cut into ¼-inch cubes) until you have 1 cup of loosely packed crumbs. Pour the crumbs into a large bowl. Add the tuna, zucchini, beaten egg, bell pepper, oregano, lemon zest, black pepper, and salt. Mix well with a fork. With your hands, form the mixture into four (½-cup-size) patties. Place them on a plate, and press each patty flat to about ¾-inch thick.
2. In a large skillet over medium-high heat, heat the oil until it's very hot, about 2 minutes.
3. Add the patties to the hot oil, then reduce the heat down to medium. Cook the patties for 5 minutes, flip with a spatula, and cook for an additional 5 minutes. Serve the patties on salad greens or whole-wheat rolls, if desired.

Per Serving
calories: 757 | fat: 72.0g | protein: 5.0g | carbs: 26.0g | fiber: 4.0g | sodium: 418mg

Mediterranean Cod Stew

Prep time: 10 minutes | Cook time: 20 minutes | Serves 6

2 tablespoons extra-virgin olive oil
2 cups chopped onion
2 garlic cloves, minced
¾ teaspoon smoked paprika
1 (14.5-ounce / 411-g) can diced tomatoes, undrained
1 (12-ounce / 340-g) jar roasted red peppers, drained and chopped
1 cup sliced olives, green or black
⅓ cup dry red wine
¼ teaspoon kosher or sea salt
¼ teaspoon freshly ground black pepper
1½ pounds (680 g) cod fillets, cut into 1-inch pieces
3 cups sliced mushrooms

1. In a large stockpot over medium heat, heat the oil. Add the onion and cook for 4 minutes, stirring occasionally. Add the garlic and smoked paprika and cook for 1 minute, stirring often. Mix in the tomatoes with their juices, roasted peppers, olives, wine, pepper, and salt, and turn the heat to medium-high. Bring the mixture to a boil. Add the cod fillets and mushrooms, and reduce the heat to medium.
2. Cover and cook for about 10 minutes, stirring a few times, until the cod is cooked through and flakes easily, and serve.

Per Serving calories: 167 | fat: 5.0g | protein: 19.0g | carbs: 11.0g | fiber: 5.0g | sodium: 846mg

Fennel Poached Cod with Tomatoes

Prep time: 10 minutes | Cook time: 20 minutes | Serves 4

1 tablespoon olive oil
1 cup thinly sliced fennel
½ cup thinly sliced onion
1 tablespoon minced garlic
1 (15-ounce / 425-g) can diced tomatoes
2 cups chicken broth
½ cup white wine
Juice and zest of 1 orange
1 pinch red pepper flakes
1 bay leaf
1 pound (454 g) cod

1. Heat the olive oil in a large skillet. Add the onion and fennel and cook for 6 minutes, stirring occasionally, or until translucent. Add the garlic and cook for 1 minute more. Add the tomatoes, chicken broth, wine, orange juice and zest, red pepper flakes, and bay leaf, and simmer for 5 minutes to meld the flavors.
2. Carefully add the cod in a single layer, cover, and simmer for 6 to 7 minutes. Transfer fish to a serving dish, ladle the remaining sauce over the fish, and serve.

Per Serving calories: 336 | fat: 12.5g | protein: 45.1g | carbs:11.0g | fiber: 3.3g | sodium: 982mg

Teriyaki Salmon

Prep time: 10 minutes | Cook time: 8 minutes | Serves 4

4 (8-ounce / 227-g) thick salmon fillets.
1 cup soy sauce
2 cups water
½ cup mirin
2 tablespoons sesame oil
4 teaspoons sesame seeds
2 cloves garlic, minced
2 tablespoons freshly grated ginger
4 tablespoons brown sugar
1 tablespoon corn starch
4 green onions, minced

1. Add the soy sauce, sesame oil, sesame seeds, mirin, ginger, water, garlic, green onions, and brown sugar to a small bowl. Mix them well. In a shallow dish place the salmon fillets and pour half of the prepared mixture over the fillets. Let it marinate for 30 minutes in a refrigerator.
2. Pour 1 cup of water into the insert of your Instant pot and place trivet inside it. Arrange the marinated salmon fillets over the trivet and secure the lid.
3. Select the Manual settings with High Pressure and 8 minutes cooking time. Meanwhile, take a skillet and add the remaining marinade mixture in it.
4. Let it cook for 2 minutes, then add the corn starch mixed with water. Stir well and cook for 1 minute.
5. Check the pressure cooker, do a Quick release if it is done.
6. Transfer the fillets to a serving platter and pour the sesame mixture over it. Garnish with chopped green chilies then serve hot.

Per Serving calories: 622 | fat: 28.6g | protein: 51.3g | carbs: 29.6g | fiber: 2.0g | sodium: 1086mg

Coconut Tangy Cod Curry

Prep time: 5 minutes | Cook time: 3 minutes | Serves 6

1 (28-ounce / 794-g) can coconut milk	2 teaspoons ground turmeric
Juice of 2 lemons	2 teaspoons ground ginger
2 tablespoons red curry paste	1 teaspoon sea salt
2 teaspoons fish sauce	1 teaspoon white pepper
2 teaspoons honey	2 pounds (907 g) codfish, cut into 1-inch cubes
4 teaspoons Sriracha	½ cup chopped fresh cilantro, for garnish
4 cloves garlic, minced	4 lime wedges, for garnish

1. Add all the ingredients, except the cod cubes and garnish, to a large bowl and whisk them well. Arrange the cod cube at the base of the Instant Pot and pour the coconut milk mixture over it. Secure the lid and hit the Manual key, select High Pressure with 3 minutes cooking time.
2. After the beep, do a Quick release then remove the lid.
3. Garnish with fresh cilantro and lemon wedges then serve.

Per Serving calories: 396 | fat: 29.1g | protein: 26.6g | carbs: 11.4g | fiber: 2.0g | sodium: 1024mg

Shrimps with Broccoli

Prep time: 5 minutes | Cook time: 10 minutes | Serves 2

2 teaspoons vegetable oil	¼ cup water
2 tablespoons corn starch	¼ cup sliced carrots
1 cup broccoli florets	3 tablespoons rice vinegar
¼ cup chicken broth	2 teaspoons sesame oil
8 ounces (227 g) large shrimp, peeled and deveined	1 tablespoon chili garlic sauce
¼ cup soy sauce	Coriander leaves to garnish
	Boiled rice or noodles, for serving

1. Add 1 tablespoon of corn starch and shrimp to a bowl. Mix them well then set it aside.
2. In a small bowl, mix the remaining corn starch, chicken broth, carrots, chili garlic sauce, rice vinegar and soy sauce together. Keep the mixture aside.
3. Select the Sauté function on your Instant pot, add the sesame oil and broccoli florets to the pot and sauté for 5 minutes. Add the water to the broccoli, cover the lid and cook for 5 minutes. Stir in shrimp and vegetable oil to the broccoli, sauté it for 5 minutes. Garnish with coriander leaves on top. Serve with rice or noodles.

Per Serving calories: 300 | fat: 16.5g | protein: 19.6g | carbs: 17.1g | fiber: 2.2g | sodium: 1241mg

Shrimp and Spaghetti Squash Bowls

Prep time: 5 minutes | Cook time: 25 minutes | Serves 4

½ cup dry white wine	1 (28-ounce / 794-g) can crushed tomatoes
¼ teaspoon crushed red pepper flakes	2 cloves garlic, minced
1 large shallot, finely chopped	2½ pounds (1.1 kg) spaghetti squash
1 pound (454 g) jumbo shrimp, peeled and deveined	1 teaspoon olive oil
	Salt and pepper, to taste
	Parsley leaves (garnish)

1. At first, sprinkle some salt and pepper over the shrimp and keep them in a refrigerator until further use.
2. Hit the Sauté function on your Instant Pot, then add the olive oil and red pepper flakes into it. Sauté for 1 minute.
3. Add the shallot and cook for 3 minutes. Then add the garlic, cook for 1 minute.
4. Add the dry wine, tomatoes, and whole spaghetti squash in the pot. Select Manual settings with medium pressure for 20 minutes. After the beep, do a Natural release. Remove the lid and the spaghetti squash.
5. Cut squash in half, remove its seed and stab with a fork to form spaghetti strands out of it. Keep them aside.
6. Select the Sauté function on your instant pot again, stir in shrimp. Mix well the shrimp with sauce.
7. To serve, top the spaghetti squash with shrimp and sauce. Garnish it with parsley.

Per Serving calories: 222 | fat: 4.4g | protein: 19.3g | carbs: 30.1g | fiber: 8.5g | sodium: 974mg

Scallop Teriyaki

Prep time: 5 minutes | Cook time: 5 minutes | Serves 6

2 pounds (907 g) jumbo sea scallops	1 cup coconut aminos
2 tablespoons olive oil	1 teaspoon ground ginger
6 tablespoons pure maple syrup	1 teaspoon garlic powder
	1 teaspoon sea salt

1. Add the olive oil to the Instant pot and heat it on the Sauté settings of your pot. Add the scallops to the pot and cook for a minute from each side.
2. Stir in all the remaining ingredients in the pot and mix them well. Secure the lid and select the Steam function to cook for 3 minutes. After the beep, do a Quick release then remove the lid. Serve hot.

Per Serving calories: 228 | fat: 5.3g | protein: 23.4g | carbs: 21.4g | fiber: 0.5g | sodium: 3664mg

Shrimp and Tomato Creole

Prep time: 20 minutes | Cook time: 7 hours 10 minutes | Serves 4

1 pound (454 g) shrimp (peeled and deveined)	1 (8-ounce / 227-g) can tomato sauce
1 tablespoon olive oil	½ teaspoon minced garlic
1 (28-ounce / 794-g) can crush whole tomatoes	¼ teaspoon ground black pepper
1 cup celery stalk (sliced)	1 tablespoon Worcestershire sauce
¾ cup chopped white onion	4 drops hot pepper sauce
½ cup green bell pepper (chopped)	Salt, to taste
	White rice for serving

1. Put the oil to the Instant Pot along with all the ingredients except the shrimp. Secure the cooker lid and keep the pressure handle valve turned to the venting position.
2. Select the Slow Cook function on your cooker and set it on medium heat. Let the mixture cook for 6 hours.
3. Remove the lid afterwards and add the shrimp to the pot.
4. Stir and let the shrimp cook for another 1 hour on Slow Cook function. Keep the lid covered with pressure release handle in the venting position. To serve, pour the juicy shrimp creole over steaming white rice.

Per Serving calories: 231 | fat: 4.8g | protein: 27.6g | carbs: 23.8g | fiber: 6.1g | sodium: 646mg

Mahi-Mahi and Tomato Bowls

Prep time: 5 minutes | Cook time: 14 minutes | Serves 3

3 (4-ounce / 113-g) mahi-mahi fillets	1 tablespoon fresh lemon juice
1½ tablespoons olive oil	Salt and freshly ground black pepper, to taste
½ yellow onion, sliced	
½ teaspoon dried oregano	1 (14-ounce / 397-g) can sugar-free diced tomatoes

1. Add the olive oil to the Instant Pot. Select the Sauté function on it. Add all the ingredient to the pot except the fillets. Cook them for 10 minutes. Press the Cancel key, then add the mahi-mahi fillets to the sauce.
2. Cover the fillets with sauce by using a spoon.
3. Secure the lid and set the Manual function at High Pressure for 4 minutes. After the beep, do a Quick release then remove the lid. Serve the fillets with their sauce, poured on top.

Per Serving calories: 265 | fat: 8.6g | protein: 39.1g | carbs: 7.0g | fiber: 3.1g | sodium: 393mg

Alfredo Tuscan Shrimp with Penne

Prep time: 5 minutes | Cook time: 5 minutes | Serves 3

1 pound (454 g) shrimp	1 cup sun-dried tomatoes
1 jar alfredo sauce	1 box penne pasta
1½ cups fresh spinach	1½ teaspoons Tuscan seasoning
	3 cups water

1. Add the water and pasta to a pot over a medium heat, boil until it cooks completely. Then strain the pasta and keep it aside. Select the Sauté function on your Instant Pot and add the tomatoes, shrimp, Tuscan seasoning, and alfredo sauce into it.
2. Stir and cook until shrimp turn pink in color.
3. Now add the spinach leaves to the pot and cook for 5 minutes.
4. Add the pasta to the pot and stir well.
5. Serve hot.

Per Serving

calories: 1361 | fat: 70.1g | protein: 55.9g | carbs: 134.4g | fiber: 19.4g | sodium: 933mg

Tuna with Shirataki Noodles

Prep time: 5 minutes | Cook time: 4 minutes | Serves 2

½ can tuna, drained	1 (14-ounce / 397-g) can cream mushroom soup
8 ounces (227 g) Shirataki noodles	2 ounces (57 g) shredded Cheddar cheese
½ cup frozen peas	1½ cups water

1. Add the water with noodles to the base of your Instant Pot.
2. Place the tuna and peas over it. Then pour the mushroom soup on top.
3. Secure the lid and cook with the Manual function at High Pressure for 4 minutes.
4. After the beep, do a Quick release then remove the lid.
5. Stir in shredded cheese to the tuna mix.
6. Serve warm.

Per Serving

calories: 362 | fat: 11.1g | protein: 19.5g | carbs: 46.5g | fiber: 1.5g | sodium: 645mg

Grits with Shrimp

Prep time: 5 minutes | Cook time: 15 minutes | Serves 8

1 tablespoon oil	24 ounces (680 g) tail-on shrimp
2 cups quick grits	
12 ounces (340 g) Parmesan cheese, shredded	2 tablespoons Old Bay seasoning
2 cups heavy cream	A pinch of ground black pepper
	4 cups water

1. Add a tablespoon of oil to the Instant Pot. Select the Sauté function for cooking.
2. Add the shrimp to the oil and drizzle old bay seasoning over it.
3. Cook the shrimp for 3-4 minutes while stirring then set them aside.
4. Now add the water, cream, and quick grits to the pot. Select the Manual function for 3 minutes at High Pressure.
5. After the beep, do a Quick release then remove the lid.
6. Add the shredded cheese to the grits then stir well.
7. Take a serving bowl, first pour in the creamy grits mixture then top it with shrimp.
8. Sprinkle black pepper on top then serve hot.

Per Serving

calories: 528 | fat: 38.6g | protein: 30.7g | carbs: 15.2g | fiber: 0.7g | sodium: 1249mg

Chapter 9

Fruits and Desserts

Rice Pudding with Roasted Orange

Prep time: 10 minutes | Cook time: 19 to 20 minutes | Serves 6

2 medium oranges	1 cup orange juice
2 teaspoons extra-virgin olive oil	1 cup uncooked instant brown rice
⅛ teaspoon kosher salt	¼ cup honey
2 large eggs	½ teaspoon ground cinnamon
2 cups unsweetened almond milk	1 teaspoon vanilla extract
	Cooking spray

1. Preheat the oven to 450°F (235°C). Spritz a large, rimmed baking sheet with cooking spray. Set aside.
2. Slice the unpeeled oranges into ¼-inch rounds. Brush with the oil and sprinkle with salt. Place the slices on the baking sheet and roast for 4 minutes. Flip the slices and roast for 4 more minutes, or until they begin to brown. Remove from the oven and set aside.
3. Crack the eggs into a medium bowl. In a medium saucepan, whisk together the milk, orange juice, rice, honey and cinnamon. Bring to a boil over medium-high heat, stirring constantly. Reduce the heat to medium- low and simmer for 10 minutes, stirring occasionally.
4. Using a measuring cup, scoop out ½ cup of the hot rice mixture and whisk it into the eggs. While constantly stirring the mixture in the pan, slowly pour the egg mixture back into the saucepan.
5. Cook on low heat for 1 to 2 minutes, or until thickened, stirring constantly. Remove from the heat and stir in the vanilla. Let the pudding stand for a few minutes for the rice to soften. The rice will be cooked but slightly chewy. For softer rice, let stand for another half hour. Top with the roasted oranges. Serve warm or at room temperature.

Per Serving
calories: 204 | fat: 6.0g | protein: 5.0g | carbs: 34.0g | fiber: 1.0g | sodium: 148mg

Cherry Walnut Brownies

Prep time: 10 minutes | Cook time: 20 minutes | Serves 9

2 large eggs	⅓ cup unsweetened dark chocolate cocoa powder
½ cup 2% plain Greek yogurt	¼ teaspoon baking powder
½ cup sugar ⅓ cup honey	¼ teaspoon salt
¼ cup extra-virgin olive oil	⅓ cup chopped walnuts
1 teaspoon vanilla extract	9 fresh cherries, stemmed and pitted
½ cup whole-wheat pastry flour	Cooking spray

1. Preheat the oven to 375°F (190°C) and set the rack in the middle of the oven. Spritz a square baking pan with cooking spray. In a large bowl, whisk together the eggs, yogurt, sugar, honey, oil and vanilla.
2. In a medium bowl, stir together the flour, cocoa powder, baking powder and salt. Add the flour mixture to the egg mixture and whisk until all the dry ingredients are incorporated. Fold in the walnuts.
3. Pour the batter into the prepared pan. Push the cherries into the batter, three to a row in three rows, so one will be at the center of each brownie once you cut them into squares. Bake the brownies for 20 minutes, or until just set. Remove from the oven and place on a rack to cool for 5 minutes. Cut into nine squares and serve.

Per Serving
calories: 154 | fat: 6.0g | protein: 3.0g | carbs: 24.0g | fiber: 2.0g | sodium: 125mg

Watermelon and Blueberry Salad

Prep time: 5 minutes | Cook time: 0 minutes | Serves 6 to 8

1 medium watermelon	2 tablespoons lemon juice
1 cup fresh blueberries	2 tablespoons finely chopped fresh mint leaves
⅓ cup honey	

1. Cut the watermelon into 1-inch cubes. Put them in a bowl.
2. Evenly distribute the blueberries over the watermelon.
3. In a separate bowl, whisk together the honey, lemon juice and mint. Drizzle the mint dressing over the watermelon and blueberries. Serve cold.

Per Serving calories: 238 | fat: 1.0g | protein: 4.0g | carbs: 61.0g | fiber: 3.0g | sodium: 11mg

Crispy Sesame Cookies

Prep time: 5 minutes | Cook time: 8 to 10 minutes | Serves 14 to 16

1 cup hulled sesame seeds	8 tablespoons almond butter
1 cup sugar	2 large eggs
	1¼ cups flour

1. Preheat the oven to 350°F (180°C).
2. Toast the sesame seeds on a baking sheet for 3 minutes. Set aside and let cool. Using a mixer, whisk together the sugar and butter. Add the eggs one at a time until well blended. Add the flour and toasted sesame seeds and mix until well blended. Drop spoonfuls of cookie dough onto a baking sheet and form them into round balls, about 1-inch in diameter, similar to a walnut.
3. Put in the oven and bake for 5 to 7 minutes, or until golden brown. Let the cookies cool for 5 minutes before serving.

Per Serving calories: 218 | fat: 12.0g | protein: 4.0g | carbs: 25.0g | fiber: 2.0g | sodium: 58mg

Mint Banana Chocolate Sorbet

Prep time: 4 hours 5 minutes | Cook time: 0 minutes | Serves 1

1 frozen banana	2 to 3 tablespoons dark chocolate chips (60% cocoa or higher)
1 tablespoon almond butter	
2 tablespoons minced fresh mint	2 to 3 tablespoons goji (optional)

1. Put the banana, butter, and mint in a food processor. Pulse to purée until creamy and smooth.
2. Add the chocolate and goji, then pulse for several more times to combine well. Pour the mixture in a bowl or a ramekin, then freeze for at least 4 hours before serving chilled.

Per Serving calories: 213 | fat: 9.8g | protein: 3.1g | carbs: 2.9g | fiber: 4.0g | sodium: 155mg

Pecan and Carrot Cake

Prep time: 15 minutes | Cook time: 45 minutes | Serves 12

½ cup coconut oil, at room temperature, plus more for greasing the baking dish	1 teaspoon baking soda
	½ teaspoon ground nutmeg
2 teaspoons pure vanilla extract	1 teaspoon ground cinnamon
¼ cup pure maple syrup 6 eggs	⅛ teaspoon sea salt
	½ cup chopped pecans
½ cup coconut flour	3 cups finely grated carrots
1 teaspoon baking powder	

1. Preheat the oven to 350°F (180°C). Grease a 13-by-9-inch baking dish with coconut oil.
2. Combine the vanilla extract, maple syrup, and ½ cup of coconut oil in a large bowl. Stir to mix well.
3. Break the eggs in the bowl and whisk to combine well. Set aside. Combine the coconut flour, baking powder, baking soda, nutmeg, cinnamon, and salt in a separate bowl. Stir to mix well. Make a well in the center of the flour mixture, then pour the egg mixture into the well. Stir to combine well. Add the pecans and carrots to the bowl and toss to mix well. Pour the mixture in the single layer on the baking dish. Bake in the preheated oven for 45 minutes or until puffed and the cake spring back when lightly press with your fingers. Remove the cake from the oven. Allow to cool for at least 15 minutes, then serve.

Per Serving calories: 255 | fat: 21.2g | protein: 5.1g | carbs: 12.8g | fiber: 2.0g | sodium: 202mg

Raspberry Yogurt Basted Cantaloupe

Prep time: 15 minutes | Cook time: 0 minutes | Serves 6

2 cups fresh raspberries, mashed	1 cantaloupe, peeled and sliced
1 cup plain coconut yogurt	½ cup toasted coconut flakes
½ teaspoon vanilla extract	

1. Combine the mashed raspberries with yogurt and vanilla extract in a small bowl. Stir to mix well.
2. Place the cantaloupe slices on a platter, then top with raspberry mixture and spread with toasted coconut.
3. Serve immediately.

Per Serving calories: 75 | fat: 4.1g | protein: 1.2g | carbs: 10.9g | fiber: 6.0g | sodium: 36mg

Apple Compote

Prep time: 15 minutes | Cook time: 10 minutes | Serves 4

6 apples, peeled, cored, and chopped	1 teaspoon ground cinnamon
¼ cup raw honey	¼ cup apple juice
	Sea salt, to taste

1. Put all the ingredients in a stockpot. Stir to mix well, then cook over medium-high heat for 10 minutes or until the apples are glazed by honey and lightly saucy. Stir constantly. Serve immediately.

Per Serving calories: 246 | fat: 0.9g | protein: 1.2g | carbs: 66.3g | fiber: 9.0g | sodium: 62mg

Peanut Butter and Chocolate Balls

Prep time: 45 minutes | Cook time: 0 minutes | Serves 15 balls

¾ cup creamy peanut butter	½ teaspoon vanilla extract
¼ cup unsweetened cocoa powder	1¾ cups maple syrup
2 tablespoons softened almond butter	

1. Line a baking sheet with parchment paper.
2. Combine all the ingredients in a bowl. Stir to mix well.
3. Divide the mixture into 15 parts and shape each part into a 1-inch ball. Arrange the balls on the baking sheet and refrigerate for at least 30 minutes, then serve chilled.

Per Serving (1 ball)
calories: 146 | fat: 8.1g | protein: 4.2g | carbs: 16.9g | fiber: 1.0g | sodium: 70mg

Spiced Sweet Pecans

Prep time: 4 minutes | Cook time: 17 minutes | Serves 4

1 cup pecan halves	½ teaspoon ground nutmeg
3 tablespoons almond butter	¼ cup raw honey
1 teaspoon ground cinnamon	¼ teaspoon sea salt

1. Preheat the oven to 350°F (180°C). Line a baking sheet with parchment paper.
2. Combine all the ingredients in a bowl. Stir to mix well, then spread the mixture in the single layer on the baking sheet with a spatula. Bake in the preheated oven for 16 minutes or until the pecan halves are well browned.
3. Serve immediately.

Per Serving calories: 324 | fat: 29.8g | protein: 3.2g | carbs: 13.9g | fiber: 4.0g | sodium: 180mg

Greek Yogurt Affogato with Pistachios

Prep time: 5 minutes | Cook time: 0 minutes | Serves 4

24 ounces (680 g) vanilla Greek yogurt	4 tablespoons chopped unsalted pistachios
2 teaspoons sugar	4 tablespoons dark chocolate chips
4 shots hot espresso	

1. Spoon the yogurt into four bowls or tall glasses.
2. Mix ½ teaspoon of sugar into each of the espresso shots.
3. Pour one shot of the hot espresso over each bowl of yogurt.
4. Top each bowl with 1 tablespoon of the pistachios and 1 tablespoon of the chocolate chips and serve.

Per Serving calories: 190 | fat: 6.0g | protein: 20.0g | carbs: 14.0g | fiber: 1.0g | sodium: 99mg

Grilled Peaches with Whipped Ricotta

Prep time: 5 minutes | Cook time: 14 to 22 minutes | Serves 4

4 peaches, halved and pitted	1 tablespoon honey
2 teaspoons extra-virgin olive oil	¼ teaspoon freshly grated nutmeg
¾ cup whole-milk Ricotta cheese	4 sprigs mint
	Cooking spray

1. Spritz a grill pan with cooking spray. Heat the grill pan to medium heat.
2. Place a large, empty bowl in the refrigerator to chill.
3. Brush the peaches all over with the oil. Place half of the peaches, cut-side down, on the grill pan and cook for 3 to 5 minutes, or until grill marks appear.
4. Using tongs, turn the peaches over. Cover the grill pan with aluminum foil and cook for 4 to 6 minutes, or until the peaches are easily pierced with a sharp knife. Set aside to cool. Repeat with the remaining peaches.
5. Remove the bowl from the refrigerator and add the Ricotta. Using an electric beater, beat the Ricotta on high for 2 minutes. Add the honey and nutmeg and beat for 1 more minute. Divide the cooled peaches among 4 serving bowls. Top with the Ricotta mixture and a sprig of mint and serve.

Per Serving calories: 176 | fat: 8.0g | protein: 8.0g | carbs: 20.0g | fiber: 3.0g | sodium: 63mg

Honey Baked Cinnamon Apples

Prep time: 5 minutes | Cook time: 20 minutes | Serves 2

1 teaspoon extra-virgin olive oil	1½ teaspoons ground cinnamon, divided
4 firm apples, peeled, cored, and sliced	2 tablespoons unsweetened almond milk
½ teaspoon salt	2 tablespoons honey

1. Preheat the oven to 375ºF (190ºC). Coat a small casserole dish with the olive oil.
2. Toss the apple slices with the salt and ½ teaspoon of the cinnamon in a medium bowl. Spread the apples in the prepared casserole dish and bake in the preheated oven for 20 minutes. Meanwhile, in a small saucepan, heat the milk, honey, and remaining 1 teaspoon of cinnamon over medium heat, stirring frequently. When it reaches a simmer, remove the pan from the heat and cover to keep warm. Divide the apple slices between 2 plates and pour the sauce over the apples. Serve warm.

Per Serving
calories: 310 | fat: 3.4g | protein: 1.7g | carbs: 68.5g | fiber: 12.6g | sodium: 593mg

Strawberries with Balsamic Vinegar

Prep time: 5 minutes | Cook time: 0 minutes | Serves 2

2 cups strawberries, hulled and sliced	2 tablespoons sugar
	2 tablespoons balsamic vinegar

1. Place the sliced strawberries in a bowl, sprinkle with the sugar, and drizzle lightly with the balsamic vinegar.
2. Toss to combine well and allow to sit for about 10 minutes before serving.

Per Serving calories: 92 | fat: 0.4g | protein: 1.0g | carbs: 21.7g | fiber: 2.9g | sodium: 5mg

Frozen Mango Raspberry Delight

Prep time: 5 minutes | Cook time: 0 minutes | Serves 2

3 cups frozen raspberries	1 peach, peeled and pitted
1 mango, peeled and pitted	1 teaspoon honey

1. Place all the ingredients into a blender and purée, adding some water as needed.
2. Put in the freezer for 10 minutes to firm up if desired. Serve chilled or at room temperature.

Per Serving

calories: 276 | fat: 2.1g | protein: 4.5g | carbs: 60.3g | fiber: 17.5g | sodium: 4mg

Grilled Stone Fruit with Honey

Prep time: 8 minutes | Cook time: 6 minutes | Serves 2

3 apricots, halved and pitted	½ cup low-fat ricotta cheese
2 plums, halved and pitted	2 tablespoons honey
2 peaches, halved and pitted	Cooking spray

1. Preheat the grill to medium heat. Spray the grill grates with cooking spray.
2. Arrange the fruit, cut side down, on the grill, and cook for 2 to 3 minutes per side, or until lightly charred and softened.
3. Serve warm with a sprinkle of cheese and a drizzle of honey.

Per Serving

calories: 298 | fat: 7.8g | protein: 11.9g | carbs: 45.2g | fiber: 4.3g | sodium: 259mg

Mascarpone Baked Pears

Prep time: 10 minutes | Cook time: 20 minutes | Serves 2

2 ripe pears, peeled	¼ teaspoon ginger
1 tablespoon plus 2 teaspoons honey, divided	¼ cup minced walnuts
1 teaspoon vanilla, divided	¼ cup mascarpone cheese
¼ teaspoon ground coriander	Pinch salt
	Cooking spray

1. Preheat the oven to 350ºF (180ºC). Spray a small baking dish with cooking spray.
2. Slice the pears in half lengthwise. Using a spoon, scoop out the core from each piece. Put the pears, cut side up, in the baking dish.
3. Whisk together 1 tablespoon of honey, ½ teaspoon of vanilla, ginger, and coriander in a small bowl. Pour this mixture evenly over the pear halves.
4. Scatter the walnuts over the pear halves.
5. Bake in the preheated oven for 20 minutes, or until the pears are golden and you're able to pierce them easily with a knife.
6. Meanwhile, combine the mascarpone cheese with the remaining 2 teaspoons of honey, ½ teaspoon of vanilla, and a pinch of salt. Stir to combine well.
7. Divide the mascarpone among the warm pear halves and serve.

Per Serving

calories: 308 | fat: 16.0g | protein: 4.1g | carbs: 42.7g | fiber: 6.0g | sodium: 88mg

Mixed Berry Crisp

Prep time: 15 minutes | Cook time: 30 minutes | Serves 2

1½ cups frozen mixed berries, thawed	1 tablespoon almond butter
1 tablespoon coconut sugar	¼ cup oats
	¼ cup pecans

1. Preheat the oven to 350ºF (180ºC). Divide the mixed berries between 2 ramekins Place the coconut sugar, almond butter, oats, and pecans in a food processor, and pulse a few times, until the mixture resembles damp sand.
2. Divide the crumble topping over the mixed berries.
3. Put the ramekins on a sheet pan and bake for 30 minutes, or until the top is golden and the berries are bubbling.
4. Serve warm.

Per Serving calories: 268 | fat: 17.0g | protein: 4.1g | carbs: 26.8g | fiber: 6.0g | sodium: 44mg

Orange Mug Cakes

Prep time: 10 minutes | Cook time: 3 minutes | Serves 2

6 tablespoons flour	2 tablespoons olive oil
2 tablespoons sugar	2 tablespoons unsweetened almond milk
1 teaspoon orange zest	2 tablespoons freshly squeezed orange juice
½ teaspoon baking powder	½ teaspoon orange extract
Pinch salt	½ teaspoon vanilla extract
1 egg	

1. Combine the flour, sugar, orange zest, baking powder, and salt in a small bowl. In another bowl, whisk together the egg, olive oil, milk, orange juice, orange extract, and vanilla extract. Add the dry ingredients to the wet ingredients and stir to incorporate. The batter will be thick.
2. Divide the mixture into two small mugs. Microwave each mug separately. The small ones should take about 60 seconds, and one large mug should take about 90 seconds, but microwaves can vary. Cool for 5 minutes before serving.

Per Serving calories: 303 | fat: 16.9g | protein: 6.0g | carbs: 32.5g | fiber: 1.0g | sodium: 118mg

Fruit and Nut Chocolate Bark

Prep time: 15 minutes | Cook time: 2 minutes | Serves 2

2 tablespoons chopped nuts	¼ cup chopped dried fruit (blueberries, apricots, figs, prunes, or any combination of those)
3 ounces (85 g) dark chocolate chips	

1. Line a sheet pan with parchment paper and set aside.
2. Add the nuts to a skillet over medium-high heat and toast for 60 seconds, or just fragrant. Set aside to cool.
3. Put the chocolate chips in a microwave-safe glass bowl and microwave on High for 1 minute.
4. Stir the chocolate and allow any unmelted chips to warm and melt. If desired, heat for an additional 20 to 30 seconds. Transfer the chocolate to the prepared sheet pan. Scatter the dried fruit and toasted nuts over the chocolate evenly and gently pat in so they stick.
5. Place the sheet pan in the refrigerator for at least 1 hour to let the chocolate harden. When ready, break into pieces and serve.

Per Serving calories: 285 | fat: 16.1g | protein: 4.0g | carbs: 38.7g | fiber: 2.0g | sodium: 2mg

Crunchy Almond Cookies

Prep time: 5 minutes | Cook time: 5 to 7 minutes | Serves 4 to 6

½ cup sugar	1½ cups all-purpose flour
8 tablespoons almond butter	1 cup ground almonds
1 large egg	

1. Preheat the oven to 375ºF (190ºC). Line a baking sheet with parchment paper.
2. Using a mixer, whisk together the sugar and butter. Add the egg and mix until combined. Alternately add the flour and ground almonds, ½ cup at a time, while the mixer is on slow.
3. Drop 1 tablespoon of the dough on the prepared baking sheet, keeping the cookies at least 2 inches apart.
4. Put the baking sheet in the oven and bake for about 5 to 7 minutes, or until the cookies start to turn brown around the edges.
5. Let cool for 5 minutes before serving.

Per Serving
calories: 604 | fat: 36.0g | protein: 11.0g | carbs: 63.0g | fiber: 4.0g | sodium: 181mg

Walnut and Date Balls

Prep time: 5 minutes | Cook time: 8 to 10 minutes | Serves 6 to 8

1 cup walnuts	14 medjool dates, pitted
1 cup unsweetened shredded coconut	8 tablespoons almond butter

1. Preheat the oven to 350ºF (180ºC).
2. Put the walnuts on a baking sheet and toast in the oven for 5 minutes.
3. Put the shredded coconut on a clean baking sheet. Toast for about 3 to 5 minutes, or until it turns golden brown. Once done, remove it from the oven and put it in a shallow bowl.
4. In a food processor, process the toasted walnuts until they have a medium chop. Transfer the chopped walnuts into a medium bowl.
5. Add the dates and butter to the food processor and blend until the dates become a thick paste. Pour the chopped walnuts into the food processor with the dates and pulse just until the mixture is combined, about 5 to 7 pulses.
6. Remove the mixture from the food processor and scrape it into a large bowl.
7. To make the balls, spoon 1 to 2 tablespoons of the date mixture into the palm of your hand and roll around between your hands until you form a ball. Put the ball on a clean, lined baking sheet. Repeat until all the mixture is formed into balls.
8. Roll each ball in the toasted coconut until the outside of the ball is coated. Put the ball back on the baking sheet and repeat.
9. Put all the balls into the refrigerator for 20 minutes before serving. Store any leftovers in the refrigerator in an airtight container.

Per Serving
calories: 489 | fat: 35.0g | protein: 5.0g | carbs: 48.0g | fiber: 7.0g | sodium: 114mg

Apple and Berries Ambrosia

Prep time: 15 minutes | Cook time: 0 minutes | Serves 4

2 cups unsweetened coconut milk, chilled
2 tablespoons raw honey

1 apple, peeled, cored, and chopped
2 cups fresh raspberries
2 cups fresh blueberries

1. Spoon the chilled milk in a large bowl, then mix in the honey. Stir to mix well.
2. Then mix in the remaining ingredients. Stir to coat the fruits well and serve immediately.

Per Serving calories: 386 | fat: 21.1g | protein: 4.2g | carbs: 45.9g | fiber: 11.0g | sodium: 16mg

Banana, Cranberry, and Oat Bars

Prep time: 15 minutes | Cook time: 40 minutes | Makes 16 bars

2 tablespoon extra-virgin olive oil
2 medium ripe bananas, mashed
½ cup almond butter
½ cup maple syrup
⅓ cup dried cranberries
1½ cups old-fashioned rolled oats

¼ cup oat flour
¼ cup ground flaxseed
¼ teaspoon ground cloves
½ cup shredded coconut
½ teaspoon ground cinnamon
1 teaspoon vanilla extract

1. Preheat the oven to 400°F (205°C). Line a 8-inch square pan with parchment paper, then grease with olive oil.
2. Combine the mashed bananas, almond butter, and maple syrup in a bowl. Stir to mix well.
3. Mix in the remaining ingredients and stir to mix well until thick and sticky.
4. Spread the mixture evenly on the square pan with a spatula, then bake in the preheated oven for 40 minutes or until a toothpick inserted in the center comes out clean.
5. Remove them from the oven and slice into 16 bars to serve.

Per Serving calories: 145 | fat: 7.2g | protein: 3.1g | carbs: 18.9g | fiber: 2.0g | sodium: 3mg

Berry and Rhubarb Cobbler

Prep time: 15 minutes | Cook time: 35 minutes | Serves 8

Cobbler:
1 cup fresh raspberries
2 cups fresh blueberries
1 cup sliced (½-inch) rhubarb pieces
1 tablespoon arrowroot powder
¼ cup unsweetened apple juice
2 tablespoons melted coconut oil
¼ cup raw honey

Topping:
1 cup almond flour
1 tablespoon arrowroot powder
½ cup shredded coconut
¼ cup raw honey
½ cup coconut oil

Make the Cobbler
1. Preheat the oven to 350°F (180°C). Grease a baking dish with melted coconut oil.
2. Combine the ingredients for the cobbler in a large bowl. Stir to mix well.
3. Spread the mixture in the single layer on the baking dish. Set aside.

Make the Topping
4. Combine the almond flour, arrowroot powder, and coconut in a bowl. Stir to mix well.
5. Fold in the honey and coconut oil. Stir with a fork until the mixture crumbled.
6. Spread the topping over the cobbler, then bake in the preheated oven for 35 minutes or until frothy and golden brown.
7. Serve immediately.

Per Serving
calories: 305 | fat: 22.1g | protein: 3.2g | carbs: 29.8g | fiber: 4.0g | sodium: 3mg

Citrus Cranberry and Quinoa Energy Bites

Prep time: 25 minutes | Cook time: 0 minutes | Makes 12 bites

2 tablespoons almond butter
2 tablespoons maple syrup
¾ cup cooked quinoa
1 tablespoon dried cranberries
1 tablespoon chia seeds

¼ cup ground almonds
¼ cup sesame seeds, toasted
Zest of 1 orange
½ teaspoon vanilla extract

1. Line a baking sheet with parchment paper.
2. Combine the butter and maple syrup in a bowl. Stir to mix well.
3. Fold in the remaining ingredients and stir until the mixture holds together and smooth.
4. Divide the mixture into 12 equal parts, then shape each part into a ball.
5. Arrange the balls on the baking sheet, then refrigerate for at least 15 minutes.
6. Serve chilled.

Per Serving (1 bite)
calories: 110 | fat: 10.8g | protein: 3.1g | carbs: 4.9g | fiber: 3.0g | sodium: 211mg

Chocolate, Almond, and Cherry Clusters

Prep time: 15 minutes | Cook time: 3 minutes | Makes 10 clusters

1 cup dark chocolate (60% cocoa or higher), chopped
1 tablespoon coconut oil

½ cup dried cherries
1 cup roasted salted almonds

1. Line a baking sheet with parchment paper.
2. Melt the chocolate and coconut oil in a saucepan for 3 minutes. Stir constantly.
3. Turn off the heat and mix in the cherries and almonds.
4. Drop the mixture on the baking sheet with a spoon. Place the sheet in the refrigerator and chill for at least 1 hour or until firm.
5. Serve chilled.

Per Serving
calories: 197 | fat: 13.2g | protein: 4.1g | carbs: 17.8g | fiber: 4.0g | sodium: 57mg

Chocolate and Avocado Mousse

Prep time: 40 minutes | Cook time: 5 minutes | Serves 4 to 6

8 ounces (227 g) dark chocolate (60% cocoa or higher), chopped
¼ cup unsweetened coconut milk
2 tablespoons coconut oil
2 ripe avocados, deseeded
¼ cup raw honey
Sea salt, to taste

1. Put the chocolate in a saucepan. Pour in the coconut milk and add the coconut oil.
2. Cook for 3 minutes or until the chocolate and coconut oil melt. Stir constantly.
3. Put the avocado in a food processor, then drizzle with honey and melted chocolate. Pulse to combine until smooth.
4. Pour the mixture in a serving bowl, then sprinkle with salt. Refrigerate to chill for 30 minutes and serve.

Per Serving

calories: 654 | fat: 46.8g | protein: 7.2g | carbs: 55.9g | fiber: 9.0g | sodium: 112mg

Coconut Blueberries with Brown Rice

Prep time: 55 minutes | Cook time: 10 minutes | Serves 4

1 cup fresh blueberries
2 cups unsweetened coconut milk
1 teaspoon ground ginger
¼ cup maple syrup
Sea salt, to taste
2 cups cooked brown rice

1. Put all the ingredients, except for the brown rice, in a pot. Stir to combine well.
2. Cook over medium-high heat for 7 minutes or until the blueberries are tender.
3. Pour in the brown rice and cook for 3 more minute or until the rice is soft. Stir constantly.
4. Serve immediately.

Per Serving

calories: 470 | fat: 24.8g | protein: 6.2g | carbs: 60.1g | fiber: 5.0g | sodium: 75mg

Blueberry and Oat Crisp

Prep time: 15 minutes | Cook time: 20 minutes | Serves 4

2 tablespoons coconut oil, melted, plus more for greasing
4 cups fresh blueberries
Juice of ½ lemon
2 teaspoons lemon zest
¼ cup maple syrup
1 cup gluten-free rolled oats
½ cup chopped pecans
½ teaspoon ground cinnamon
Sea salt, to taste

1. Preheat the oven to 350°F (180°C). Grease a baking sheet with coconut oil.
2. Combine the blueberries, lemon juice and zest, and maple syrup in a bowl. Stir to mix well, then spread the mixture on the baking sheet.
3. Combine the remaining ingredients in a small bowl. Stir to mix well. Pour the mixture over the blueberries mixture.
4. Bake in the preheated oven for 20 minutes or until the oats are golden brown.
5. Serve immediately with spoons.

Per Serving

calories: 496 | fat: 32.9g | protein: 5.1g | carbs: 50.8g | fiber: 7.0g | sodium: 41mg

Glazed Pears with Hazelnuts

Prep time: 10 minutes | Cook time: 20 minutes | Serves 4

4 pears, peeled, cored, and quartered lengthwise
1 cup apple juice
1 tablespoon grated fresh ginger
½ cup pure maple syrup
¼ cup chopped hazelnuts

1. Put the pears in a pot, then pour in the apple juice. Bring to a boil over medium-high heat, then reduce the heat to medium-low. Stir constantly.
2. Cover and simmer for an additional 15 minutes or until the pears are tender.
3. Meanwhile, combine the ginger and maple syrup in a saucepan. Bring to a boil over medium-high heat. Stir frequently. Turn off the heat and transfer the syrup to a small bowl and let sit until ready to use.
4. Transfer the pears in a large serving bowl with a slotted spoon, then top the pears with syrup.
5. Spread the hazelnuts over the pears and serve immediately.

Per Serving

calories: 287 | fat: 3.1g | protein: 2.2g | carbs: 66.9g | fiber: 7.0g | sodium: 8mg

Lemony Blackberry Granita

Prep time: 10 minutes | Cook time: 0 minutes | Serves 4

1 pound (454 g) fresh blackberries
1 teaspoon chopped fresh thyme
¼ cup freshly squeezed lemon juice
½ cup raw honey
½ cup water

1. Put all the ingredients in a food processor, then pulse to purée.
2. Pour the mixture through a sieve into a baking dish. Discard the seeds remain in the sieve.
3. Put the baking dish in the freezer for 2 hours. Remove the dish from the refrigerator and stir to break any frozen parts.
4. Return the dish back to the freezer for an hour, then stir to break any frozen parts again.
5. Return the dish to the freezer for 4 hours until the granita is completely frozen.
6. Remove it from the freezer and mash to serve.

Per Serving

calories: 183 | fat: 1.1g | protein: 2.2g | carbs: 45.9g | fiber: 6.0g | sodium: 6mg

Lemony Tea and Chia Pudding

Prep time: 30 minutes | Cook time: 0 minutes | Serves 3 to 4

2 teaspoons matcha green tea powder (optional)
2 tablespoons ground chia seeds
1 to 2 dates
2 cups unsweetened coconut milk
Zest and juice of 1 lime

1. Put all the ingredients in a food processor and pulse until creamy and smooth.
2. Pour the mixture in a bowl, then wrap in plastic. Store in the refrigerator for at least 20 minutes, then serve chilled.

Per Serving

calories: 225 | fat: 20.1g | protein: 3.2g | carbs: 5.9g | fiber: 5.0g | sodium: 314mg

Sweet Spiced Pumpkin Pudding

Prep time: 2 hours 10 minutes | Cook time: 0 minutes | Serves 6

1 cup pure pumpkin purée	½ teaspoon ground ginger
2 cups unsweetened coconut milk	Pinch cloves
1 teaspoon ground cinnamon	¼ cup pure maple syrup
¼ teaspoon ground nutmeg	2 tablespoons chopped pecans, for garnish

1. Combine all the ingredients, except for the chopped pecans, in a large bowl. Stir to mix well.
2. Wrap the bowl in plastic and refrigerate for at least 2 hours.
3. Remove the bowl from the refrigerator and discard the plastic. Spread the pudding with pecans and serve chilled.

Per Serving
calories: 249 | fat: 21.1g | protein: 2.8g | carbs: 17.2g | fiber: 3.0g | sodium: 46mg

Mango and Coconut Frozen Pie

Prep time: 1 hour 10 minutes | Cook time: 0 minutes | Serves 8

Crust:	Filling:
1 cup cashews	2 large mangoes, peeled and chopped
½ cup rolled oats	½ cup unsweetened shredded coconut
1 cup soft pitted dates	1 cup unsweetened coconut milk
	½ cup water

1. Combine the ingredients for the crust in a food processor. Pulse to combine well.
2. Pour the mixture in an 8-inch springform pan, then press to coat the bottom. Set aside.
3. Combine the ingredients for the filling in the food processor, then pulse to purée until smooth.
4. Pour the filling over the crust, then use a spatula to spread the filling evenly. Put the pan in the freeze for 30 minutes.
5. Remove the pan from the freezer and allow to sit for 15 minutes under room temperature before serving.

Per Serving (1 slice)
calories: 426 | fat: 28.2g | protein: 8.1g | carbs: 14.9g | fiber: 6.0g | sodium: 174mg

Mini Nuts and Fruits Crumble

Prep time: 15 minutes | Cook time: 15 minutes | Serves 6

Topping:	Filling:
¼ cup coarsely chopped hazelnuts	6 fresh figs, quartered
1 cup coarsely chopped walnuts	2 nectarines, pitted and sliced
1 teaspoon ground cinnamon	1 cup fresh blueberries
Sea salt, to taste	2 teaspoons lemon zest
1 tablespoon melted coconut oil	½ cup raw honey
	1 teaspoon vanilla extract

Make the Topping
1. Combine the ingredients for the topping in a bowl. Stir to mix well. Set aside until ready to use.

Make the Filling:
2. Preheat the oven to 375ºF (190ºC).
3. Combine the ingredients for the fillings in a bowl. Stir to mix well.
4. Divide the filling in six ramekins, then divide and top with nut topping.
5. Bake in the preheated oven for 15 minutes or until the topping is lightly browned and the filling is frothy.
6. Serve immediately.

Per Serving
calories: 336 | fat: 18.8g | protein: 6.3g | carbs: 41.9g | fiber: 6.0g | sodium: 31mg

Cozy Superfood Hot Chocolate

Prep time: 5 minutes | Cook time: 8 minutes | Serves 2

2 cups unsweetened almond milk	1 teaspoon ground cinnamon
1 tablespoon avocado oil	1 teaspoon ground ginger
1 tablespoon collagen protein powder	1 teaspoon vanilla extract
2 teaspoons coconut sugar	½ teaspoon ground turmeric
2 tablespoons cocoa powder	Dash salt
	Dash cayenne pepper (optional)

1. In a small saucepan over medium heat, warm the almond milk and avocado oil for about 7 minutes, stirring frequently.
2. Fold in the protein powder, which will only properly dissolve in a heated liquid.
3. Stir in the coconut sugar and cocoa powder until melted and dissolved.
1. Carefully transfer the warm liquid into a blender, along with the cinnamon, ginger, vanilla, turmeric, salt, and cayenne pepper (if desired). Blend for 15 seconds until frothy.
4. Serve immediately.

Per Serving
calories: 217 | fat: 11.0g | protein: 11.2g | carbs: 14.8g | fiber: 6.0g | sodium: 202mg

Chapter 10

Sauces, Dips, and Dressings

Creamy Cucumber Dip

Prep time: 10 minutes | Cook time: 0 minutes | Serves 6

1 medium cucumber, peeled and grated
¼ teaspoon salt
1 cup plain Greek yogurt
2 garlic cloves, minced
1 tablespoon extra-virgin olive oil
1 tablespoon freshly squeezed lemon juice
¼ teaspoon freshly ground black pepper

1. Place the grated cucumber in a colander set over a bowl and season with salt. Allow the cucumber to stand for 10 minutes. Using your hands, squeeze out as much liquid from the cucumber as possible. Transfer the grated cucumber to a medium bowl.
2. Add the yogurt, garlic, olive oil, lemon juice, and pepper to the bowl and stir until well blended.
3. Cover the bowl with plastic wrap and refrigerate for at least 2 hours to blend the flavors.
4. Serve chilled.

Per Serving (¼ cup)

calories: 47 | fat: 2.8g | protein: 4.2g | carbs: 2.7g | fiber: 0g | sodium: 103mg

Italian Dressing

Prep time: 5 minutes | Cook time: 0 minutes | Serves 12

½ cup extra-virgin olive oil
¼ cup red wine vinegar
1 teaspoon dried Italian seasoning
1 teaspoon Dijon mustard
¼ teaspoon salt
¼ teaspoon freshly ground black pepper
1 garlic clove, minced

1. Place all the ingredients in a mason jar and cover. Shake vigorously for 1 minute until completely mixed.
2. Store in the refrigerator for up to 1 week.

Per Serving (1 tablespoon)

calories: 80 | fat: 8.6g | protein: 0g | carbs: 0g | fiber: 0g | sodium: 51mg

Ranch-Style Cauliflower Dressing

Prep time: 10 minutes | Cook time: 0 minutes | Serves 8

2 cups frozen cauliflower, thawed
½ cup unsweetened plain almond milk
2 tablespoons apple cider vinegar
2 tablespoons extra-virgin olive oil
1 garlic clove, peeled
2 teaspoons finely chopped fresh parsley
2 teaspoons finely chopped scallions (both white and green parts)
1 teaspoon finely chopped fresh dill
½ teaspoon onion powder
½ teaspoon Dijon mustard
½ teaspoon salt
¼ teaspoon freshly ground black pepper

1. Place all the ingredients in a blender and pulse until creamy and smooth.
2. Serve immediately, or transfer to an airtight container to refrigerate for up to 3 days.

Per Serving (2 tablespoons)

calories: 41 | fat: 3.6g | protein: 1.0g | carbs: 1.9g | fiber: 1.1g | sodium: 148mg

Asian-Inspired Vinaigrette

Prep time: 5 minutes | Cook time: 0 minutes | Serves 2

¼ cup extra-virgin olive oil
3 tablespoons apple cider vinegar
1 garlic clove, minced
1 tablespoon peeled and grated fresh ginger
1 tablespoon chopped fresh cilantro
1 tablespoon freshly squeezed lime juice
½ teaspoon sriracha

1. Add all the ingredients in a small bowl and stir to mix well.
2. Serve immediately, or store covered in the refrigerator and shake before using.

Per Serving

calories: 251 | fat: 26.8g | protein: 0g | carbs: 1.8g | fiber: 0.7g | sodium: 3mg

Not Old Bay Seasoning

Prep time: 10 minutes | Cook time: 0 minutes | Makes about ½ cup

3 tablespoons sweet paprika
1 tablespoon mustard seeds
2 tablespoons celery seeds
2 teaspoons freshly ground black pepper
1½ teaspoons cayenne pepper
1 teaspoon red pepper flakes
½ teaspoon ground ginger
½ teaspoon ground nutmeg
½ teaspoon ground cinnamon
¼ teaspoon ground cloves

1. Mix together all the ingredients in an airtight container until well combined.
2. You can store it in a cool, dry, and dark place for up to 3 months.

Per Serving (1 tablespoon)

calories: 26 | fat: 1.9g | protein: 1.1g | carbs: 3.6g | fiber: 2.1g | sodium: 3mg

Tzatziki

Prep time: 15 minutes | Cook time: 0 minutes | Serves 4 to 6

½ English cucumber, finely chopped	1 garlic clove, finely minced
1 teaspoon salt, divided	1 to 2 tablespoons chopped fresh dill
1 cup plain Greek yogurt	1 teaspoon red wine vinegar
8 tablespoons olive oil, divided	½ teaspoon freshly ground black pepper

1. In a food processor, pulse the cucumber until puréed. Place the cucumber on several layers of paper towels lining the bottom of a colander and sprinkle with ½ teaspoon of salt. Allow to drain for 10 to 15 minutes. Using your hands, squeeze out any remaining liquid.
2. In a medium bowl, whisk together the cucumber, yogurt, 6 tablespoons of olive oil, garlic, dill, vinegar, remaining ½ teaspoon of salt, and pepper until very smooth.
3. Drizzle with the remaining 2 tablespoons of olive oil. Serve immediately or refrigerate until ready to serve.

Per Serving calories: 286 | fat: 29.0g | protein: 3.0g | carbs: 5.0g | fiber: 0g | sodium: 615mg

Harissa Sauce

Prep time: 10 minutes | Cook time: 20 minutes | Makes 3 to 4 cups

1 large red bell pepper, deseeded, cored, and cut into chunks	2 tablespoons tomato paste
	1 tablespoon tamari
1 yellow onion, cut into thick rings	1 teaspoon ground cumin
	1 tablespoon Hungarian paprika
4 garlic cloves, peeled	
1 cup vegetable broth	

1. Preheat the oven to 450°F (235°C). Line a baking sheet with parchment paper.
2. Place the bell pepper on the prepared baking sheet, flesh-side up, and space out the onion and garlic around the pepper.
3. Roast in the preheated oven for 20 minutes. Transfer to a blender.
4. Add the vegetable broth, tomato paste, tamari, cumin, and paprika. Purée until smooth. Served chilled or warm.

Per Serving (¼ cup)
calories: 15 | fat: 1.0g | protein: 1.0g | carbs: 3.0g | fiber: 1.0g | sodium: 201mg

Pineapple Salsa

Prep time: 10 minutes | Cook time: 0 minutes | Serves 6 to 8

1 pound (454 g) fresh or thawed frozen pineapple, finely diced, juices reserved	1 bunch cilantro or mint, leaves only, chopped
	1 jalapeño, minced (optional)
1 white or red onion, finely diced	Salt, to taste

1. Stir together the pineapple with its juice, onion, cilantro, and jalapeño (if desired) in a medium bowl. Season with salt to taste and serve.
2. The salsa can be refrigerated in an airtight container for up to 2 days.

Per Serving
calories: 55 | fat: 0.1g | protein: 0.9g | carbs: 12.7g | fiber: 1.8g | sodium: 20mg

Garlic Lemon-Tahini Dressing

Prep time: 5 minutes | Cook time: 0 minutes | Serves 8 to 10

½ cup tahini	1 garlic clove, finely minced
¼ cup extra-virgin olive oil	2 teaspoons salt
¼ cup freshly squeezed lemon juice	

1. In a glass mason jar with a lid, combine the tahini, olive oil, lemon juice, garlic, and salt. Cover and shake well until combined and creamy.
2. Store in the refrigerator for up to 2 weeks.

Per Serving
calories: 121 | fat: 12.0g | protein: 2.0g | carbs: 3.0g | fiber: 1.0g | sodium: 479mg

Creamy Grapefruit and Tarragon Dressing

Prep time: 5 minutes | Cook time: 0 minutes | Serves 4 to 6

½ cup avocado oil mayonnaise	½ teaspoon salt
	Zest and juice of ½ grapefruit
2 tablespoons Dijon mustard	¼ teaspoon freshly ground black pepper
1 teaspoon dried tarragon or 1 tablespoon chopped fresh tarragon	1 to 2 tablespoons water (optional)

1. In a large mason jar with a lid, combine the mayonnaise, Dijon, tarragon, grapefruit zest and juice, salt, and pepper and whisk well with a fork until smooth and creamy. If a thinner dressing is preferred, thin out with water.
2. Serve immediately or refrigerate until ready to serve.

Per Serving
calories: 86 | fat: 7.0g | protein: 1.0g | carbs: 6.0g | fiber: 0g | sodium: 390mg

Vinaigrette

Prep time: 5 minutes | Cook time: 0 minutes | Makes 1 cup

½ cup extra-virgin olive oil	½ teaspoon salt
¼ cup red wine vinegar	½ teaspoon freshly ground black pepper
1 tablespoon Dijon mustard	
1 teaspoon dried rosemary	

1. In a cup or a mansion jar with a lid, combine the olive oil, vinegar, mustard, rosemary, salt, and pepper and shake until well combined.
2. Serve chilled or at room temperature.

Per Serving
calories: 124 | fat: 14.0g | protein: 0g | carbs: 1.0g | fiber: 0g | sodium: 170mg

Ginger Teriyaki Sauce

Prep time: 5 minutes | Cook time: 0 minutes | Serves 2

¼ cup pineapple juice	1 tablespoon grated fresh ginger
¼ cup low-sodium soy sauce	
2 tablespoons packed coconut sugar	1 tablespoon arrowroot powder or cornstarch
	1 teaspoon garlic powder

1. Whisk the pineapple juice, soy sauce, coconut sugar, ginger, arrowroot powder, and garlic powder together in a small bowl.
2. Store in an airtight container in the fridge for up to 5 days.

Per Serving
calories: 37 | fat: 0.1g | protein: 1.1g | carbs: 12.0g | fiber: 0g | sodium: 881mg

Aioli

Prep time: 5 minutes | Cook time: 0 minutes | Makes ½ cup

½ cup plain Greek yogurt
2 teaspoons Dijon mustard
½ teaspoon hot sauce
¼ teaspoon raw honey
Pinch salt

1. In a small bowl, whisk together the yogurt, mustard, hot sauce, honey, and salt.
2. Serve immediately or refrigerate in an airtight container for up to 3 days.

Per Serving calories: 47 | fat: 2.5g | protein: 2.1g | carbs: 3.5g | fiber: 0g | sodium: 231mg

Parsley Vinaigrette

Prep time: 5 minutes | Cook time: 0 minutes | Makes about ½ cup

½ cup lightly packed fresh parsley, finely chopped
⅓ cup extra-virgin olive oil
3 tablespoons red wine vinegar
1 garlic clove, minced
¼ teaspoon salt, plus additional as needed

1. Place all the ingredients in a mason jar and cover. Shake vigorously for 1 minute until completely mixed.
2. Taste and add additional salt as needed.
3. Serve immediately or serve chilled.

Per Serving (1 tablespoon)

calories: 92 | fat: 10.9g | protein: 0g | carbs: 0g | fiber: 0g | sodium: 75mg

Hot Pepper Sauce

Prep time: 10 minutes | Cook time: 20 minutes | Makes 4 cups

1 red hot fresh chiles, deseeded
2 dried chiles
2 garlic cloves, peeled
½ small yellow onion, roughly chopped
2 cups water
2 cups white vinegar

1. Place all the ingredients except the vinegar in a medium saucepan over medium heat. Allow to simmer for 20 minutes until softened. Transfer the mixture to a food processor or blender. Stir in the vinegar and pulse until very smooth. Serve immediately or transfer to a sealed container and refrigerate for up to 3 months.

Per Serving (2 tablespoons) calories: 20 | fat: 1.2g | protein: 0.6g | carbs: 4.4g | fiber: 0.6g | sodium: 12mg

Lemon-Tahini Sauce

Prep time: 10 minutes | Cook time: 0 minutes | Makes 1 cup

½ cup tahini
1 garlic clove, minced
Juice and zest of 1 lemon
½ teaspoon salt, plus more as needed
½ cup warm water, plus more as needed

1. Combine the tahini and garlic in a small bowl.
2. Add the lemon juice and zest and salt to the bowl and stir to mix well. Fold in the warm water and whisk until well combined and creamy. Feel free to add more warm water if you like a thinner consistency. Taste and add more salt as needed. Store the sauce in a sealed container in the refrigerator for up to 5 days.

Per Serving (¼ cup)

calories: 179 | fat: 15.5g | protein: 5.1g | carbs: 6.8g | fiber: 3.0g | sodium: 324mg

Peri-Peri Sauce

Prep time: 10 minutes | Cook time: 5 minutes | Serves 4

1 tomato, chopped
1 red onion, chopped
1 red bell pepper, deseeded and chopped
1 red chile, deseeded and chopped
4 garlic cloves, minced
2 tablespoons extra-virgin olive oil
Juice of 1 lemon
1 tablespoon dried oregano
1 tablespoon smoked paprika
1 teaspoon sea salt

1. Process all the ingredients in a food processor or a blender until smooth. Transfer the mixture to a small saucepan over medium-high heat and bring to a boil, stirring often.
2. Reduce the heat to medium and allow to simmer for 5 minutes until heated through. You can store the sauce in an airtight container in the refrigerator for up to 5 days.

Per Serving calories: 98 | fat: 6.5g | protein: 1.0g | carbs: 7.8g | fiber: 3.0g | sodium: 295mg

Peanut Sauce with Honey

Prep time: 5 minutes | Cook time: 0 minutes | Serves 4

¼ cup peanut butter
1 tablespoon peeled and grated fresh ginger
1 tablespoon honey
1 tablespoon low-sodium soy sauce
1 garlic clove, minced
Juice of 1 lime
Pinch red pepper flakes

1. Whisk together all the ingredients in a small bowl until well incorporated. Transfer to an airtight container and refrigerate for up to 5 days.

Per Serving calories: 117 | fat: 7.6g | protein: 4.1g | carbs: 8.8g | fiber: 1.0g | sodium: 136mg

Cilantro-Tomato Salsa

Prep time: 10 minutes | Cook time: 0 minutes | Serves 6

2 or 3 medium, ripe tomatoes, diced
1 serrano pepper, seeded and minced
½ red onion, minced
¼ cup minced fresh cilantro
Juice of 1 lime
¼ teaspoon salt, plus more as needed

1. Place the tomatoes, serrano pepper, onion, cilantro, lime juice, and salt in a small bowl and mix well. Taste and add additional salt, if needed. Store in an airtight container in the refrigerator for up to 3 days.

Per Serving (¼ cup) calories: 17 | fat: 0g | protein: 1.0g | carbs: 3.9g | fiber: 1.0g | sodium: 83mg

Cheesy Pea Pesto

Prep time: 5 minutes | Cook time: 0 minutes | Serves 4

½ cup fresh green peas
½ cup grated Parmesan cheese
¼ cup extra-virgin olive oil
¼ cup pine nuts
¼ cup fresh basil leaves
2 garlic cloves, minced
¼ teaspoon sea salt

1. Add all the ingredients to a food processor or blender and pulse until the nuts are chopped finely.
2. Transfer to an airtight container and refrigerate for up to 2 days. You can also store it in ice cube trays in the freezer for up to 6 months.

Per Serving calories: 247 | fat: 22.8g | protein: 7.1g | carbs: 4.8g | fiber: 1.0g | sodium: 337mg

Guacamole

Prep time: 10 minutes | Cook time: 0 minutes | Serves 6

2 large avocados
¼ white onion, finely diced
1 small, firm tomato, finely diced
¼ cup finely chopped fresh cilantro
2 tablespoons freshly squeezed lime juice
¼ teaspoon salt
Freshly ground black pepper, to taste

1. Slice the avocados in half and remove the pits. Using a large spoon to scoop out the flesh and add to a medium bowl.
2. Mash the avocado flesh with the back of a fork, or until a uniform consistency is achieved. Add the onion, tomato, cilantro, lime juice, salt, and pepper to the bowl and stir to combine.
3. Serve immediately, or transfer to an airtight container and refrigerate until chilled.

Per Serving (¼ cup)

calories: 81 | fat: 6.8g | protein: 1.1g | carbs: 5.7g | fiber: 3.0g | sodium: 83mg

Lentil-Tahini Dip

Prep time: 10 minutes | Cook time: 15 minutes | Makes 3 cups

1 cup dried green or brown lentils, rinsed
2½ cups water, divided
⅓ cup tahini
1 garlic clove
½ teaspoon salt, plus more as needed

1. Add the lentils and 2 cups of water to a medium saucepan and bring to a boil over high heat.
2. Once it starts to boil, reduce the heat to low, and then cook for 14 minutes, stirring occasionally, or the lentils become tender but still hold their shape. You can drain any excess liquid.
3. Transfer the lentils to a food processor, along with the remaining water, tahini, garlic, and salt and process until smooth and creamy.
4. Taste and adjust the seasoning if needed. Serve immediately.

Per Serving (¼ cup)

calories: 100 | fat: 3.9g | protein: 5.1g | carbs: 10.7g | fiber: 6.0g | sodium: 106mg

Lemon-Dill Cashew Dip

Prep time: 10 minutes | Cook time: 0 minutes | Makes 1 cup

¾ cup cashews, soaked in water for at least 4 hours and drained well
¼ cup water
Juice and zest of 1 lemon
2 tablespoons chopped fresh dill
¼ teaspoon salt, plus more as needed

1. Put the cashews, water, lemon juice and zest in a blender and blend until smooth.
2. Add the dill and salt to the blender and blend again.
3. Taste and adjust the seasoning, if needed.
4. Transfer to an airtight container and refrigerate for at least 1 hour to blend the flavors.
5. Serve chilled.

Per Serving (1 tablespoon)

calories: 37 | fat: 2.9g | protein: 1.1g | carbs: 1.9g | fiber: 0g | sodium: 36mg

Homemade Blackened Seasoning

Prep time: 10 minutes | Cook time: 0 minutes | Makes about ½ cup

2 tablespoons smoked paprika
2 tablespoons garlic powder
2 tablespoons onion powder
1 tablespoon sweet paprika
1 teaspoon dried dill
1 teaspoon freshly ground black pepper
½ teaspoon ground mustard
¼ teaspoon celery seeds

1. Add all the ingredients to a small bowl and mix well.
2. Serve immediately, or transfer to an airtight container and store in a cool, dry and dark place for up to 3 months.

Per Serving (1 tablespoon)

calories: 22 | fat: 0.9g | protein: 1.0g | carbs: 4.7g | fiber: 1.0g | sodium: 2mg

Basil Pesto

Prep time: 5 minutes | Cook time: 0 minutes | Makes 1 cup

2 cups packed fresh basil leaves
3 garlic cloves, peeled
½ cup freshly grated Parmesan cheese
½ cup extra-virgin olive oil
⅓ cup pine nuts
Kosher salt and freshly ground black pepper, to taste

1. Place all the ingredients, except for the salt and pepper, in a food processor. Pulse a few times until smoothly puréed. Season with salt and pepper to taste.
2. Store in an airtight container in the fridge for up to 2 weeks.

Per Serving

calories: 100 | fat: 10.2g | protein: 2.2g | carbs: 1.2g | fiber: 0g | sodium: 72mg

Orange-Garlic Dressing

Prep time: 5 minutes | Cook time: 0 minutes | Serves 2

¼ cup extra-virgin olive oil
1 orange, zested
2 tablespoons freshly squeezed orange juice
¾ teaspoon za'atar seasoning
1 teaspoon garlic powder
½ teaspoon salt
¼ teaspoon Dijon mustard
Freshly ground black pepper, to taste

1. Whisk together all ingredients in a bowl until well combined. Serve immediately or refrigerate until ready to serve.

Per Serving calories: 287 | fat: 26.7g | protein: 1.2g | carbs: 12.0g | fiber: 2.1g | sodium: 592mg

Creamy Cider Yogurt Dressing

Prep time: 5 minutes | Cook time: 0 minutes | Serves 2

1 cup plain, unsweetened, full-fat Greek yogurt
½ cup extra-virgin olive oil
½ lemon, juiced
1 tablespoon chopped fresh oregano
1 tablespoon apple cider vinegar
½ teaspoon dried parsley
½ teaspoon kosher salt
¼ teaspoon garlic powder
¼ teaspoon freshly ground black pepper

1. In a large bowl, whisk all ingredients to combine.
2. Serve chilled or at room temperature.

Per Serving calories: 407 | fat: 40.7g | protein: 8.3g | carbs: 3.8g | fiber: 0.5g | sodium: 382mg

Basic French Vinaigrette

Prep time: 5 minutes | Cook time: 0 minutes | Serves 2

3 tablespoons apple cider vinegar

2 tablespoons minced shallot (or 1 tablespoon minced red onion)

1 tablespoon balsamic vinegar

½ teaspoon dried thyme

1 teaspoon Dijon mustard

¼ cup olive oil

Salt and black pepper, to taste

1. Stir together the apple cider vinegar, shallot, and balsamic vinegar in a medium jar with a tight-fitting lid. Allow to sit for 5 minutes.
2. Stir in the mustard and thyme. Whisk in the olive oil in a slow, steady stream and season to taste with salt and pepper.
3. Store in an airtight container in the fridge for up to 5 days.

Per Serving

calories: 256 | fat: 27.1g | protein: 0.3g | carbs: 3.4g | fiber: 0.4g | sodium: 207mg

Appendix 1 Measurement Conversion Chart

VOLUME EQUIVALENTS(DRY)

US STANDARD	METRIC (APPROXIMATE)
1/8 teaspoon	0.5 mL
1/4 teaspoon	1 mL
1/2 teaspoon	2 mL
3/4 teaspoon	4 mL
1 teaspoon	5 mL
1 tablespoon	15 mL
1/4 cup	59 mL
1/2 cup	118 mL
3/4 cup	177 mL
1 cup	235 mL
2 cups	475 mL
3 cups	700 mL
4 cups	1 L

VOLUME EQUIVALENTS(LIQUID)

US STANDARD	US STANDARD (OUNCES)	METRIC (APPROXIMATE)
2 tablespoons	1 fl.oz.	30 mL
1/4 cup	2 fl.oz.	60 mL
1/2 cup	4 fl.oz.	120 mL
1 cup	8 fl.oz.	240 mL
1 1/2 cup	12 fl.oz.	355 mL
2 cups or 1 pint	16 fl.oz.	475 mL
4 cups or 1 quart	32 fl.oz.	1 L
1 gallon	128 fl.oz.	4 L

TEMPERATURES EQUIVALENTS

FAHRENHEIT(F)	CELSIUS(C) (APPROXIMATE)
225 °F	107 °C
250 °F	120 °C
275 °F	135 °C
300 °F	150 °C
325 °F	160 °C
350 °F	180 °C
375 °F	190 °C
400 °F	205 °C
425 °F	220 °C
450 °F	235 °C
475 °F	245 °C
500 °F	260 °C

WEIGHT EQUIVALENTS

US STANDARD	METRIC (APPROXIMATE)
1 ounce	28 g
2 ounces	57 g
5 ounces	142 g
10 ounces	284 g
15 ounces	425 g
16 ounces (1 pound)	455 g
1.5 pounds	680 g
2 pounds	907 g

<u>Appendix 2   Dirty Dozen and Clean Fifteen</u>

The Environmental Working Group (EWG) is a nonprofit, nonpartisan organization dedicated to protecting human health and the environment Its mission is to empower people to live healthier lives in a healthier environment. This organization publishes an annual list of the twelve kinds of produce, in sequence, that have the highest amount of pesticide residue-the Dirty Dozen-as well as a list of the fifteen kinds ofproduce that have the least amount of pesticide residue-the Clean Fifteen.

THE DIRTY DOZEN		THE CLEAN FIFTEEN	
• The 2016 Dirty Dozen includes the following produce. These are considered among the year's most important produce to buy organic:		• The least critical to buy organically are the Clean Fifteen list. The following are on the 2016 list:	
Strawberries	Spinach	Avocados	Papayas
Apples	Tomatoes	Corn	Kiw
Nectarines	Bell peppers	Pineapples	Eggplant
Peaches	Cherry tomatoes	Cabbage	Honeydew
Celery	Cucumbers	Sweet peas	Grapefruit
Grapes	Kale/collard greens	Onions	Cantaloupe
Cherries	Hot peppers	Asparagus	Cauliflower
		Mangos	
• *The Dirty Dozen list contains two additional itemskale/collard greens and hot peppers-because they tend to contain trace levels of highly hazardous pesticides.*		• *Some of the sweet corn sold in the United States are made from genetically engineered (GE) seedstock. Buy organic varieties of these crops to avoid GE produce.*	

Appendix 3 Index

Leave a Review

As an independent author with a small marketing budget, reviews are my livelihood on this platform. If you enjoyed this book, I'd appreciate it if you could leave your honest feedback.

I read EVERY single review because I love the feedback from MY readers!

Thank you for staying with me.

Made in the USA
Monee, IL
20 February 2022